# Professional and Student Portfolios for Physical Education

## Vincent J. Melograno, PhD

Cleveland State University

**Human Kinetics**

**Library of Congress Cataloging-in-Publication Data**

Melograno, Vincent.
    Professional and student portfolios for physical education /
Vincent J. Melograno.
        p.    cm.
    Includes bibliographical references.
    ISBN 0-88011-809-1
    1. Physical fitness--Testing.    2. Portfolios in education.
I. Title.
GV436.5.M45    1998
796'.07'7--dc21                                      97-45626
                                                      CIP

ISBN: 0-88011-809-1

**Acquisitions Editor:** Scott Wikgren; **Developmental Editor:** Laura Casey Mast; **Assistant Editor:** Cynthia McEntire; **Editorial Assistants:** Laura Ward Majersky, Laura Seversen, Jennifer Simmons; **Copyeditor:** Allen Gooch; **Proofreader:** Kathy Bennett; **Graphic Designer:** Robert Reuther; **Graphic Artist:** Kathy Fuoss; **Photo Editor:** Boyd LaFoon; **Cover Designer:** Jack Davis; **Cover Photographer (bottom):** Human Kinetics/Tom Roberts; **Interior Photographer:** Photos on pages 1, 79, 82, 87, 159, and 169 courtesy of Instructional Media Services, Cleveland State University, Cleveland, OH and Shaker Heights City School District, Shaker Heights, OH. Photos on pages 11, 16, 19, 28, 37, 42 (and top cover photo), 92, 108, and 162 courtesy of Instructional Media Services, Cleveland State University and Department of Health, Physical Education, Recreation, and Dance, Cleveland State University, Cleveland, OH.; **Illustrator:** Tom Roberts; **Printer:** United Graphics

Printed in the United States of America        10  9  8  7  6  5  4  3

**Human Kinetics**
Web site: www.humankinetics.com

*United States:* Human Kinetics, P.O. Box 5076, Champaign, IL 61825-5076
800-747-4457
e-mail: humank@hkusa.com

*Canada:* Human Kinetics, 475 Devonshire Road, Unit 100, Windsor, ON N8Y 2L5
800-465-7301 (in Canada only)
e-mail: hkcan@mnsi.net

*Europe:* Human Kinetics, P.O. Box IW14, Leeds LS16 6TR, United Kingdom
+44 (0)113 278 1708
e-mail: humank@hkeurope.com

*Australia:* Human Kinetics, 57A Price Avenue, Lower Mitcham, South Australia 5062
08  8277 1555
e-mail: liahka@senet.com.au

*New Zealand:* Human Kinetics, P.O. Box 105-231, Auckland Central
09-309-1890
e-mail: hkp@ihug.co.nz

For my wonderful, loving family:
Nan & Pop; Mom & Dad; Eddie;
Laura; Craig & Charlene; Janet & Scott;
Denise, Scott, Tyler, & Victoria;
Debbie, Dan, & Christina; and Doreen & Mark.

# Contents

# Preface

Teaching practices and student learning of the past are not adequate to meet the demands of the 21st century. The roots of a redesign of teaching and learning for the next century have been planted and established through a challenging, national standards movement. Emerging from this effort are explicit standards for both teachers and students. The questions that arise are, "What knowledge and skills are essential for effective teaching?" and "What should students know and be able to do as a result of their education?" As higher and more demanding expectations are placed on students, the need for professionals capable of teaching to achieve these standards becomes more essential. In other words, student standards must be matched by teacher standards.

The standards-based reform of teaching and learning is evident in physical education. The *National Standards for Beginning Physical Education Teachers* (Tannehill et al., 1995) evolved out of work by the Interstate New Teacher Assessment and Support Consortium (INTASC). The consortium's *Model Standards for Beginning Teacher Licensing and Development: A Resource for State Dialogue* (Darling-Hammond, 1992) presented teachers as reflective, inquiry-oriented professionals who are cognizant of equity and diversity issues, competent in their subject matter, and able to select instructional strategies best suited to the varying needs of their students. The physical education teacher standards parallel this framework.

Explicit standards for K-12 students in physical education were developed through a series of projects. The National Association for Sport and Physical Education (NASPE) completed an outcomes project that resulted in a definition of the "physically educated person." This effort was followed by a set of attendant outcomes and benchmark statements for grades kindergarten, 2, 4, 6, 8, 10, and 12 in the publication *Outcomes of Quality Physical Education Programs* (Franck et al., 1992). About the same time, developmentally appropriate practices were advanced by the Council on Physical Education for Children (COPEC) that maximize opportunities for learning and success for all children (Graham et al., 1992). Then, the NASPE appointed a standards and assessment task force to develop content standards and assessment material based on the *Outcomes* document. Work of the task force was published in *National Standards for Physical Education: A Guide to Content and Assessment* (Rink et al., 1995). The document established content standards for the physical education school program and teacher-friendly guidelines for assessment.

Concomitant to the standards-based reform in education is the growing dissatisfaction with traditional forms of assessment. The trend is toward authentic forms of assessment that rely on more naturalistic, performance-based approaches instead of highly inferential estimates provided by the group-administered, objectively scored, and normatively interpreted standardized tests. Authentic assessment applies to both students and teachers and is structured to provide evidence of real-life samples of learning and classroom performance, respectively. In physical education, multiple-choice, machine-scored tests or standardized sport skill or fitness tests do not seem to be good indicators of what students really learned. Likewise, multiple-choice tests of basic skills and general knowledge seem woefully inadequate to measure teaching skill. Thus, assessment systems are needed to document the degree to which established student and teacher standards are met, specific to physical education. That is the purpose of this book.

The pendulum of alternative educational assessment has swung toward a portfolio format. In general terms, a portfolio is a purposeful, integrated collection of artifacts showing effort, progress, or achievement in one or more aspects. The type of portfolio that a teacher or student will use depends on the needs the portfolio serves. Because portfolios feature work samples over time, they are well suited to demonstrate student growth and learning. They can also be used by teachers, for example, to document the implementation and success of a new instructional strategy.

Given the national focus on learning and teaching standards, it follows that any accompanying assessment system correspond to established standards. Therefore, *Professional and Student Portfolios for Physical Education* provides both teacher and student portfolio systems based on teacher standards and K-12 content standards, respectively. It presents practical, step-by-step procedures and tips on how to organize portfolio systems. These systems can be used from the beginning to the end of one's career as a physical educator. The full continuum of professional involvement is covered as follows:

• Professional portfolio systems are presented for preservice teachers to help them become "beginning" physical education teachers. The book is recommended to higher education personnel in the business of teacher training. A portfolio system is suggested for a preservice teacher education program in physical education.

• Student portfolio systems are detailed and illustrated. Practicing physical education teachers will find the book useful because comprehensive student portfolio systems are outlined across the K-12 physical education spectrum.

• The same practicing teachers will also discover the value of portfolios to grow professionally and to help maintain teaching effectiveness. A portfolio system is suggested for use at the inservice level.

The principles and concepts underlying these portfolio systems are treated in four chapters.

**Chapter 1: Gateway to Portfolios**—The demand for greater educational effectiveness and accountability is analyzed with respect to teaching and learning. Various educational trends are explored as contexts for the authentic assessment movement. A rationale is offered for portfolios as the means for validating the standards-based reform of teaching and learning in physical education.

**Chapter 2: Preservice Professional Portfolios**—To integrate and interrelate the knowledge and skills learned in a teacher education program, a portfolio scheme is proposed. General guidelines are provided for organizing a preservice professional portfolio around a set of standards for the beginning physical education teacher. Processes for implementing portfolio assessment are also identified, along with guidelines for management and assembly. Required and optional artifacts are suggested for the introductory, working, presentation, and employment portfolios. Finally, formative and summative evaluation procedures are described and illustrated. A sample portfolio system is included for a preservice teacher education program

**Chapter 3: Student Portfolios**—A multifaceted approach is recommended for designing student portfolio systems appropriate for K-12 school physical education programs. The framework for developing portfolios includes six phases: (1) determine purposes and types, (2) organize and plan logistics, (3) select items, (4) reflect and self-assess, (5) conduct conferences, and (6) evaluate. Exemplary materials are provided for established content standards in physical education. Sample portfolio systems are included for the high school, middle school, and elementary school levels.

**Chapter 4: Inservice Professional Portfolios**—Procedures are presented on how to organize a professional portfolio for inservice physical education teachers. Various purposes are suggested to document professional accomplishments. Organization and management strategies are offered for working and showcase portfolios. Guidelines are also provided for collecting and selecting items and for evaluating one's own portfolio. A sample portfolio system is included for use at the inservice level.

# Acknowledgments

This book reflects the contributions of many others including teachers, students, colleagues, and other authors in the area of authentic assessment. In particular, I owe a debt of gratitude to Jane Zaharias, Cleveland State University, who really introduced me to portfolio assessment. Her willingness to share ideas and materials got me interested in teaching, writing, and talking about professional and student portfolios. In addition, Jane has always been a source of professional and personal support, and for that I will always be thankful.

Appreciation is also extended to Scott Wikgren, acquisitions editor, HK Academic Book Division, who enthusiastically endorsed this writing from beginning to end. His professional style and personable manner are his trademarks. Scott is a distinct asset to the HK team.

Special thanks and respect are reserved for Laura Casey Mast, my developmental editor, whose dedication and commitment to this book were truly remarkable. Her tireless energy and high quality of work were evident during all phases of editing, production, and marketing. I am extremely proud to be one of Laura's authors.

*Vincent Melograno*

# Gateway
# to Portfolios

As expectations become more demanding about what students should know and be able to do as a result of their education, so do the knowledge and skill requirements essential for effective teaching. Standards for students must be matched by standards for teachers. So, how do we document that both student standards and teacher standards are being met?

# INTRODUCTION

Demands for greater educational effectiveness that began in the early 1980s have resulted in widespread educational reform. This chapter traces the wave of reform initiatives that is still going strong today, including the redesign of learning and teaching. It explores the national standards movement and analyzes the trend toward more authentic forms of assessment. Both are discussed relative to their impact on learning and teaching. In combination, standards-based assessment of both students and teachers offers a new vision for the future of physical education. Finally, a rationale is offered for using portfolios to validate established student and teacher standards in physical education.

# REDESIGN OF LEARNING AND TEACHING STANDARDS

In the 1980s, a federal report titled *A Nation at Risk: The Imperative of Educational Reform* (National Commission on Excellence in Education, 1983) raised public concern about the condition of education in the United States. Overall, the quality of education was rated as poor. Supposedly, students were not learning and teachers were not teaching effectively. As a result, the 1980s saw massive school improvement efforts through legislation at all levels, school effectiveness projects, and instructional intervention approaches. Many so-called reforms that became popular included magnet schools, proficiency testing, school choice, alternative schools, vouchers, charter schools, and year-round schools.

Just three years after *A Nation at Risk,* another pivotal report was issued, titled *A Nation Prepared: Teachers for the 21st Century* (Carnegie Task Force on Teaching as a Profession, 1986). One of its recommendations led to the creation of the National Board for Professional Teaching Standards (NBPTS) in 1987. The mission of the NBPTS was to (1) establish high and rigorous standards for what accomplished teachers should know and be able to do, (2) develop and operate a national, voluntary system to assess and certify teachers who meet these standards, and (3) advance related education reforms for the purpose of improving student learning in American schools (National Board for Professional Teaching Standards, 1994).

Along with taking on these school restructuring efforts, teachers were also expected to respond to forces that operate in the larger culture (e.g., substance abuse, changes in family patterns, sexually transmitted diseases, ethnic and linguistic diversity, economic inequities, and abused children). Some hopeful changes in education included these features:

- *Culturally responsive pedagogy*—teaching that considers cultural differences; includes skills needed to accommodate the diversity found in cross-cultural school settings; eliminates discriminatory practices; and promotes multicultural understanding through movement.

- *Inclusive education*—places and instructs all students in regular settings regardless of the type or severity of disability and uses teams of professionals representing different specialties, including motor development.

- *Knowledge-based approaches*—subject matter mastery is fundamental to one's ability to solve problems, think, or be creative; includes body of knowledge in physical education (e.g., exercise physiology, kinesiology, motor learning, and sport psychology).

- *Developmentally appropriate practices*—principles of child and adolescent development are applied; depends on age appropriateness (predictable sequences of growth and change) and individual appropriateness (pattern and timing of growth); recognizes each learner's changing abilities to move while accommodating previous movement experiences, fitness and skill levels, and body size.

- *Outcomes-based education*—student success is reflected in "goals reached"; outcomes are linked with objectives and then with assessment measures; includes outcome statements and grade-level benchmarks (competencies) that define the physically educated person.

An overwhelming set of expectations, it seemed, had been placed on schools in general and on students and teachers in particular. It prompted a historic education summit in 1989 involving the president and the nation's governors. Educational goals were adopted and a National Education Goals Panel was established to measure their progress. *America 2000: An Education Strategy* (U.S. Department of Education, 1991) provided the elements needed to ensure that students would be prepared to function in a diverse society and to compete in a global economy. The goals stated that, by the year 2000, (1) children will enter school ready to learn, (2) the high school graduation rate will be 90 percent, (3) students will leave 4th, 8th, and 12th grades having demonstrated competency in challenging subject matter, (4) teachers will receive the professional development needed to help students reach the other goals, (5) U.S. students will be first in the world in math and science, (6) every adult will be literate, (7) schools will be free of drugs and violence, and (8) schools will promote partnerships to increase parent involvement.

The other critical element of the education equation—the teacher—was not forgotten. The Interstate New Teacher Assessment and Support Consortium (INTASC) developed model standards for teachers (Darling-Hammond, 1992). Because of the general applicability of the standards for teachers of all disciplines and all levels, many professional societies, state departments of education, and university schools of education have used the standards in their attempts to define teaching excellence.

Ultimately, the shift toward student and teacher competencies led to passage of the federal Goals 2000: Educate America Act (PL 103-227) in March 1994. With educational standards written into law, a national standards movement emerged. Through the National Education Standards Improvement Council (NESIC), students would be expected to achieve the standards, given adequate support and sustained effort. Voluntary content standards were developed on a kindergarten through 12th grade (K-12) continuum across various school subjects, including physical education. In addition, a National Commission on Teaching & America's Future was appointed in 1994. After two years of intense study, it concluded "... that the reform of elementary and secondary education depends first and foremost on restructuring its foundation—the teaching profession" (National Commission on Teaching & America's Future, 1996, p. 5). The commission recommended that rigorous standards be developed and enforced for teacher preparation, initial licensing, and continuing development.

Clearly, student learning and teaching practices of the past are not adequate to meet the demands of the 21st century. The roots of a redesign of both learning and teaching have been planted and established through the challenging national standards movement. Standards are the cornerstone of educational reform. The questions that arise are, "What should students know and be able to do as a result of their physical education program?" and "What knowledge and skills are essential for effective teaching in physical education?" The following sections explore some answers to these questions.

## Content Standards for K–12 Physical Education

Explicit standards for the physical education school program evolved through a series of projects. The Council on Physical Education for Children (COPEC) provided a set of developmentally appropriate practices that maximize opportunities for learning and success for all children (Graham, Castenada, Hopple, Manross, & Sanders, 1992). About the same time, the outcomes project of the National Association for Sport and Physical Education (NASPE) defined the physically educated person. The definition, consisting of five major focus areas, was expanded to 20 outcome statements. This was followed by a set of attendant benchmark statements for grades kindergarten, 2, 4, 6, 8, 10, and 12 in the publication *Outcomes of Quality Physical Education Programs* (Franck et al., 1992). These are each part of the definition and its corresponding outcomes:

### A Physically Educated Person*

*HAS learned skills necessary to perform a variety of physical activities.*

1. Moves using concepts of body awareness, space awareness, effort, and relationships.
2. Demonstrates competence in a variety of manipulative, locomotor, and nonlocomotor skills.
3. Demonstrates competence in combinations of manipulative, locomotor, and nonlocomotor skills performed individually and with others.
4. Demonstrates competence in many different forms of physical activity.

*Reprinted from *Outcomes of Quality Physical Education Programs* (1992) with permission from the National Association for Sport and Physical Education (NASPE), 1900 Association Drive, Reston, VA 20191-1599.

5. Demonstrates proficiency in a few forms of physical activity.

6. Has learned how to learn new skills.

*IS physically fit.*

7. Assesses, achieves, and maintains physical fitness.

8. Designs safe, personal fitness programs in accordance with principles of training and conditioning.

*DOES participate regularly in physical activity.*

9. Participates in health enhancing physical activity at least three times a week.

10. Selects and regularly participates in lifetime physical activities.

*KNOWS the implications of and the benefits from involvement in physical activities.*

11. Identifies the benefits, costs, and obligations associated with regular participation in physical activity.

12. Recognizes the risk and safety factors associated with regular participation in physical activity.

13. Applies concepts and principles to the development of motor skills.

14. Understands that wellness involves more than being physically fit.

15. Knows the rules, strategies, and appropriate behaviors for selected physical activities.

16. Recognizes that participation in physical activity can lead to multicultural and international understanding.

17. Understands that physical activity provides the opportunity for enjoyment, self-expression, and communication.

*VALUES physical activity and its contributions to a healthful lifestyle.*

18. Appreciates the relationships with others that result from participation in physical activity.

19. Respects the role that regular physical activity plays in the pursuit of lifelong health and well-being.

20. Cherishes the feelings that result from regular participation in physical activity.

Then, NASPE appointed a standards and assessment task force to develop content standards and assessment material based on the *Outcomes* publication. Work of the task force was published in *National Standards for Physical Education: A Guide to Content and Assessment* (Rink et al., 1995). The document established content standards for the physical education school program (grades kindergarten, 2, 4, 6, 8, 10, and 12) and teacher-friendly guidelines for assessing the content standards. It was designed to expand and complement, not replace, the *Outcomes* publication. A general description of each content standard follows.

**A physically educated person**

1. demonstrates competency in many movement forms and proficiency in a few movement forms,

2. applies movement concepts and principles to the learning and development of motor skills,

3. exhibits a physically active lifestyle,

4. achieves and maintains a health-enhancing level of physical fitness,

5. demonstrates responsible personal and social behavior in physical activity settings,

6. demonstrates understanding and respect for differences among people in physical education settings, and

7. understands that physical activity provides opportunities for enjoyment, challenge, self-expression, and social interaction.

In an ambitious project conducted by the Mid-continent Regional Educational Laboratory, the literature on content standards and benchmarks was synthesized. For physical education, information was integrated from numerous sources including the *Outcomes* and *Standards* documents from the NASPE. This systematic identification and articulation process led to publication of *Content Knowledge: A Compendium of Standards and Benchmarks for K-12 Education* (Kendall & Marzano, 1996). The physical education content standards and corresponding benchmarks for four levels (grades K-2, 3-6, 7-8, 9-12) appear in table 1.1. They provide the answer to "What should students know and be able to do as a result of their physical education program?" These standards and benchmarks will be used in chapter 3 to facilitate the organization of student portfolios.

-------TABLE 1.1-------

# K–12 Physical Education Content Standards and Benchmarks

| PRIMARY: GRADES K-2 |
| --- |

**Uses a variety of basic and advanced movement forms**
- Uses a variety of basic locomotor movements (e.g., running, skipping, hopping, galloping, sliding)
- Uses a variety of basic non-locomotor skills (e.g., bending, twisting, stretching, turning, lifting)
- Uses a variety of basic object control skills (e.g., underhand & overhand throw, catch, hand dribble, foot dribble, kick and strike)
- Uses simple combinations of fundamental movement skills (e.g., locomotor, non-locomotor, object control, body control, rhythmical skills)
- Uses control in weight-bearing activities on a variety of body parts (e.g., jumping and landing using combinations of one and two foot take-offs and landings)
- Uses control in balance activities on a variety of body parts (e.g., one foot, one hand and one foot, hands and knees, headstands)
- Uses control in travel activities on a variety of body parts (e.g., travels in backward direction and changes direction quickly and safely, without falling; changes speeds and directions in response to various rhythms; combines traveling patterns to music)
- Uses smooth transitions between sequential motor skills (e.g., running into a jump)
- Uses locomotor skills in rhythmical patterns (e.g., even, uneven, fast, slow)

**Uses movement concepts and principles in the development of motor skills**
- Understands a vocabulary of basic movement concepts (e.g., personal space, high/low levels, fast/slow speeds, light/heavy weights, balance, twist)
- Understands terms that describe a variety of relationships with objects (e.g., over/under, behind, alongside, through)
- Uses concepts of space awareness and movement control with a variety of basic skills (e.g., running, hopping, skipping) while interacting with others
- Understands the critical elements of a variety of basic movement patterns such as throwing (e.g., the ready position, arm preparation, step with leg opposite the throwing arm, follow-through, accuracy of throw)
- Uses feedback to improve performance (e.g., peer/coach review)
- Understands the importance of practice in learning skills

**Understands the benefits and costs associated with participation in physical activity**
- Understands the health benefits of physical activity (e.g., good health, physical endurance)

**Understands how to monitor and maintain a health-enhancing level of physical fitness**
- Engages in basic activities that cause cardiorespiratory exertion (e.g., running, galloping, skipping, hopping)
- Knows how to measure cardiorespiratory fitness (e.g., listening to heartbeat, counting pulse rate)
- Knows the physiological indicators (e.g., perspiration, increased heart rate and breathing rate) that accompany moderate to vigorous physical activity
- Engages in activities that develop muscular strength and endurance (e.g., climbing, hanging, taking weight on hands)
- Engages in activities that require flexibility (e.g., stretching toward the toes while in the sit-and-reach position, moving each joint through its full range of motion)
- Knows how body composition influences physical fitness levels (e.g., proportion of lean body mass to fat body mass)
- Knows similarities and differences in body height, weight, and shape

**Understands the social and personal responsibility associated with participation in physical activity**
- Follows rules and procedures (e.g., playground, classroom, gymnasium) with little reinforcement
- Uses equipment and space safely and properly (e.g., takes turns using equipment, puts equipment away when not in use)
- Understands the purpose of rules in games
- Understands the social contributions of physical activity (e.g., learning to cooperate and interact with others, having a role in team sports)
- Works cooperatively (e.g., takes turns, is supportive, assists partner) with another to complete an assigned task
- Understands the elements of socially acceptable conflict resolution in physical activity settings (e.g., cooperation, sharing, consideration)
- Understands the importance of playing, cooperating, and respecting others regardless of personal differences (e.g., gender, ethnicity, disability) during physical activity

*(continued)*

---TABLE 1.1---
## *(continued)*

---

### UPPER ELEMENTARY: GRADES 3-6

**Uses a variety of basic and advanced movement forms**
- Uses mature form in object control skills (e.g., underhand and overhand throw, catch, hand dribble, foot dribble, kick and strike, batting, punt, pass)
- Uses basic sport-specific skills for a variety of physical activities (e.g., basketball chest pass, soccer dribble, fielding a softball with a glove)
- Uses mature form and appropriate sequence in combinations of fundamental locomotor, object control, and rhythmical skills that are components of selected modified games, sports, and dances (e.g., combining steps to perform certain dances; combining running, stopping, throwing, shooting, kicking for sideline soccer)
- Uses mature form in balance activities on a variety of apparatuses (e.g., balance board, large apparatus, skates)
- Uses beginning strategies for net and invasion games (e.g., keeping object going with partner using striking pattern, placing ball away from opponent in a racket sport, hand and foot dribble while preventing an opponent from stealing the ball in basketball)

**Uses movement concepts and principles in the development of motor skills**
- Uses information from a variety of internal and external sources to improve performance (e.g., group projects, student journal, self-assessment, peer and coach review)
- Understands principles of practice and conditioning that improve performance
- Understands proper warm-up and cool-down techniques and reasons for using them
- Uses basic offensive and defensive strategies in unstructured game environments (e.g., limited rules, modified equipment, small numbers of participants)

**Understands the benefits and costs associated with participation in physical activity**
- Knows about opportunities for participation in physical activities both in and out of school (e.g., recreational leagues, intramural sports, clubs)
- Chooses physical activities based on a variety of factors (e.g., personal interests and capabilities, perceived social and physical benefits, challenge and enjoyment)
- Knows factors that inhibit physical activity (e.g., substance abuse)
- Knows how to modify activities to be more health-enhancing (e.g., walking instead of riding, taking the stairs rather than the elevator)
- Understands detrimental effects of physical activity (e.g., muscle soreness, overuse injuries, over-training, temporary tiredness, and discovering inability)
- Understands activities that provide personal challenge (e.g., risk-taking, adventure, and competitive activities)

**Understands how to monitor and maintain a health-enhancing level of physical fitness**
- Engages in activities that develop and maintain cardiorespiratory fitness (e.g., timed or distance walk/run and other endurance activities at specified heart rate)
- Engages in activities that develop and maintain muscular strength (e.g., push-ups, pull-ups, curl-ups, isometric strength activities, jump rope)
- Engages in activities that develop and maintain flexibility of the major joints (e.g., sit and reach, trunk twists, and arm-shoulder stretches)
- Knows the effects of physical activity and nutrition on body composition
- Knows how to monitor intensity of exercise (e.g., heart rate, breathing rate, perceived exertion, and recovery rate)
- Meets health-related fitness standards for appropriate level of a standardized physical fitness test (e.g., aerobic capacity, body composition, muscle strength, endurance, and flexibility)
- Knows the characteristics of a healthy lifestyle (e.g., daily health-enhancing physical activity, proper nutrition)
- Uses information from fitness assessments to improve selected fitness components (e.g., cardiorespiratory endurance, muscular strength and endurance, flexibility, and body composition)
- Participates in moderate to vigorous physical activity in a variety of settings (e.g., gymnastics clubs, community sponsored youth sports)

**Understands the social and personal responsibility associated with participation in physical activity**
- Knows how to develop rules, procedures, and etiquette that are safe and effective for specific activity situations
- Works in a group to accomplish a set goal in both cooperative and competitive activities
- Understands the role of physical activities in learning more about others of like and different backgrounds (e.g., gender, culture, ethnicity, disability)

*(continued)*

---TABLE 1.1---

# (continued)

- Understands the physical challenges faced by people with disabilities (e.g., wheelchair basketball, dancing with a hearing disability)
- Understands the origins of different sports and how they have evolved

## MIDDLE SCHOOL/JUNIOR HIGH: GRADES 7-8

**Uses a variety of basic and advanced movement forms**
- Uses intermediate sport-specific skills for individual, dual, and team sports
- Uses intermediate sport-specific skills for dance and rhythmical activities
- Uses intermediate sport-specific skills for outdoor activities

**Uses movement concepts and principles in the development of motor skills**
- Understands principles of training and conditioning for specific physical activities
- Understands the critical elements of advanced movement skills (e.g., such as a racing start in freestyle swimming)
- Uses basic offensive and defensive strategies in a modified version of a team and individual sport
- Understands movement forms associated with highly skilled physical activities (e.g., moves that lead to successful serves, passes, and spikes in an elite volleyball game)

**Understands the benefits and costs associated with participation in physical activity**
- Understands long-term physiological benefits of regular participation in physical activity (e.g., improved cardiovascular and muscular strength, improved flexibility and body composition)
- Understands long-term psychological benefits of regular participation in physical activity (e.g., healthy self-image, stress reduction, strong mental and emotional health)

**Understands how to monitor and maintain a health-enhancing level of physical fitness**
- Engages in more advanced activities that develop and maintain cardiorespiratory endurance (e.g., timed or distance walk/run and other endurance activities at specified heart rate/heart rate recovery)
- Engages in more advanced activities that develop and maintain muscular strength and endurance (e.g., calisthenics activities, resistance, and weight training)
- Engages in more advanced levels of activity that develop and maintain flexibility
- Understands the role of exercise and other factors in weight control and body composition
- Understands basic principles of training that improve physical fitness (e.g., threshold, overload, specificity, frequency, intensity, duration, and mode of exercise)
- Meets health-related fitness standards for appropriate level of a standardized physical fitness test (e.g., aerobic capacity, body composition, muscle strength, endurance, and flexibility)
- Knows how to interpret the results of physical fitness assessments and use the information to develop individual fitness goals
- Knows how to differentiate the body's response to physical activities of various exercise intensities (e.g., measurement of heart rate, resting heart rate, heart rate reserve; taking pulse at rest and during exercise)

**Understands the social and personal responsibility associated with participation in physical activity**
- Understands the importance of rules, procedures, and safe practice in physical activity settings
- Understands proper attitudes toward both winning and losing
- Knows the difference between inclusive (e.g., changing rules of activity to include less skilled players) and exclusionary (e.g., failing to pass ball to less skilled players) behaviors in physical activity settings
- Understands physical activity as a vehicle for self-expression (e.g., dance, gymnastics, and various sport activities)
- Understands the concept that physical activity (e.g., sport, games, dance) is a microcosm of modern culture and society

## HIGH SCHOOL: GRADES 9-12

**Uses a variety of basic and advanced movement forms**
- Uses advanced sport-specific skills in selected physical activities (e.g., aquatics, dance, outdoor pursuits, individual, dual, and team sports and activities)
- Uses skills in complex rather than modified versions of physical activities (e.g., more players or participants, rules and strategies)

(continued)

—————————————————————————TABLE 1.1—————————————————————————

## *(continued)*

**Uses movement concepts and principles in the development of motor skills**
- Understands the biomechanical concepts that govern different types of movement (e.g., gymnastics skills)
- Understands how sport psychology affects the performance of physical activities (e.g., the effect of anxiety on performance)
- Understands the physiological principles governing fitness maintenance and improvement (e.g., overload principle, law of specificity)
- Uses offensive and defensive strategies and appropriate rules for sports and other physical activities

**Understand the benefits and costs associated with participation in physical activity**
- Understands factors that impact the ability to participate in physical activity (e.g., type of activity, cost, available facilities, equipment required, personnel involved)
- Understands how various factors (e.g., age, gender, race, ethnicity, socioeconomic status, and culture) affect physical activity preferences and participation
- Understands the potentially dangerous consequences and outcomes from participation in physical activity (e.g., physical injury, potential conflicts with others)

**Understands how to monitor and maintain a health-enhancing level of physical fitness**
- Knows personal status of cardiorespiratory endurance
- Knows personal status of muscular strength and endurance of the arms, shoulders, abdomen, back, and legs
- Knows personal status of flexibility of the joints of the arms, legs, and trunk
- Knows personal status of body composition
- Meets health-related fitness standards for appropriate level of a physical fitness test (e.g., aerobic capacity, body composition, muscle strength, endurance, and flexibility)
- Knows how to monitor and adjust activity levels to meet personal fitness needs
- Understands how to maintain an active lifestyle throughout life (e.g., participate regularly in physical activities that reflect personal interests)
- Designs a personal fitness program that is based on the basic principles of training and encompasses all components of fitness (e.g., cardiovascular and respiratory efficiency, muscular strength and endurance, flexibility, and body composition)

**Understands the social and personal responsibility associated with participation in physical activity**
- Uses leadership and follower roles, when appropriate, in accomplishing group goals in physical activities
- Works with others in a sport activity to achieve a common goal (e.g., winning a team championship)
- Understands how participation in physical activity fosters awareness of diversity (e.g., cultural, ethnic, gender, physical)
- Includes persons of diverse backgrounds and abilities in physical activity
- Understands the history and purpose of international competitions (e.g., Olympics, Special Olympics, Pan American Games, World Cup Soccer)
- Understands the role of sport in a diverse world (e.g., the influence of professional sport in society, the usefulness of dance as an expression of multiculturalism, the affect of age and gender on sport participation patterns)
- Understands the concept of "sportsmanship" and the importance of responsible behavior while participating in physical activities

*Note.* Kendall, J.S., & Marzano, R.J. (1996). *Content Knowledge: A Compendium of Standards and Benchmarks for K-12 Education.* Aurora, CO: Mid-continent Regional Educational Laboratory. Reprinted with permission of McREL, 1997.

## Standards for Physical Education Teachers

Efforts to establish standards and policy that affect the quality of teachers in training (preservice) and continuing professional development (inservice) have been noteworthy. For beginning teacher licensing, performance standards were developed by the Interstate New Teacher Assess-ment and Support Consortium, a group of more than 30 state and professional organizations formed under the auspices of the Council of Chief State School Officers. The consortium's model standards present teachers as reflective, inquiry-oriented professionals who are cognizant of equity and diversity issues, competent in their subject matter, and able to select instructional strategies best suited to the varying needs of their students (Darling-Hammond, 1992). The designated headings for the 10 standards are (1) knowledge of subject matter, (2) knowledge of human development and learning, (3) adaptation of instruction for individual needs, (4) multiple instructional strategies, (5) classroom motivation and management skills, (6) communication skills, (7) instructional planning skills, (8) assessment of student learning, (9) professional commitment and responsibility, and (10) partnerships (Campbell, Cignetti, Melenyzer, Nettles, & Wyman, 1997).

The standards-based reform of teaching physical education is likewise significant. NASPE's beginning teacher standards task force produced a set of standards (Tannehill et al., 1995) that parallels the earlier INTASC framework. The following list of standards and descriptions for beginning teachers provides the answer to "What knowledge and skills are essential for effective teaching in physical education?" These standards will be used in chapter 2 to facilitate the organization of preservice professional portfolios.

## Standards for Beginning Physical Education Teachers*

*Standard 1:* **Content knowledge**

Understands physical education content, disciplinary concepts, and tools of inquiry related to the development of a physically educated person

*Standard 2:* **Growth and development**

Understands how individuals learn and develop and can provide opportunities that support their physical, cognitive, social, and emotional development

*Standard 3:* **Diverse learners**

Understands how individuals differ in their approaches to learning and creates appropriate instruction adapted to diverse learners

*Standard 4:* **Management and motivation**

Uses an understanding of individual and group motivation and behavior to create a learning environment that encourages positive social interaction, active engagement in learning, and self-motivation

*Standard 5:* **Communication**

Uses knowledge of effective verbal, nonverbal, and media communication techniques to foster inquiry, collaboration, and engagement in physical activity settings

*Standard 6:* **Planning and instruction**

Plans and implements a variety of developmentally appropriate instructional strategies to develop physically educated individuals

*Standard 7:* **Learner assessment**

Understands and uses formal and informal assessment strategies to foster physical, cognitive, social, and emotional development of learners in physical activity

*Standard 8:* **Reflection**

Is a reflective practitioner who evaluates the effects of his/her actions on others (e.g., learners, parents/guardians, and other professionals in the learning community) and seeks opportunities to grow professionally

*Standard 9:* **Collaboration**

Fosters relationships with colleagues, parents/guardians, and community agencies to support learners' growth and well-being

For experienced teachers, five core propositions were advanced by the National Board for Professional Teaching Standards (1994). Teachers who demonstrate the high level of knowledge, skills, dispositions, and commitments reflected in these principles go the heart of the National Board's perspective on accomplished teaching, regardless of subject field. The following list of core propositions for practicing teachers provides the answer to "What knowledge and skills are essential for effective teaching?" These propositions will be used in chapter 4 to facilitate the organization of inservice professional portfolios.

*Core Proposition 1:* Teachers are committed to students and their learning.

*Core Proposition 2:* Teachers know the subjects they teach and how to teach those subjects to students.

*Core Proposition 3:* Teachers are responsible for managing and monitoring student learning.

---

*Reprinted from *National Standards for Beginning Physical Education Teachers* (1995) with permission from the National Association for Sport and Physical Education (NASPE), 1900 Association Drive, Reston, VA 20191-1599.

*Core Proposition 4:* Teachers think systematically about their practice and learn from experience.

*Core Proposition 5:* Teachers are members of learning communities.

# AUTHENTIC ASSESSMENT TREND

One result of the educational reform movement is the focus on clearly developed, publicly stated standards that are linked to assessment. This redesign of learning and teaching has exposed, however, the dissatisfaction with traditional forms of assessment—multiple-choice tests, group-administered achievement tests, and standardized skill tests. These kinds of assessment make it nearly impossible to measure the broad range of skills and competencies represented by established standards.

Although society has been oriented toward standardized achievement tests, the readiness for change is apparent. Alternatives have centered on more naturalistic, performance-based approaches. They measure not only knowledge and skills but also other outcomes such as attitudes, motivation, social conduct, and values. Evaluation that scans this full spectrum of learning reflects the trend toward authentic assessment (Perrone, 1991). Actual exhibits and work samples of student performance serve as the measure of learning instead of the highly inferential estimates provided by the objective scoring and normative interpretation of tests.

Authentic assessment is usually thought to be the process of gathering evidence about students' levels of achievement. However, collecting authentic information about teachers' performance is just as valuable. Clearly, the concept applies to both students and teachers in which assessment is structured around real-life samples of learning and actual classroom performance, respectively. In physical education, use of multiple-choice, machine-scored tests or standardized sport skill or fitness tests do not seem to be good indicators of what students really learn. Likewise, multiple-choice tests of basic skills and general knowledge seem woefully inadequate to measure teaching skill. Thus, authentic techniques are needed to assess the degree to which established student and teacher standards are met, specific to physical education. That is the purpose of the following sections.

## Measuring Student Learning

An assessment is considered authentic if the student demonstrates the desired behavior in real-life situations rather than in artificial or contrived settings. Teachers want more practical, relevant assessment tools to measure what students really know and are able to do. With traditional testing, teachers may know that students are learning, but that is often not what is being measured, nor do the tests seem to facilitate learning. Instead, students respond to prompts or perform tasks that have no worthwhile, real-life, or authentic counterpart. Standardized measures of motor ability, fitness parameters, sport skills, knowledge, and psychosocial traits may be objective and reliable, but they may fail to measure authentic outcomes of interest to the teacher and students.

Probably the most difficult part of authentic assessment is determining an appropriate real-life context in which to conduct learning tasks. But that is the challenge of this new vision of assessment. An example might be helpful. One outcome of a physical fitness unit could be that students are able to develop a personalized program. Traditional assessment might involve written tests of understanding, summaries of articles about fitness programs, and an essay about a case study. These measures are not wrong, but there is a question of whether students are moving toward broader outcomes. In contrast, a group project could be structured to (1) evaluate the fitness needs of teachers and staff at the school, (2) design custom fitness programs for these individuals, (3) provide training on how to safely and effectively engage in fitness activities, and (4) monitor the individuals as they progress through their programs. The teacher serves as a facilitator. Students present oral synopses and reflections of their challenges and successes at each stage of the process. Feedback is given to students during the process so that learning takes place during the assessment (Rink et al., 1995).

Traditional testing also focuses too much on whether students get correct answers. When students take a multiple-choice test on offensive strategies in soccer, a teacher does not know which students select the correct answer because they truly understand the principle of switching, which students understand the principle but make a careless recording mistake, or which ones have no idea and guess correctly. Multiple-choice tests also lead to multiple-choice teaching—an

Authentic assessment of swim strokes is determined during a real, in-class swimming competition using a performance checklist.

emphasis on acquisition of facts and predetermined answers.

Using authentic assessment and allowing performance in naturalistic settings require students to actually demonstrate knowledge or skills. Students in math, for example, could show their understanding of interest rates by comparison shopping for a used car loan and identifying the best deal. The teacher would know whether a student really understands the concept of interest, can calculate it, and can perform mathematical operations accurately. To illustrate further, students could demonstrate their understanding of English grammar by editing a poorly written passage (Rudner & Boston, 1994). In physical education, performance in naturalistic game settings (e.g., volleyball bump pass when returning a "real" serve) could be assessed using an observation rating sheet instead of performance at a testing station (e.g., volleyball bump pass from a partner toss).

Authentic assessment provides other benefits over conventional, norm-based measures. It is nonstigmatizing, it enhances motivation, it assists teachers with decision making, and it is effective for reporting accomplishments and progress to

families. Traditional grades may be replaced with anecdotal records, performance samples, and student profiles. Despite new attempts to restructure report cards that emphasize performance, social skills, higher-order thinking, and other meaningful outcomes, traditional As, Bs, Cs, Ds, and Fs still dominate as the "weapon of choice." Teachers can pass judgment with the stroke of a pen or the "bubble" of a scantron computer sheet (Burke, 1994).

The various forms of authentic assessment seem to have common goals: to capitalize on the actual work of students, to enhance teacher and student involvement in evaluation, and to satisfy the accountability need prompted by school reform (Chittenden, 1991). Furthermore, these performance-based assessments can be longitudinal (across grade levels), multidimensional (physical, intellectual, social, emotional), and individually modifiable (wide range of student variability) (Meisels, Dichtelmiller, Dorfman, Jablon, & Marsden, 1993). This broadened view of assessment coincides with holistic approaches to teaching, including recommended practice in physical education. Regarding assessment, developmentally appropriate practice in physical education means that "teacher decisions are based primarily on ongoing individual assessment of children as they participate in physical education class activities (formative evaluation) and not on the basis of a single test score (summative evaluation)" (Graham et al., 1992, p. 7).

Although these approaches are intended to promote a better alignment of instruction and assessment, they entail new roles for teachers and students in the evaluation process (Chittenden, 1991; Melograno, 1997). However, in physical education, these roles may not be entirely new

because a performance-based approach is used for what is typically evaluated (e.g., motor abilities, sports skills, game strategies, fair play). A variety of techniques is available for conducting authentic assessment. Although a particular technique may not be entirely new, an authentic context is needed for its use in the whole teaching-learning process. It is not simply tacked on to the end of a learning segment. Therefore, selected options are described and illustrated in table 1.2. The examples show how authentic as-

---

TABLE 1.2

### Authentic Assessment for Physical Education

| OPTIONS | DESCRIPTIONS | EXAMPLES |
|---|---|---|
| **Peer review** | One student observes another student's performance, compares and contrasts performance against teacher's criteria (critical elements), draws conclusions, and communicates results (verbal, non-verbal, or written feedback). | Student "A" watches student "B" during a tennis game; using a criteria task sheet, five forehand strokes are observed; six "points to look for" are rated +, ✓, or — for each stroke. |
| **Log** | Performance of specific behaviors over a certain time period is recorded by individual students, small groups, or whole class to show changes, sequences, choices, feelings, progress, and/or participation. | Fitness calendar is maintained for three months showing aerobic and strength training workout schedule, weekly changes from baseline data, and status of target goals at midpoint and end point. |
| **Group project** | Several students work cooperatively to solve a problem, learn a skill, concept, or generalization, engage in shared discovery, or carry out a series of performance tasks in an atmosphere of interdependence and accountability. | In groups of 5 or 6, students design an obstacle course of straight, curved, and zigzag pathways using wands, ropes, and other manipulative objects; pathways must connect; students must decide what locomotor movements to use in traveling the various pathways. |
| **Individual project** | With the guidance of a teacher, a student pursues an area of interest and takes responsibility for completing the following tasks: building a scenario, determining goals, planning a program of participation to achieve outcomes, and implementing the plan to the completion of the goals. | With "discovering my roots" as the theme, student presents a game, dance, or other physical activity associated with his/her origins; project includes reading activities, interviews, written or art expressions, and demonstration of selected activities complete with costumes, equipment, and/or music. |
| **Role playing** | Students pretend they are a particular person in order to solve a problem or act out a real-world situation; allows students to re-create (simulate) or act out issues in interpersonal relations such as social events, personal concerns, values, problem behaviors, or social skills. | Students are given this scenario. You are at a basketball game where your best friend's sister plays for the opposing team. Another friend from your school makes disruptive noises when the other team shoots free throws, boos the officials, and makes derogatory remarks to the other team. What would you say to this friend? Create a dialogue. |
| **Reflection** | Students engage in the thoughtful examination of the learning process in order to plan, monitor, assess, and improve their own performance and their own thinking. | Small groups design and perform a movement sequence that uses matching and mirroring movements; students respond in writing to the questions: What was easy about working together? Difficult? What should be changed about working together? How was your performance affected? |

*(continued)*

-TABLE 1.2-

## *(continued)*

| OPTIONS | DESCRIPTIONS | EXAMPLES |
|---|---|---|
| **Self-evaluation** | Students make critical and valid assessments of their own abilities by rating their performance for comparison with individual target goals, peer standards, teacher-established criteria, or all of these. | Following a segment on throwing different objects (e.g., Frisbees, Nerf balls, deck tennis rings, footballs), students identify the number of different objects thrown, describe the types of throwing patterns used, and complete a self-check skill performance rating scale. |
| **Event task** | A performance task is written broadly enough (loosely structured) so that there are many solutions or possible answers, it captures the interest of students, and it replicates or simulates a real-world experience. | Students watch a tape of an athletic performance and discuss, in writing, the space awareness concepts athletes used during their performances. They answer these questions: What did the athletes do at a high, medium, or low level? What kinds of pathways did they use? Directions? What kind of space did they move in? Give examples of how athletes use these concepts. |
| **Observation** | Teacher uses different tools to record information about students' performance or behavior (live observation or video analysis), such as anecdotal notes, narrative descriptions, rating scales, checklist, frequency index scales, or scoring rubrics. | Students choreograph their own dance routine. Using a scoring rubric, the teacher watches the routine and rates the following criteria on a scale of 1 to 5: rhythm with music, creativity, fluidity, and diversity. Critical elements for each criterion are built into the rubric. |
| **Portfolio** | Students exhibit samples of their work or performance data in a collection of artifacts that show effort, progress, or achievement over a certain time period. | Second-graders are given a sheet that has a picture of a child with body parts labeled. Students color with crayon those body parts at a low level, medium level, and high level in red, blue, and yellow, respectively. The sheet is placed in the student's portfolio. |

*Note.* Information for this table was derived from the following sources: *National Standards for Physical Education: A Guide to Content and Assessment* (Rink et al., 1995), *Designing the Physical Education Curriculum* (Melograno, 1996), and *Teaching for Outcomes in Elementary Physical Education: A Guide for Curriculum and Assessment* (Hopple, 1995).

sessments serve as a measure of real student learning.

When information is gathered in reference to established student standards, and serves as a guide to teaching, it can enhance learning as well as measure it. Teachers have known that the time spent on assessment does not always yield the desired educational benefits. How often have we heard from a student, "That test didn't really show what I can do!" The inadequacy of standardized, group-based assessment begs for an alternative. Authentic assessment offers an approach that is context-responsive—real learning that is found in naturalistic settings.

## Documenting Effective Teaching

Traditional evaluation of teaching suffers much the same way as traditional testing of students.

For example, goals conferences with supervisors and/or principals, formal observations by peers, supervisors, and/or principals, or self-evaluation of goals do not seem to be good measures of a teacher's knowledge and skills. Like student testing, more naturalistic, performance-based approaches are needed that document real teaching effectiveness. Knowledge tests for an initial teaching license also lack an authentic quality. And, minimum passing scores are usually so low that there is no effective standard for entry (National Commission on Teaching & America's Future, 1996).

Authentic systems for assessing the skills of teachers in their own setting should be linked to established teacher standards. As discussed earlier, a distinction is made between beginning teachers (initial license) and experienced teachers (advanced certification). Nearly all the standards overlap in some manner. For example, the management standards may differ in degree, but beginning and experienced teachers are expected nonetheless to create a teaching environment conducive to learning. Also, both beginning and experienced teachers are expected to engage in reflection but are likely to draw on different sources to improve their practice.

For beginning teachers, the Educational Testing Service (ETS) developed assessments ranging from entry into teacher education to actual classroom teaching. *The Praxis Series: Professional Assessments for Beginning Teachers* (ETS, 1992) offers measures of academic skills, subject knowledge, and classroom performance. Of particular significance is *Praxis III: Classroom Performance Assessments—Orientation Guide* (ETS, 1995), a system for assessing the skills of beginning teachers in their own classroom settings. Its framework of knowledge and skills includes assessment criteria (standards), scoring rules, and the assessment process. *Praxis III* uses three assessment methods: (1) direct observation of a lesson or instructional event, (2) review of written documentation by the teacher that conveys a sense of the general classroom context and the students as well as information about the lesson, and (3) semistructured interviews before and after the observation to explore the teacher's decisions and practices.

Four interrelated domains comprise the framework of knowledge and skills: (1) organizing content knowledge for student learning, (2) creating an environment for student learning, (3) teaching for student learning, and (4) teacher professionalism. Criteria for each domain are used to assess teaching performance, and each criterion represents a critical aspect of teaching. The 19 criteria covering the domains are in table 1.3. The results of *Praxis III* are considered to yield an authentic assessment of teaching effectiveness.

For experienced teachers, the National Board for Professional Teaching Standards developed and operates a national, voluntary system to assess and certify teachers who meet its standards. The standards (NBPTS, 1994) presented earlier (pages 9-10) establish what accomplished teachers should know and be able to do. Like *Praxis III*, advanced certification by NBPTS requires the assessment of teachers' competencies in real classroom settings.

The two-part assessment process is authentic in nature. First, teachers complete a portfolio in their classroom composed of student work, videotapes, and other teaching artifacts. The student work samples and videos are supported by commentaries on the goals and purposes of instruction, the effectiveness of the practice, reflections on what occurred, and the rationale for professional judgments. Second, exercises conducted at an assessment center are designed to complement the portfolio and are organized around challenging teaching issues. Teachers are given an opportunity to demonstrate knowledge, skills, and abilities in situations across the age range and topics of the certificate field (NBPTS, 1996).

Formal involvement in the *Praxis III* and NBPTS teacher assessment systems may not be feasible for all teachers. However, the information presented in this chapter should be sufficient for determining teacher effectiveness based on practical and relevant measures. This information should motivate beginning and practicing physical education teachers to seek the best way to document their real knowledge and skills.

# ROLE OF PORTFOLIOS IN STANDARDS-BASED ASSESSMENT

Given the national focus on learning and teaching standards, it follows that attempts to assess students and teachers should correspond to any established standards. A strong case has been made that such assessments should be authentic in nature. Therefore, assessment systems are needed that merge standards and authentic qualities. The pendulum of alternative educational assessment has swung toward a portfolio format (Melograno, 1994). Although relatively new to education, portfolios have been used for a long time by commercial artists, journalists, architects, photographers, models, and other professionals to showcase achievement and skills.

In general, a portfolio is a purposeful, integrated collection of actual exhibits and work samples showing effort, progress, or achievement in one or more areas. It presents a broad, genuine picture of student learning or teacher performance and allows all concerned to have input (ongoing feedback). Portfolios are not made of anything and everything. Item selection is a key phase of the portfolio process.

The type of portfolio that a teacher uses depends on the needs that the portfolio serves. Portfolios feature artifacts collected over time, so they are well suited for demonstrating student growth

---

TABLE 1.3
## Teacher Performance Assessment Criteria

---

### DOMAIN A: ORGANIZING CONTENT KNOWLEDGE FOR STUDENT LEARNING

A1: Becoming familiar with relevant aspects of students' background knowledge and experiences

A2: Articulating clear learning goals for the lesson that are appropriate for the students

A3: Demonstrating an understanding of the connections between the content that was learned previously, the current content, and the content that remains to be learned in the future

A4: Creating or selecting teaching methods, learning activities, and instructional materials or other resources that are appropriate for the students and that are aligned with the goals of the lesson

A5: Creating or selecting evaluation strategies that are appropriate for the students and that are aligned with the goals of the lesson

---

### DOMAIN B: CREATING AN ENVIRONMENT FOR STUDENT LEARNING

B1: Creating a climate that promotes fairness

B2: Establishing and maintaining rapport with students

B3: Communicating challenging learning expectations to each student

B4: Establishing and maintaining consistent standards of classroom behavior

B5: Making the physical environment as safe and conducive to learning as possible

---

### DOMAIN C: TEACHING FOR STUDENT LEARNING

C1: Making learning goals and instructional procedures clear to students

C2: Making content comprehensive to students

C3: Encouraging students to extend their thinking

C4: Monitoring students' understanding of content through a variety of means, providing feedback to students to assist learning, and adjusting learning activities as the situation demands

C5: Using instructional time effectively

---

### DOMAIN D: TEACHER PROFESSIONALISM

D1: Reflecting on the extent to which the learning goals were met

D2: Demonstrating a sense of efficacy

D3: Building professional relationships with colleagues to share teaching insights and to coordinate learning activities for students

D4: Communicating with parents or guardians about student learning

---

*Note.* Educational Testing Service (1995). *Praxis III: Classroom Performance Assessments—Orientation Guide.* Princeton, NJ. Reprinted by permission of Educational Testing Service, the copyright owner.

and achievement of standards. For example, an array of artifacts could be used to indicate the extent to which students "understand how to monitor and maintain a health-enhancing level of physical fitness," such as exercise logs, nutrition journals, self-check rating scales, workout schedules, and charts showing the diagnosis and prescription of weight-training routines. Likewise, portfolios can be used by preservice and inservice teachers to document teaching effectiveness in reference to standards. Any number of products could reveal, for example, that teachers truly "recognize individual differences in their students and adjust their practices accordingly," such as lesson plans that outline multiple outcomes, individualized class materials, samples of student work, videotapes depicting alternative strategies, and written teacher behavior analyses and reflections.

## Student Portfolios

Portfolio assessment offers a dynamic, visual presentation of a student's abilities, strengths, and areas of needed improvement over time. Students must be involved in selecting and judging the quality of their own work, including self-reflection. With portfolios, traditional teaching roles may not work. Teachers need to facilitate, guide, and offer choices rather than inform, direct, and predetermine priorities. Partnerships are established among teacher, students, and parents.

Some teachers look at portfolios and say, "I have too many students and not enough time." However, portfolios demand a high level of student responsibility in self-management, self-assessment, and peer conferences and evaluation. If students are guided toward a system of portfolios, restrictions of time and too many students are minimized. Partners, small groups, and self-directed tasks can reduce the seemingly high student-teacher ratios. Obviously, the system needs to be well planned and organized.

As portfolio data are collected, progress should be reported at regular intervals to parents, administrators, and others. Information gathering should be based on multiple methods (e.g., observations, performance samples, test-like procedures). The following guidelines and strategies create the framework for a student portfolio system. In chapter 3, these aspects are developed in greater detail, specific to K-12 physical education programming.

**Purposes.** Some general purposes for creating portfolios are to keep track of students' progress, have students assess their own accomplishments, determine the extent to which standards have been achieved, and help parents understand their child's effort and progress. Purposes specific to physical education might be to help students practice a healthy lifestyle, determine personal growth in an adventure-outdoor program, and communicate students' strengths and areas of needed improvement in gross and fine motor skills.

**Organization and Management.** Strategies are needed for making decisions about construction (e.g., file folders inside an accordion file, pocket folders, hanging files, boxes), storage (e.g., milk crates, file cabinets, shelves, drawers, covered cereal boxes), who should have access to the portfolios (e.g., peers, parents, other teachers), and how the portfolios will be set up and reviewed to avoid a large accumulation of materials.

**Item Selection.** Usually, students' first items are "baseline" samples collected through preassessment. Selection criteria should reflect the purpose of the portfolios and possibly include "something that shows improvement," "something that was

Portfolio feedback can be obtained through conferences with a small group of peers.

hard to do," and/or the "best" or "most representative" skill. Item variety provides students with selection options, thus enabling them to establish standards by which their work can be evaluated. In addition to student decisions, some teacher and administrator selections may become part of the total portfolio picture, including preinstruction inventories, journals, task sheets, student reflections, self-assessment checklists, projects, logs, independent study contracts, rating scales, videotapes, peer reviews, teachers' anecdotal statements, parent observations and comments, skill tests, and written tests.

**Evaluation.** Portfolios should be evaluated relative to student standards. Conventional symbols (grades, scores) have been abandoned by some teachers in favor of ways that describe, analyze, discuss, annotate, and confer. Other aspects of evaluation include reflection on portfolios (self, peers, parents), conferences (individual, small group of peers, parents), and progress reports (rubrics, narrative statements, descriptive labels).

## Professional Portfolios

To demonstrate teaching competence, teachers need creative ways to present themselves to others. For prospective teachers, these people might include education professors, field supervisors, cooperating teachers, school principals, or state department of education personnel. For practicing teachers, these people might include teaching peers, department heads, subject matter supervisors, school principals, and parents. Regardless of whether teachers are beginners or have experience, they have a common goal of becoming effective professionals.

Most professionals want all their knowledge and experiences to count when they are evaluated. Excellent teachers are characteristically similar in that they seek ongoing professional training, remain current about educational research, read professional writings, attend workshops, ask questions of others, refine their practice, and try out new ideas, reflect on the results, and discard or adapt the ideas. However, the same teachers often have difficulty in demonstrating how these various experiences fit into their pattern of professional competency (Campbell et al., 1997).

The professional portfolio can be a convincing, empowering tool that brings sense to a wealth of experiences. It is not just a scrapbook of teaching memorabilia, but it is an authentic representation of teaching performance. The professional portfolio is an organized, standards-based, goal-driven documentation of one's professional growth and achieved competence in the complex act of teaching (Campbell et al., 1997). Although it is a collection of documents, the professional portfolio is tangible evidence of the wide range of knowledge, dispositions, and skills that one possesses as a growing professional. The strategies and guidelines that create the framework for a professional portfolio system follow. In chapters 2 and 4, these aspects are developed in greater detail for preservice and inservice physical education teachers, respectively.

**Type.** There are at least five kinds of professional portfolios. The introductory portfolio introduces the teacher as a person and as a future or present teaching professional. It serves as a catalyst for self-reflection and continual sharing of ideas and insights. The working portfolio is the ongoing systematic collection of professional exhibits that form the basis for self-assessment and goal setting. The presentation portfolio offers artifacts that best reflect one's achieved competence, individuality, and creativity as a professional physical educator. It is selective and streamlined. The employment portfolio focuses on artifacts to enhance job placement. The showcase portfolio includes a limited number of items to exhibit growth over time and to serve a particular professional purpose.

**Organization and Management.** Regardless of the type of portfolio, it should be organized around the set of standards being sought. Advanced organizers should be considered, depending on teaching status, that might serve as the primary goal of the portfolio, such as getting a job, contributing to the school's mission, creating a "symbol" of professional excellence, qualifying for merit, or achieving advanced certification. Storage options for working portfolios include a large file box, cardboard banker's boxes, several large notebooks divided into sections, or file drawers in a cabinet. For presentation portfolios, notebooks, expanding files, folders, or portfolio satchels are common. The teacher assumes responsibility for his or her own storage.

**Artifacts.** Where possible, exhibits should be selected representing more than one standard. Each section of the portfolio should be labeled with an abbreviated title for the standard. For each artifact, a brief rationale should be included (e.g., reflection cover sheet). The type and goal of the portfolio will determine required and optional artifacts, including case studies, computer programs, lesson plans, thematic units, professional development plans, journals, meetings and workshops log, peer critiques, projects, samples from student portfolios, student contracts, custom-made materials, and unit plans.

**Evaluation.** Portfolios should be evaluated relative to the established standards. Scoring rubrics are commonly used for assessing the whole portfolio for completeness, creativity, diversity of selections, reflectiveness, and accuracy. Critical elements of each teacher standard should serve as the criteria against which individual artifacts are judged.

# CLOSING STATEMENT

Content standards and benchmarks for what students should know and be able to do in grades kindergarten through 12 physical education programs were presented. The knowledge and skills essential for effective teaching in physical education were also identified in a standards-based format for beginning and practicing teachers. In addition, the process of authentic assessment was applied to students and teachers where assessment is centered on real-life work samples and actual classroom performance, respectively. These approaches focused on more naturalistic, performance-based situations. And, portfolios were justified as the method of authentic assessment to document that student standards and preservice and inservice teacher standards are being met.

# chapter 2

# Preservice Professional Portfolios

Prospective teachers need more authentic, broad-based ways to show their professional competence. A transcript of grades, a score on a written exam, and the number of hours spent in field experiences seem woefully inadequate as measures of teaching skill. So, what is the best way to document the achievement of professional education outcomes?

# INTRODUCTION

Teacher education programs face a challenge in this era of standards-based assessment. Competent graduates are confronted with a highly competitive job market, and they must convey to others the knowledge and skills acquired in something as complex as teaching. This chapter proposes a scheme—the preservice professional portfolio—that can integrate, interrelate, and communicate the knowledge and skills acquired in a teacher education program. First, to help determine the uses of portfolios, various purposes and types of preservice professional portfolios are outlined. Then, the standards for the beginning physical education teacher are recommended as the basis for organizing these portfolios. In addition, processes for implementing portfolio assessment are provided, as well as guidelines to assist preservice teachers in portfolio management and assembly. Required and optional artifacts are also suggested when selecting items for the different types of portfolios. Lastly, portfolio evaluation procedures that serve formative and summative purposes are described and illustrated. To synthesize this information, a sample preservice professional portfolio system is presented at the end of the chapter.

# DETERMINING USES OF PORTFOLIOS

Any successful program of study includes a systematic way to determine the progress of individual students and the effect of the program across the broad spectrum of student development. Before introducing portfolios into an evaluation system, primary and secondary purposes should be determined. Some hard questions need to be answered. Why involve preservice teachers in the ongoing process of gathering artifacts of their work throughout a semester, year, or entire teacher education program? How are the portfolios going to be used? What is the real purpose of this assessment tool? What are the potential uses, overuses, and abuses of portfolios for assessment purposes and beyond (Burke, Fogarty, & Belgrad, 1994)?

## Primary and Secondary Purposes

Imagine the difficulty in selecting items for a portfolio with no sense of what the portfolio is to represent. The professional portfolio is a flexible and powerful tool that can serve multiple purposes. The primary purpose of the portfolio developed by *preservice* teachers is to verify the wide range of knowledge, skills, and dispositions acquired through coursework, clinical and field experiences, community involvements, and student teaching. This primary reason is supported by several secondary purposes.

**Help Teachers Grow Professionally.** Preservice teachers can learn to assess their own progress as teachers. When they review and reflect on their accomplishments, they engage in a self-assessment process that fosters lifelong professional development. Strengths and weaknesses are revealed so that preservice teachers can monitor their own growth. They also learn that this cumulative process is just as valuable as the product (exhibits and work samples).

**Provide for Program Review.** Teacher education faculty can keep track of individual preservice teacher development and determine the overall success of the teacher training program. Feedback is needed about the goals and objectives of the teacher education program. Gathering various work samples in a sequential manner yields valuable information that serves as the basis for making curriculum improvement decisions.

**Satisfy Licensing or Certification Requirements.** Compelling evidence of teacher competence is becoming more necessary to meet licensing or certification requirements. Accountability for the range of abilities possessed by the preservice teacher includes the authentic, broad-based, and impartial assessments found in a professional portfolio.

**Enhance Employment Opportunities.** Employers require that prospective teachers be able to demonstrate teaching competence in concrete ways. The information derived from actual exhibits and work samples can be used during the job interview process in which reviews by superintendents, supervisors, principals, department heads, teachers, and even school board members are likely.

## Types of Portfolios

Once the primary and secondary purposes for implementing a preservice professional portfolio system are determined, then consideration should be given to what type of portfolios can best achieve these purposes. The following types can be used in any combination to fulfill the purposes of the portfolio. They will be covered again in subsequent sections of this chapter that deal with portfolio management and assembly, selection of items, and evaluation.

**Introductory Portfolio.** This type of personal portfolio introduces the individual as a person and as a future teaching professional in physical education. It serves as a catalyst for self-reflection and continual sharing of ideas and insights throughout the teacher education program.

**Working Portfolio.** This ongoing systematic collection of selected work samples is compiled from courses and evidence (exhibits) of school/community activities. The working portfolio is the framework for self-assessment and goal setting. It provides a basis for formative evaluation throughout the teacher education program at planned intervals.

**Presentation Portfolio.** This includes samples of work that best reflect one's competence, individuality, and creativity as a professional physical educator. The presentation portfolio should be selective and streamlined. It is used during the teacher education program to satisfy different purposes (e.g., field course requirement, clinical experiences, poster-like session) and audiences (e.g., faculty, cooperating teachers, peers). In addition, it provides for formative evaluation depending on how it is used and when.

**Employment Portfolio.** This type of portfolio provides a rich overview of the personality and abilities of the preservice physical education teacher. It focuses on selected artifacts to enhance job placement, and it may be customized to a particular school. The employment portfolio offers a basis for summative evaluation.

# ORGANIZATION AROUND STANDARDS

Regardless of purpose or type, professional portfolios need an organizational scheme that is clear and meaningful. Portfolios could be organized around goals, competencies, or outcome statements available through professional societies, state departments of education, and college teacher education programs. For example, the INTASC standards (pages 8-9), developed by a consortium of state and professional organizations, and the standards of the National Board for Professional Teaching Standards (pages 9-10) are generally applicable for teachers of all disciplines and all levels. They could serve as the basis for organizing the professional portfolio.

The teacher education curriculum models being developed for accreditation purposes are also useful. Preservice professional portfolios could be organized logically around the set of themes, goals, and/or competencies normally contained in these models. To illustrate, the teacher education program at Wichita State University was designed to produce beginning teachers who can demonstrate certain knowledge and skills within the theme, "The teacher is a professional, nurturing instructor/manager, who is both knowledgeable of the discipline(s) and sensitive to the needs of the learner." Specific goal statements were identified as targets for the professional, instructor, and manager roles that teachers are expected to demonstrate (Wichita State University College of Education, 1995). These goals were used for organizing the professional portfolio.

The art and science of teaching is complex and cannot be easily reduced to a universal set of behavioral categories. Yet the goals, competencies, or outcome statements established by professional organizations attempt to do the same thing—determine the knowledge, skills, and dispositions that define excellent teachers. Dispositions refer to one's fundamental attitudes, beliefs, and assumptions about teaching and learning. Charting and demonstrating professional competence through a portfolio requires some system of organization. Therefore, everything collected for preservice professional portfolios—except possibly the introductory portfolio—should be organized around whatever standards are chosen. Because of their widespread acceptance, the standards of the NASPE's *National Standards for Beginning Physical Education Teachers* (Tannehill et al., 1995) are recommended for organizing the preservice professional portfolio.

The beginning physical education teacher standards were identified and described (page 9). The artifacts selected should provide tangible evidence that each standard has been met. They should document the knowledge that has been gained, skills that have been mastered, and dispositions that are characteristic of the preservice teacher. Although artifacts cannot conclusively prove the attainment of knowledge, skills, and dispositions, they can include achieved competence (Campbell et al., 1997). The knowledge, skills, and dispositions that support each standard are outlined in table 2.1. They will be used

—————TABLE 2.1—————

# Knowledge, Skills, and Dispositions for Teaching Standards

## STANDARD 1: CONTENT KNOWLEDGE

The teacher understands physical education content, disciplinary concepts, and tools of inquiry related to the development of a physically educated person.

**Knowledge**
- Critical elements and sequencing of basic motor skills
- Concepts and strategies related to physical activity and fitness and how to incorporate into other subject areas
- The relationship among physical activity, fitness, and health
- Historical, philosophical, sociological, and psychological factors associated with diverse physical activities
- The organic, skeletal, and neuromuscular structures of the human body, how these systems adapt to physical activity, and how they contribute to motor performance, fitness, and wellness
- Concepts, assumptions, debates, and processes of inquiry central to the study of physical activity
- Appropriate instructional cues, and prompts for basic motor skills and physical activity

**Skills**
- Demonstrates basic motor skills and physical activities with competence
- Applies disciplinary concepts and principles to skillful movement and physical activity
- Incorporates interdisciplinary learning experiences that allow learners to integrate knowledge, skills, and methods of inquiry from multiple subject areas
- Supports and encourages learner expression through movement

**Dispositions**
- Believes physical activity and fitness are important to the health and well-being of individuals
- Has enthusiasm for the importance of physical education as a means of developing a physically educated person
- Seeks to keep abreast of new ideas and understandings in disciplines related to physical education and education
- Believes that physical activity can foster self expression, development, and learning

## STANDARD 2: GROWTH AND DEVELOPMENT

The teacher understands how individuals learn and develop and can provide opportunities that support their physical, cognitive, social, and emotional development.

**Knowledge**
- How learning and development occur—how learners grow and develop, become physically fit, construct knowledge, and acquire skills
- Physical, cognitive, social, and emotional development and their influence on learning and how to address these factors when making instructional decisions
- Expected developmental progressions and ranges of individual variation and can identify levels of readiness
- The value of practice opportunities for growth and development

**Skills**
- Assess individual and group performance in order to design safe instruction that meets learner developmental needs in the physical, cognitive, social, and emotional domains
- Stimulates learner reflection on prior knowledge, experiences, and skills and encourages them to assume responsibility for their own learning

**Dispositions**
- Appreciates and promotes physical activity in the overall growth and development of learners
- Appreciates individual variations in growth and development and is committed to helping learners become competent and self-confident

## STANDARD 3: DIVERSE LEARNERS

The teacher understands how individuals differ in their approaches to learning and creates appropriate instruction adapted to diverse learners.

**Knowledge**
- Differences in approaches to learning and physical performance (e.g., different learning styles, multiple intelligences, and performance modes) and can design instruction that uses learners' strengths as the basis for growth

(continued)

TABLE 2.1
*(continued)*

- Areas of special need including physical and emotional challenges, learning disabilities, sensory difficulties, and language barriers (e.g., English as a second language)
- How learning is influenced by individual experiences, talents, and prior learning, as well as culture, family, and community values

**Skills**

- Selects and implements developmentally appropriate instruction that is sensitive to the multiple needs, learning styles, and experiences of learners
- Uses appropriate strategies, services, and resources to meet special and diverse learning needs
- Creates a learning environment that respects and incorporates learners' personal, family, cultural, and community experiences

**Dispositions**

- Believes that all learners can develop motor skills, feel successful, and enjoy physical activity
- Appreciates and values human diversity and shows respect for varied talents and perspectives
- Is committed to helping learners become physically educated in personally meaningful ways
- Seeks to understand and is sensitive to learners' families, communities, cultural values, and experiences as they relate to physical activity

### STANDARD 4: MANAGEMENT AND MOTIVATION

The teacher uses an understanding of individual and group motivation and behavior to create a safe learning environment that encourages positive social interaction, active engagement in learning, and self-motivation.

**Knowledge**

- Developmentally appropriate practices to motivate learners to participate in physical activity
- Strategies to teach learners to use behavior change techniques
- Strategies to help learners demonstrate responsible personal and social behavior that promotes positive relationships and a productive environment in physical activity settings
- The principles of effective management and a variety of strategies to promote equitable and meaningful learning in physical activity settings
- Factors related to intrinsic motivation and strategies to help learners become self-motivated

**Skills**

- Uses a variety of developmentally appropriate practices to motivate learners to participate in physical activity inside and outside of the school
- Uses strategies to promote mutual respect, support, safety, and cooperative participation
- Uses managerial and instructional routines that create smoothly functioning learning experiences
- Organizes, allocates, and manages resources (e.g., time, space, equipment, activities, and teacher attention) to provide active and equitable learning experiences

**Dispositions**

- Accepts responsibility for establishing a positive climate in the physical education setting and school environment
- Believes that providing opportunities for learners' input into instructional decisions increases their commitment to learning
- Recognizes the importance of positive peer relationships in establishing a climate for learning
- Recognizes the value of intrinsic motivation to lifelong participation in physical activity
- Is committed to using appropriate motivational strategies to meet the needs of individuals

### STANDARD 5: COMMUNICATION

The teacher uses knowledge of effective verbal, nonverbal, and media communication techniques to foster inquiry, collaboration, and engagement in physical activity settings.

**Knowledge**

- Communication techniques
- Appropriate verbal and nonverbal cues and when to use them in the teaching of physical activity
- How ethnic, cultural, economic, ability, gender, and environmental differences affect communication
- How to use computers and other technologies to communicate and network
- Strategies for building a community of learners within a physical activity setting

*(continued)*

---TABLE 2.1---

### *(continued)*

- Strategies for communicating with school colleagues, parents, and the community (e.g., PTA, advisory committees, and conferences)

**Skills**

- Communicates in ways that demonstrate sensitivity to ethnic, cultural, economic, ability, gender, and environmental differences
- Communicates managerial and instructional information in a variety of ways (e.g., bulletin boards, music, task cards, posters, and video)
- Communicates with school colleagues, parents/guardians, and the community through open houses, faculty meetings, newsletters, and conferences
- Models communication strategies (e.g., restating ideas and making connections, active listening, sensitivity to the effects of messages and the nonverbal cues given and received)

**Disposition**

- Recognizes the importance of communication skills and being informed of technological advances
- Appreciates the cultural dimensions of communication and seeks to foster sensitive interactions with and among learners
- Is committed to communicating with school colleagues, parents/guardians, and the community
- Is committed to serving as a role model

### STANDARD 6: PLANNING AND INSTRUCTION

The teacher plans and implements a variety of developmentally appropriate instructional strategies to develop physically educated individuals.

**Knowledge**

- Learning theory and current curricular models
- Contextual issues to consider when planning instruction (e.g., instructional materials, individual interests, needs and aptitudes, and community resources)
- How to design instructional sequences and learning experiences that maximize learner participation and success
- The uses of a variety of equipment, materials, human, and technological resources (e.g., computers, audiovisual technologies, videotapes and disks, local experts, and print resources) to enhance learning in a safe environment
- Principles, techniques, advantages, and limitations of various instructional strategies (e.g., cooperative learning, direct instruction, discovery learning, independent study, and interdisciplinary instruction)
- Safety issues to consider when planning and implementing instruction (e.g., environmental checks for equipment, field, and movement space; contraindicated exercises and body positions; basic first aid and CPR)

**Skills**

- Can identify program goals
- Selects instructional strategies based on developmental levels, learning styles, program goals, and safety issues
- Applies disciplinary and pedagogical knowledge in developing safe learning experiences
- Selects teaching resources and curriculum materials for their comprehensiveness, accuracy, usefulness, and safety
- Uses curricula that encourage learners to see, question, and interpret physical activity from diverse perspectives
- Designs and implements learning experiences that are safe, appropriate, realistic, and relevant based on principles of effective instruction (e.g., that activate learners' prior knowledge, anticipate preconceptions, encourage exploration and problem solving, and build on skills and experiences)
- Uses demonstrations and explanations to capture key components and link them to learners' experiences in physical activity
- Helps learners incorporate problem-solving and critical-thinking strategies in the process of becoming a physically educated person
- Chooses varied roles in the instructional process based on the content, purpose of instruction, and the needs of learners (e.g., model, assessor, monitor, facilitator)
- Creates short- and long-term plans that are linked to learner needs and performance, and adapts plans to ensure learner progress, motivation, and safety
- Models instructional strategies that facilitate learning in physical activity settings (e.g., manages, informs, checks for learner understanding, draws connections, uses visual, aural, and kinesthetic cues, and is sensitive to learner responses)

*(continued)*

—TABLE 2.1—
# *(continued)*

- Asks questions and poses scenarios to stimulate interactive learning opportunities (e.g., helps students articulate ideas/thinking, promotes risk taking/problem solving, facilitates factual recall, encourages convergent/divergent thinking, stimulates curiosity)

**Dispositions**
- Values short- and long-term planning to reach curricular goals
- Values the use of multiple instructional strategies to develop competence, cooperation, and higher order learning in physical activity settings
- Believes that plans must be open to revision based on student needs and changing circumstances
- Is committed to using learner strengths as a basis for planning instruction
- Is committed to continual learning about pedagogical content knowledge and its impact on learning
- Believes that the safety of students is the first priority in any movement setting

## STANDARD 7: LEARNER ASSESSMENT

The teacher understands and uses formal and informal assessment strategies to foster physical, cognitive, social, and emotional development of learners in physical activity.

**Knowledge**
- Characteristics, uses, advantages, and limitations of different types of assessment (e.g., criterion and norm-referenced, formative and summative, motor performance and physical fitness, portfolio and authentic assessments)
- How to select and use developmentally appropriate assessment strategies and instruments congruent with physical activity learning goals
- Measurement issues, such as validity, reliability, and bias
- The use of assessment as an integral part of instruction to provide feedback to learners
- How to use and interpret learner performance data to inform instructional decisions and report progress

**Skills**
- Uses a variety of formal and informal assessment techniques to assess learner progress (e.g., criterion and norm-referenced, formative and summative, motor performance and physical fitness, portfolio and authentic assessments)
- Uses assessment strategies to involve learners in self-assessment
- Maintains records of learner performance and can communicate learner progress based on appropriate indicators

**Dispositions**
- Values ongoing assessment to identify learner needs and ability
- Recognizes that a variety of assessment strategies are necessary

## STANDARD 8: REFLECTION

The teacher is a reflective practitioner who evaluates the effects of his/her actions on others (e.g., learners, parents/guardians, and other professionals in the learning community) and seeks opportunities to grow professionally.

**Knowledge**
- A variety of self-assessment and problem-solving strategies for reflecting on practice and its influences on learning
- Literature on teaching physical education and resources available for professional development (e.g., journals, associations, and development activities)

**Skills**
- Reflects upon and revises practice based on observation of learners
- Consults professional literature, colleagues, and other resources to develop as a learner and a teacher
- Participates in the professional physical education community and within the broader educational field
- Reflects on the appropriateness of program design on the development of physically educated individuals

**Dispositions**
- Is committed to ongoing self-reflection, assessment, and learning
- Values critical thinking and self-directed learning
- Is committed to seeking, developing, and refining practices to address individual needs of learners
- Recognizes responsibility for engaging in and supporting appropriate professional practices

*(continued)*

————————————————————TABLE 2.1————————————————————
## *(continued)*

| STANDARD 9: COLLABORATION |
|---|

The teacher fosters relationships with colleagues, parent/guardians, and community agencies to support learners' growth and well-being.

**Knowledge**

- How schools and organizations function within the larger community context relative to physical education
- The influence of nonschool factors on learning and engagement in physical activity (e.g., family circumstances, community settings, health and economic conditions)
- Laws related to learner rights and teacher responsibilities (e.g., equity, inclusion, confidentiality, privacy, and child abuse)
- Issues related to the functions of schools (e.g., school culture, inclusion, school-based management)

**Skills**

- Acts as an advocate in the school and community to promote a variety of physical activity opportunities
- Consults with counselors and other professionals in community agencies
- Identifies and uses community resources to enhance physical activity opportunities
- Establishes productive partnerships with parents/guardians to support learner growth and well-being
- Is sensitive and responsive to signs of distress and seeks help as needed and appropriate
- Participates in collegial activities to make the school a productive learning environment

**Dispositions**

- Values collaborating with teachers of other subject matter areas
- Is willing to consult with others regarding the total well-being and education of learners
- Respects learners' privacy and the confidentiality of information
- Is willing to work with others to improve the overall working environment

Reprinted from *National Standards for Beginning Physical Education Teachers* (1995) with permission from the National Association for Sport and Physical Education (NASPE), 1900 Association Drive, Reston, VA 20191-1599.

in subsequent sections of this chapter that deal with portfolio management and assembly, selection of items, and evaluation.

# PROCESSES FOR IMPLEMENTATION

The preservice professional portfolio should be a cumulative record of professional growth and achieved competence. It is the thread running throughout the entire teacher education program. Therefore, a systematic process is needed to collect, select, and evaluate appropriate portfolio entries. Various checkpoints and periodic reviews are possible to (1) determine whether expectations have been approximated or achieved at key intervals, (2) decide whether preservice teachers can continue, and (3) plan future directions within the remaining program elements. The system should also include some way to introduce the portfolio assessment model and a means for bringing closure to the process.

The preservice portfolio model will vary from one institution to another depending on philoso-

phy, program structure, faculty commitment, advising procedures, and preservice teachers' attitudes. The processes for implementation are usually based on some combination of advisers, courses, committees, and program phases. Whether the portfolio model involves advisers, courses, committees, and/or program phases, other common aspects of assessment should be built into the process (i.e., training, presentations, reflection, self-assessment, conferences).

## Adviser Directed

Preservice teachers are normally assigned an academic adviser who could also serve as portfolio adviser. Advisers would guide their advisees through the various stages of portfolio development. When the adviser is assigned, portfolio guidelines (e.g., handbook) could be given to the preservice teacher at that time. To begin the process, the preservice teacher might be required to submit an introductory portfolio at an early advising session. During the teacher education program, the adviser might be expected to (1) confer about the portfolio system, (2) discuss criteria for earning satisfactory ratings, (3) help select portfolio entries, and (4) evaluate portfolios at predetermined checkpoints, including the employment portfolio.

## Course Affiliated

Development of the various types of professional portfolios (i.e., introductory, working, presentation, employment) could be linked with selected key courses in the teacher education program. Factors to consider are the nature of the course, timing of the course in the program, and instructor. Stages of the preservice professional portfolio become part of the individual courses and are graded by the instructor as part of course requirements. For example, a sophomore level course such as "Introduction to Physical Education, Fitness, and Sport" could include distribution of and orientation to the entire portfolio model (e.g., handbook). Preservice teachers could develop and present their introductory portfolios. Other late sophomore, junior, and early senior year courses could be affiliated with the cumulative development of the working and presentation portfolios. Finally, the employment (exit) portfolio could be required as part of a course that is completed along with student teaching such as "Gateway to the Profession" or "Senior Seminar."

## Committee Oversight

A group of faculty, school personnel, and/or preservice teachers could assume ultimate responsibility for overseeing the portfolio system. Upon application to the teacher education program, preservice teachers could receive portfolio guidelines (e.g., handbook). As part of the screening process, preservice teachers might be required to submit an introductory portfolio. One criterion for admittance could be satisfactory review by a portfolio committee of one's introductory portfolio. Periodic feedback would also be provided by the committee throughout the teacher education program, including the employment portfolio.

## Program Phases

Teacher education programs are often structured around various kinds of segments, such as (1) blocks (e.g., preprofessional, I, II, III), (2) course groupings (e.g., professional core, forms of movement, major field theory/content, planned electives), (3) practical experiences (e.g., clinical/field,

practicum/internship, student teaching), or (4) knowledge bases (e.g., organizing content knowledge, creating a learning environment, teaching for learning, professionalism). The collection, selection, reflection, presentation, and evaluation of portfolio documents could be associated with any of these program segments. However, it would still be necessary to decide whether an adviser, course instructor, and/or committee would direct the portfolio development within each program segment.

## Training

Those directing the portfolio process (i.e., advisers, course instructors, and/or committee members) *and* preservice teachers should receive formal portfolio training. Preservice teachers could be trained at the time the portfolio system is introduced (e.g., required general advising session, selected introductory course). Training should include a set of guidelines, illustrative artifacts, and sample portfolios. In addition, the basic skills of self-management, reflection, self-assessment, peer review, and conferences should be developed during the training. For persons directing the portfolio process, comprehensive training could be conducted for those who are new to the system, and a training update could be held for those who are experienced.

## Presentations

Preservice teachers should be afforded several opportunities to present their portfolios to different kinds of audiences, in a variety of forums, and at key stages of the teacher education program. For example, the different types of portfolios could be presented orally in a one-on-one situation with an adviser, instructor, or peer, to a small group of peers, or to an entire class. They could also be presented in a poster-like session at which faculty and peer feedback is provided. Toward the end of the teacher education program, the portfolio could be presented in a job interview simulation that is conducted by a role-playing team of employers.

## Reflection

At a minimum, preservice teachers should thoughtfully examine each artifact selected for the working, presentation, and employment portfolios. Each piece should be labeled to reveal its meaning and value to the entire portfolio with reference to the teacher standards. By reflecting

The presentation portfolio can be displayed in a poster-like session.

on why an artifact is included, preservice teachers get to know why an artifact was chosen for a particular standard. The artifact should not be summarized. Instead, the preservice teacher should try to answer certain questions: What is the artifact? Why is it filed under this standard? What does it say about my growing competence? A sample reflection cover sheet appears in figure 2.1. Other kinds of reflections will be described in the subsequent section of this chapter that deals with the selection of items.

## Self-Assessment

In contrast to piece-by-piece reflection, preservice teachers need to review the entire collection of artifacts with reference to their short- and long-term goals and how the portfolio adheres to the teacher standards. This phase can be an informal self-check to make sure they are on the right track and to determine what changes might be needed. Preservice teachers should look for "holes"—standards that are not well documented by artifacts. The standards should be kept in mind as the teacher completes courses or professional activities. Consideration should be given to how an assignment, an article critique, a personal journal, or any number of school or community activities could help a standard that

needs work. The preservice teacher should look for ways to document a "missing" standard. The artifacts self-assessment checklist shown in figure 2.2 can help preservice teachers identify standards that are well documented ("Good"), standards that are satisfactorily evidenced ("OK"), and standards for which goals and artifacts are needed along with a target completion date ("Artifacts needed"). Other forms of self-assessment will be covered in the subsequent section of this chapter that deals with selection of items.

## Conferences

A natural progression in the portfolio process is to share the finished product with others. A portfolio conference offers a chance to "connect" with others using the portfolio as the basis for discussion. While presentations were described as portfolio exhibitions, conferences provide a chance for meaningful dialogue with other preservice teachers, advisers, instructors, and/or school personnel. In planning for conferences, the following questions should be answered: What will the goals be? What reflections do preservice teachers need to engage in? What questions should be prepared for the conference? When will it be held? At the conference, some basic ques-

**Reflection Cover Sheet**

Name: _____ Date: _____

Standard #: _____ Title: _____

Name of Artifact: _____

Course/Activity: _____

Rationale Statement: _____

_____

_____

_____

_____

_____

_____

_____

_____

_____

_____

**Figure 2.1** Format for reflecting on individual pieces selected for the preservice professional portfolio.

tions include, What have you learned about yourself by putting together your portfolio? What artifacts are you particularly proud of and why? If you could publish one thing in your portfolio, what would it be and why? What areas of your teaching performance need further improvement? How do you feel about your role as a professional teacher?

# MANAGEMENT AND ASSEMBLY

Ultimately, the preservice teacher assumes responsibility for organizing, maintaining, and storing the professional portfolio throughout the assessment process. Decisions about method of construction, how and where to store portfolios, and how often to "manage" portfolios depend on the type of portfolio. Clearly, preservice teachers need a plan to handle the logistics of the portfolio process. Although there are many ways to manage and assemble portfolios, several specific storage options and organizational techniques can help in developing the plan.

## Storage Options

Because preservice teachers are responsible for storing their own portfolios, the "container" for collecting artifacts is a matter of personal preference. Possibilities include notebooks, expanding and accordion files, large file boxes, folders, satchels, pockets for electronic documents, large notebooks divided into sections, and file drawers in a cabinet. The type of portfolio will likely determine the most practical way to store portfolio items. For example, the introductory portfolio is a scaled-down version of a complete portfolio. The number of artifacts is relatively small, so an accordion file or cardboard box is all that may be needed. By contrast, the working portfolio requires space considerations because the number of artifacts is high.

The presentation portfolio should not be cumbersome or unwieldy. Sample pages from a large project might replace the entire project. A large notebook or accordion file is all that may be needed. Finally, the employment portfolio should be a succinct representation of one's teaching competence. A limited number of carefully

## Artifacts Self-Assessment Checklist

Name: _____ Date: _____

| Standard | Good | OK | Artifacts Needed |
|---|---|---|---|
| #1. Content knowledge | | | Goal:<br><br>Target Date: |
| #2. Growth and development | | | Goal:<br><br>Target Date: |
| #3. Diverse learners | | | Goal:<br>Target Date: |
| #4. Management and motivation | | | Goal:<br>Target Date: |
| #5. Communication | | | Goal:<br>Target Date: |
| #6. Planning and instruction | | | Goal:<br>Target Date: |
| #7. Learner assessment | | | Goal:<br>Target Date: |
| #8. Reflection | | | Goal:<br>Target Date: |
| #9. Collaboration | | | Goal:<br>Target Date: |

**Figure 2.2** The artifacts self-assessment checklist can be used by preservice teachers to determine overall status of the portfolio.

selected items should be included in a "professional" container, such as a portfolio satchel. Easy access for employers should be built in.

## Organizational Techniques

Preservice teachers may be good at collecting work samples and exhibits, but they may not be able to organize all the materials. Several organizational tools have proved to be effective. Although many of these ideas may seem like common sense, not everyone is good at managing loose ends, particularly something as comprehensive as a portfolio system. These people should benefit from some of these simple organizational suggestions.

- Dividers—Whatever kind of container is used, divided notebook folders or divider pages can be used to separate artifacts according to the teaching standards or by any other category that makes sense (e.g., courses, program phases, incomplete works, finished works). A filing system should be created so that the standards are easily identified. Each section could be labeled with a shortened version of the standard.

- Color codes—To facilitate easier management, colored dots or colored files could be used to code entries in the portfolio. Artifacts could also be coded using different color markers. A code for the colors needs to be included.

- Artifact registry—Using a sheet for each standard, preservice teachers could record the date, item, and reason for either adding or removing an item. Because the registry is supposed to chronicle when and why items are removed and/or replaced, preservice teachers engage in a dynamic form of reflection.

- Work log—For a long-term project like a portfolio, a biography of work could show the evolution of the portfolio. This would help in making necessary changes or shifting directions. The log could be as simple as a dated entry that traces all activities and decisions associated with the portfolio.

- Index—An alphabetical index of items could be compiled as the portfolio evolves. Such an organizational tool would help in the cross-referencing of artifacts that represent more than one standard and vice versa.

The index could be placed in the front of the portfolio like a table of contents.

- Post-it™ Notes—Artifacts need to be cataloged so that ideas are not lost over time. A Post-it™ Note or index card could be attached to each artifact to identify the standard and could include a brief statement explaining why the artifact was collected. Specific descriptors from the standard statement may help later in connecting the artifact to the standard. Using a Post-it™ Note or index card protects original works.

## Type of Portfolio

In the same manner that the various types of portfolios may be stored differently, each type of portfolio may be managed differently. With the introductory portfolio, preservice teachers should introduce themselves to the profession as revealed by personal characteristics and professional goals. These aspects serve as the basis for managing the portfolio. Artifacts could be assembled that are keyed to the following topics: (1) relationships with family, friends, and professionals, (2) personal interests or hobbies, (3) teaching and professional experiences, and (4) reasons for wanting to be a physical education teacher.

Although the other types of portfolios—working, presentation, and employment—should be organized around the teaching standards, they are managed and assembled quite differently. Even the required and optional artifacts for each type of portfolio will vary, as shown in the next chapter section on item selection. For the working portfolio, anything should be collected that relates to a standard, even if not required or eventually selected as an optional piece. Preservice teachers should continually look for ways to document standards, particularly those that may need improvement.

For the presentation portfolio, less is more. Artifacts could represent more than one standard. Artifacts should be selected from both those that were required for the working portfolio and those that were optional. Each section should be labeled with an abbreviated title for the standard so that someone viewing the portfolio will know what it means. A rationale for choosing the artifact should be included. The reflection cover sheet suggested previously in figure 2.1 could be used for this purpose.

The employment portfolio may be the first impression an employer has of the preservice teacher. Spelling, grammar, and neatness should be carefully checked. Because employers do not have a great deal of time to peruse portfolios, the overall presentation should be consistent and artifacts should be easy to follow. In addition to the teaching standards, artifacts should exemplify the kind of position being sought (e.g., elementary school, high school).

# SELECTION OF ITEMS

The selection of portfolio items is the next consideration for the preservice professional portfolio. The actual selection strategy is closely linked to any established criteria (i.e., teacher standards) and the type of portfolio (i.e., introductory, working, presentation, employment). It also depends on the processes being used (i.e., advisers, courses, committees, program phases). As artifacts are created and selected, confidentiality should be maintained. Names or other identifying information should be avoided when referring to students or teachers.

Selecting portfolio items involves decision making associated with several key questions: **What** items should be included? **How** will items be selected? **Who** will select items? **When** will items be selected? The primary focus of this chapter section is to outline the range of possibilities for what items could be included. This section also describes the basic processes of reflection and self-assessment, offers suggestions for required and optional artifacts, and provides a design for analyzing artifacts. How items are selected relates directly to whether or not they demonstrate a preservice teacher's ability to meet the beginning teacher standards. Any combination of preservice teacher, adviser, course instructor, committee member, and school personnel may be involved in selecting items. When items are selected depends on where the types of portfolios are integrated throughout the teacher education program.

## Basic Processes

Most required and optional artifacts will be derived from courses, clinical and field experiences, and school and community activities. Before looking at these kinds of artifacts, commonly referred to as work samples or exhibits, two processes are reviewed that can yield other kinds of artifacts—reflection and self-assessment. The information introduced previously (pages 27-28) is expanded here because of the value of developing reflection and self-assessment artifacts for the professional portfolio. Emphasis has been placed on the *process* of portfolio assessment, not just its products. Therefore, the preservice teacher must actively participate in selecting items *and* must determine the merits of the items through reflection and self-assessment.

**Reflection Artifacts.** In addition to the reflection cover sheets shown in figure 2.1 (page 29) that might accompany each work sample and exhibit, more extensive reflection artifacts would enhance the working, presentation, and employment portfolios. These reflections could include reflective stems for individual pieces, such as (1) This is my favorite piece because . . ., (2) If I could do this piece over again, I would . . ., (3) This piece will impress other teachers because . . ., (4) Other preservice teachers liked this piece because . . ., and (5) This piece was my greatest challenge because . . . Preservice teachers can also ask themselves questions to help "bridge" individual items into the entire portfolio as they contemplate their selections. Some bridging questions include, Why should I choose this piece? What are its strengths and weaknesses? Why is it important? How does it fit into what I already have? What if I took it out? How will others react to it? In addition, reflection artifacts should be related to the teacher standards. Artifacts could be generated representing an overall reflection on each standard. Reflective questions to consider for this kind of artifact, specific to each standard, are identified in table 2.2.

**Self-Assessment Artifacts.** The sample checklist in figure 2.2 for reviewing the teacher standards represents an informal self-check of the entire collection of items. It might appear in the working portfolio, but it would not likely be included in the presentation and employment portfolios. More formal self-assessment artifacts would provide additional insight into the collection of items. For example, preservice teachers could look at the whole portfolio and rate, on a scale of one to three, whether they have met criteria for quality work. Criteria might include several of the following areas: accuracy of information, completeness, connection to standards, creativity, diversity of items, insightfulness, organization, and visual appeal. Preservice teachers should also assess their strengths and weaknesses with respect to the teacher standards and

## TABLE 2.2

# Reflective Questions for Teacher Standards

| STANDARD | DESCRIPTION | REFLECTIVE QUESTIONS |
|---|---|---|
| #1. Content knowledge | Understands physical education content, disciplinary concepts, and tools of inquiry related to the development of a physically educated person | • What special insights did I develop about the physical education discipline?<br>• What area of physical education would I like to study in greater depth?<br>• What special project (e.g., report, experiment, learning experience, unit plan) added to my knowledge of physical education?<br>• What person (e.g., instructor, adviser, supervisor, teacher) left me with an indelible impression about physical education?<br>• What aspects of physical education need the greatest emphasis in elementary schools? Middle or junior high schools? High schools? |
| #2. Growth and development | Understands how individuals learn and develop and can provide opportunities that support their physical, cognitive, social, and emotional development | • How do I help learners in their physical, cognitive, social, and emotional development?<br>• What developmentally appropriate practices do I rely on most in teaching physical education?<br>• How do I know that learners are developmentally ready to engage in physical education activities? |
| #3. Diverse learners | Understands how individuals differ in their approaches to learning and creates appropriate instruction adapted to diverse learners | • What do I understand about my own culture?<br>• What are some ways that I have used to learn about the students I teach?<br>• What experiences have I had that affect teaching and learning in diverse environments?<br>• What are some characteristics of teachers who work effectively in diverse classrooms?<br>• What skills do I need to develop to work effectively in diverse classrooms?<br>• What experiences have I had in the role of a minority and how did this help my understanding of diversity? |
| #4. Management and motivation | Uses an understanding of individual and group motivation and behavior to create a safe learning environment that encourages positive social interaction, active engagement in learning, and self-motivation | • How have I successfully motivated learners to participate in physical activity?<br>• What managerial and instructional routines create smoothly functioning learning experiences?<br>• How do I establish a positive climate in the physical education setting and school environment?<br>• What strategies are best for promoting mutual respect, support, safety, and cooperative participation in physical education? |
| #5. Communication | Uses knowledge of effective verbal, nonverbal, and media communication techniques to foster inquiry, collaboration, and engagement in physical activity settings | • Is my communication clear, and how do I check for understanding?<br>• What communication strategies do I model that have proven successful?<br>• How do I communicate with school colleagues, parents, and the community?<br>• How do ethnic, cultural, economic, ability levels, gender, and environmental differences affect the ways I communicate in the physical education setting? |

*(continued)*

—TABLE 2.2—

*(continued)*

| STANDARD | DESCRIPTION | REFLECTIVE QUESTIONS |
|---|---|---|
| #6. Planning and instruction | Plans and implements a variety of developmentally appropriate instructional strategies to develop physically educated individuals | • What are my primary program goals and desired outcomes in physical education?<br>• What instructional strategies do I prefer to maximize learner participation and success?<br>• If a lesson is not successful, what do I do to improve my teaching the next time?<br>• What principles of effective instruction do I try to build into my teaching routine? motivation, and safety?<br>• How do I adapt plans to ensure learner progress, motivation, and safety? |
| #7. Learner assessment | Understands and uses formal and informal assessment strategies to foster physical, cognitive, social, and emotional development of learners in physical activity | • How do I integrate assessment into my physical education instruction?<br>• What are my favorite formal and informal assessment techniques?<br>• What assessment strategies would I like to really develop for my physical education setting?<br>• What kinds of learner performance data should be reported for physical education? |
| #8. Reflection | Is a reflective practitioner who evaluates the effects of his/her actions on others (e.g., learners, parents/guardians, and other professionals in the learning community) and seeks opportunities to grow professionally | • How has my philosophy of education and physical education changed during the teacher education program?<br>• What have I read or heard that has influenced my ideas about teaching physical education?<br>• What experiences have significantly affected my teaching philosophy?<br>• What are my primary reasons for wanting to teach physical education? |
| #9. Collaboration | Fosters relationships with colleagues, parents/guardians, and community agencies to support learners' growth and well-being | • What are my personal characteristics that make me an effective team member?<br>• How do schools function within the larger community context relative to physical education?<br>• What do I find difficult about working with other teachers?<br>• How do I encourage students to work together in the physical education setting?<br>• What partnership activities with parents/guardians do I think will be most effective?<br>• What personal skills should I improve to make me a better advocate for physical education in the school and community? |

then set short-term and long-term goals accordingly. They should analyze their attributes in terms of the knowledge, skills, and dispositions as detailed in table 2.1. The form in figure 2.3 could be used to generate self-assessment artifacts for each standard. In addition, any of the scoring rubrics presented in the subsequent section of this chapter that deals with evaluation could be used by preservice teachers to assess their own portfolios.

## Required Artifacts

Theoretically, the number of *required* portfolio items could range from all to none. Requiring all items would stifle preservice teachers. Because portfolio assessment promotes reflection, self-assessment, individual choice, initiative, and autonomy, preservice teachers should develop ownership and responsibility along with a sense of "voice" in selecting portfolio items. On the

## Self-Assessment of Teacher Standards

Name: _____ Date: _____

Standard #: _____ Title: _____

| | | |
|---|---|---|
| **My strengths** | Knowledge | |
| | Skills | |
| | Dispositions | |
| **My problem areas** | Knowledge | |
| | Skills | |
| | Dispositions | |

| Short-term goals | Target date |
|---|---|
| 1. | |
| 2. | |
| 3. | |

| Long-term goals | Target date |
|---|---|
| 1. | |
| 2. | |
| 3. | |

**Figure 2.3** Form that can be used by preservice teachers to produce a self-assessment artifact for each teacher standard.

other hand, requiring no items would leave too much to chance. Some items are absolutely essential for a properly constructed portfolio, particularly one that is organized around a set of teacher standards. For these reasons, some combination of required and optional artifacts is recommended. The actual ratio will vary according to the purposes, types, and processes of the portfolio system in place.

In determining what should be required, consideration should be given to the link between established teacher standards and the artifacts selected to represent these standards. For example, the working portfolio not only could require a set number of artifacts for each standard, but it also could prescribe the nature of these artifacts (e.g., unit plan to document planning and instruction). The presentation portfolio would be limited further in terms of what kinds of artifacts are required from the working portfolio and how many. The following are possible artifacts that could be required for each standard.

*Standard 1:* **Content Knowledge**

- Project titled "Contributions of Physical Activity" from a foundations course dealing with the principles, history, and philosophy of physical education
- Readings list organized by the subdisciplines of human movement (e.g., exercise physiology, kinesiology and biomechanics, motor learning, control, and development, sport sociology, sport psychology, sport pedagogy, and the sport humanities)

*Standard 2:* **Growth and Development**

- Research paper on the developmental stages children follow in learning to throw, catch, and strike objects
- Criteria checklists showing task analyses and progressions for basic tennis skills (e.g., forehand, backhand, serve)

*Standard 3:* **Diverse Learners**

- Anecdotal notes that focus on different learning styles in physical education from a series of field experiences in multicultural school settings
- Learning contracts for three middle school students as part of a voluntary, after-school tutoring program for children who are physically challenged

*Standard 4:* **Management and Motivation**

- Written rules and procedures for conduct-

ing a high school elective course titled "Personalized Health-Related Fitness"
- Videotape demonstrating ability to gain students' cooperation, help students solve problems with peers, and promote self-management among students

*Standard 5:* **Communication**

- Log of activities during student teaching documenting interactions with school colleagues, parents, and the community
- Photographs showing various communication techniques (e.g., posters, bulletin boards, newsletter, conferences) used in the role of a part-time coach

*Standard 6:* **Planning and Instruction**

- Lesson plans (three) representing critical thinking (cognitive), cooperative learning (affective), and locomotor skills development (psychomotor) from a senior-level methods course
- Teacher-made materials (e.g., task cards, worksheets, rating scales) for a three-week thematic unit plan titled "Learning to Move Through Discovery"

*Standard 7:* **Learner Assessment**

- Case study of a middle school student showing the characteristics, uses, advantages, and limitations of different kinds of assessment (e.g., proficiency tests, motor performance measures, portfolio assessment)
- Summary and critique of an article on the advantages and disadvantages of criterion-referenced and norm-referenced assessment in physical education

*Standard 8:* **Reflection**

- Journal of observations from an elementary school field experience focusing on the development of physically educated students
- Copy of questions and answers used in a conference with a student and his/her parent to discuss the student's progress report

*Standard 9:* **Collaboration**

- Letter and certificate of appreciation for conducting a lunch-hour intramural program during student teaching
- Essay from a senior seminar on the "Influence of Nonschool Factors on Learning and Engagement in Physical Activity"

Another important factor to consider when deciding on required artifacts is the types of preservice professional portfolios. Introductory, working, presentation, and employment portfolios are characteristically different. They serve different purposes, and they are reviewed by different audiences. For example, the working portfolio is all-inclusive documentation of knowledge and skills, and it is assembled primarily for adviser and/or instructor review. The employment portfolio, however, should be streamlined toward enhancing job placement, and it targets prospective employers. Although some work samples and exhibits may be selected for all the portfolios, other kinds of items may be required that are essential for each type of portfolio. Possible items that could be required for each type of portfolio include the following:

### Introductory Portfolio

1. Relationships with family, friends, and professionals (e.g., photographs, cards or letters, mementos, keepsakes, meaningful gift)
2. Personal interests or hobbies (e.g., tapes or CDs, ticket stubs, items from a collection, list of favorite books, leisure sport statistics)
3. Teaching and professional experiences (e.g., custom-made materials, coaching hand-

book, journal entries, note or letter from parent or former student, employer evaluations)
4. Reasons for wanting to be a physical education teacher (e.g., reflections, statement of philosophy, list of professional goals, essay on a controversial topic)

### Working Portfolio

1. Index
2. Artifacts representing each teacher standard
3. Reflection cover sheets for each artifact (figure 2.1, page 29)
4. Artifacts self-assessment checklist (figure 2.2, page 30)
5. Reflection artifacts on teacher standards (table 2.2, pages 33-34)
6. Artifacts analysis chart (figure 2.4, page 40)

### Presentation Portfolio

1. Creative cover (e.g., "Traveling on a Journey Toward Teaching")
2. Table of contents
3. Artifacts representing each teacher standard selected from the working portfolio

Reflection cover sheets are needed for each artifact in the working portfolio.

4. Reflection cover sheets for each artifact (figure 2.1, page 29) selected from the working portfolio

5. Self-assessment of teacher standards (figure 2.3, page 35)

**Employment Portfolio**

1. Table of contents

2. Cover letter (i.e., introduce yourself, tell why you are a good job candidate, describe some pertinent experiences, point out areas of portfolio that are exemplary)

3. Biographical sketch

4. Resume

5. Philosophy of education statement

6. Certification/licensing documents (e.g., copy of certificate, teacher exam scores, transcripts)

7. Letters of recommendation (e.g., adviser, faculty, supervisors, employers)

8. List of relevant courses (i.e., title, credits, grade, teacher standards to which course relates)

9. Student teaching evaluations (i.e., supervisor, cooperating teacher)

10. Reflection artifacts on teacher standards (table 2.2, pages 33-34)

11. Artifacts representing the teacher standards selected from the working and presentation portfolios

12. Evaluations of working and presentation portfolios by advisers, instructors, and/or committees

## Optional Artifacts

Optional artifacts can be collected as part of the working portfolio. Particular consideration should be given to school and/or community activities. Many of them may ultimately be selected for the presentation and employment portfolios in accordance with previous guidelines. Reference to the teacher standards should always be a factor in making selection decisions. To show the range of options that exists, several kinds of artifacts are listed and explained. Each contains a brief definition and the teacher standards it may reflect. These do not exhaust all the possibilities that exist as artifacts.

1. **Anecdotal records**—notes taken during teaching or through personal observation about students' cognitive, affective, or psychomotor development; documents growth and development (standard #2), planning and instruction (#6), or learner assessment (#7).

2. **Article summary/critique**—review of article from a professional journal in connection with a teacher standard; documents potentially any of the teacher standards.

3. **Case study**—in-depth examination of an *anonymous* student's development over a certain time period; documents growth and development (#2), diverse learners (#3), or learner assessment (#7).

4. **Computer programs**—includes software used or incorporated into teaching; documents content knowledge (#1), management and motivation (#4), or planning and instruction (#6).

5. **Curriculum plans**—comprehensive program designs reflecting what it is to be a learner, how learning is acquired, and how learning is verified; documents diverse learners (#3), management and motivation (#4), communication (#5), planning and instruction (#6), or learner assessment (#7).

6. **Essays**—written papers on topics pertinent to relevant education topics; documents potentially any of the teacher standards.

7. **Evaluations**—performance assessments from clinical experiences, field experiences, student teaching, and jobs; documents potentially any of the teacher standards.

8. **Goal statements**—provides information about the direction one wants to take professionally and the means for getting there; documents potentially any of the teacher standards.

9. **Honors**—letters, awards, or certificates that verify outstanding contributions; documents communication (#5) or collaboration (#9).

10. **Instructional materials**—custom-made teaching aids (e.g., transparencies, charts, videotapes, games, manipulations); documents planning and instruction (#6).

11. **Journals**—ongoing record of experiences that includes dates, times, and reflections; documents potentially any of the teacher standards.

12. **Lesson plans**—execution of instructional planning, including objectives, activities, procedures, resources, time lines, and evaluation; documents growth and development (#2), diverse learners (#3), management and motivation (#4),

communication (#5), planning and instruction (#6), or learner assessment (#7).

13. **Photographs**—shows teacher competence and accomplishments that cannot be physically included in a portfolio; documents diverse learners (#3), management and motivation (#4), communication (#5), planning and instruction (#6), or collaboration (#9).

14. **Projects**—products resulting from endeavors that involve problem solving or researching current topics; documents potentially any of the teacher standards.

15. **Readings list**—identification of professional readings, including reactions to issues and concepts; documents potentially any of the teacher standards.

16. **Technology resources**—samples of materials representing how state-of-the-art technology is incorporated into teaching (e.g., information retrieval via the Internet, E-mail uses, interactive video, cable and electronic television); documents content knowledge (#1), communication (#5), planning and instruction (#6), or collaboration (#9).

17. **Unit plans**—integrated plan for instruction on a topic covering several days or weeks, including goals, objectives, content outline, learning activities, and evaluation procedures; documents growth and development (#2), diverse learners (#3), management and motivation (#4), communication (#5), planning and instruction (#6), or learner assessment (#7).

18. **Videotapes**—recording of actual teaching episodes in clinical, field, and/or work settings; documents diverse learners (#3), management and motivation (#4), communication (#5), planning and instruction (#6), or learner assessment (#7).

## Artifacts Analysis

In addition to the management and assembly guidelines offered previously in this chapter, preservice teachers need to "manage" the documentation of the teacher standards. Each artifact selected for the working, presentation, and/or employment portfolio should be analyzed to help determine (1) standards that need work, (2) overreliance on some kinds of artifacts, and (3) need to diversify artifacts. The artifacts analysis chart in figure 2.4 can be used for this purpose. Check marks and/or dates could be entered to record the range of artifacts in support of the nine teacher standards.

# EVALUATION OF PORTFOLIOS

Suggestions for self-reflection and self-assessment were previously outlined. The focus is on *self*-analysis. However, if preservice teachers are to become fully involved in evaluating their growth and competence, then they also need to communicate the contents of their portfolios to others and receive evaluative feedback. Whether portfolios are facilitated through advisers, courses, and/or committees, results of formal and informal evaluation should be provided at planned intervals.

The professional portfolio documents a preservice teacher's growth and competence throughout a teacher education program. If it truly represents an ongoing, cumulative development of knowledge, skills, and dispositions, then feedback and evaluation should also be ongoing and cumulative. Continual review is undamental to portfolio assessment. Key checkpoints are also inherent to any teacher education program, such as admission, continuation decisions, entry to field experiences, and exit from student teaching. They represent the progressive stages of professional training. Normally, a process-level review is carried out at each stage that might include program course requirements and grade point average minimums. Therefore, it should be clear that periodic reviews are not only essential but also natural to a system of portfolio assessment and a teacher education program.

Because the portfolio is tied to accountability, and is itself an evaluation tool, individual artifacts and/or the whole portfolio should be evaluated according to established standards. Also, criteria should be referenced to the portfolio's *content* and *quality*. Guidelines for the formative and summative evaluation of preservice professional portfolios recognize these criteria.

## Formative Evaluation

When information is sought to help decide how to adjust or improve performance during a learning process, evaluation serves a formative value. The working and presentation portfolios are primarily associated with formative evaluation. For example, with working portfolios that are linked to key courses, feedback and evaluation could include peer reflection, peer conferences, instructor conferences, and grading by the instructor as

| Kind of artifact (e.g., curriculum plan) | Name of artifact (e.g., thematic unit on "Teamwork") | Teacher standard | | | | | | | | |
|---|---|---|---|---|---|---|---|---|---|---|
| | | 1 | 2 | 3 | 4 | 5 | 6 | 7 | 8 | 9 |
| | | | | | | | | | | |
| | | | | | | | | | | |
| | | | | | | | | | | |
| | | | | | | | | | | |
| | | | | | | | | | | |
| | | | | | | | | | | |
| | | | | | | | | | | |
| | | | | | | | | | | |
| | | | | | | | | | | |
| | | | | | | | | | | |
| | | | | | | | | | | |
| | | | | | | | | | | |

**Figure 2.4**  The artifacts analysis chart is used to manage the documentation of each teacher standard.

part of course requirements. For the presentation portfolio, additional feedback and evaluation could be received from peers, faculty, and advisers during a poster-like session that is organized within a key course.

Various feedback and evaluation constructs can serve a formative purpose, including peer reflection, conferences, and performance rating. They are applicable to both working and presentation portfolios, and they can be used in systems guided by advisers, course instructors, and/or committees.

**Peer Reflection.** Preservice teachers are deeply involved in their own portfolio development and are therefore qualified to review the work of other preservice teachers and provide feedback. In fact, they could even select items they feel should be included in another teacher's portfolio. However, it is important that preservice teachers who pro-

---

**Peer Reflection Sheet**

Date: _____

To: _____

From: _____

Please review the attached items that are included in my professional portfolio and provide feedback. Thanks!

1. What teacher standard is documented the most effectively? Why?

2. What teacher standard is documented the least effectively? Why?

3. What artifacts really made an impression on you? Why?

4. What artifact do you feel needs the most work? Why?

5. What is your overall impression of the organization and presentation of artifacts?

Signed: _____ Date: _____

---

**Figure 2.5** Format for peer reflection on the working or presentation portfolio.

vide the feedback be trained in how to (1) offer constructive or encouraging words, (2) disagree with an idea rather than with the person, and (3) assess the quality of work based on the established standards. The sample peer reflection sheet that appears in figure 2.5 could be applied in several ways. It could be used to provide a direct review of someone else's portfolio or to provide feedback in reaction to a portfolio presentation to a small group of peers, to an entire class, or through a poster-like session.

**Conferences.** Previously, conducting a conference was described as a general portfolio process in which preservice teachers shared their feelings about their portfolios. Conferences also serve a formative evaluation purpose. Preservice teachers receive and discuss information about their portfolios. The focus is on the teacher standards and their documentation, regardless of who is providing the feedback. Sometimes, there is a reluctance to use direct personal communication as a legitimate form of assessment because it is considered too subjective. However, conferences can yield assessment data when structured prop-

erly. Preservice teachers would have the opportunity to refine and clarify their abilities and to respond to others. Through conferences, they become more thoughtful and truly reflective in evaluating outcomes and setting goals. Upon review of the preservice teacher's working and/or presentation portfolio, feedback from peers, advisers, instructors, committee members, and/or school personnel could be structured around answers to the following scenarios.

The part of the portfolio I like best is _____ because . . .

The part I'm not really clear about is _____ because . . .

The part you need to tell me more about is . . .

You could improve your portfolio by . . .

My overall impression is . . .

**Performance Rating.** During the formative evaluation phase, the preservice teacher needs specific feedback about the teacher standards. The working portfolio represents the broadest view of the preservice teacher's growing competence and serves as the underlying framework for the presentation portfolio. As a result, a more formal rating of the portfolio should be conducted by advisers, course instructors, and/or committees. If the portfolio system is linked to courses, it may be necessary to convert ratings into a letter grade. Because the teacher standards serve as the basis for organizing the professional portfolio, they are central to any scheme that has meaningful feedback as its goal. The rating form in figure 2.6 can be used to evaluate working and presentation portfolios.

## Summative Evaluation

Evaluation of a summative nature is used to decide the extent to which "learners" have been successful in mastering final outcomes (standards). Because the employment portfolio is viewed as the final or exit portfolio, it is subject to summative evaluation protocols. However, any feedback and evaluation format must recognize the purposes of the employment portfolio—to synthesize the knowledge, skills, and dispositions of the preservice teacher and enhance job placement. Information about the employment portfolio can be received from peers, but the primary feedback and evaluation source should be experienced professionals (e.g., advisers, faculty, committee members, school personnel).

Various feedback and evaluation constructs can serve a summative purpose, including conferences, simulation, and performance rating. These constructs can be used in portfolio systems guided by advisers, course instructors, and/or committees.

**Conferences.** The format of conferences for summative purposes is basically the same as the format for formative evaluation. However, the focus is different because the employment portfolio is different from the working and presentation portfolios in terms of purpose, organization, and presentation. Regardless of who is involved in the conferences, discussion should be centered on how effectively preservice teachers document their competence as fully qualified, professionally mature beginning physical education teachers. Upon review of the employment portfolio by peers, advisers, instructors, committee members, and/or school personnel, conferences could be structured around a comparison of the preservice teacher's perceptions and the conference participants' opinion regarding the following areas: (1) overall strengths as a physical education teacher,

The employment portfolio is the focus for the simulated job interview.

# Portfolio Rating Form

Name: _____ Date: _____

**Directions:** Use the following scale to rate each portfolio item according to the criteria below.

4 = Outstanding      3 = Good      2 = Satisfactory      1 = Fair      0 = Poor

**Organization:** Follows directions; completeness of items; clear layout; overall creativity
**Form and quality:** Writing mechanics; expressiveness; visual appeal; spelling, punctuation, and grammar
**Evidence of understanding:** Explicit demonstration of standard's knowledge, skills, and dispositions; application of ideas

| Standard/Items | Organization | Form and quality | Evidence of understanding |
|---|---|---|---|
| #1. Content knowledge | | | |
| Reflection artifact on standard | _____ | _____ | _____ |
| Reflection cover sheets | _____ | _____ | _____ |
| Required artifacts: | | | |
| Name: _____ | _____ | _____ | _____ |
| Name: _____ | _____ | _____ | _____ |
| Optional artifacts: | | | |
| Name: _____ | _____ | _____ | _____ |
| Name: _____ | _____ | _____ | _____ |
| #2. Growth and development | | | |
| Reflection artifact on standard | _____ | _____ | _____ |
| Reflection cover sheets | _____ | _____ | _____ |
| Required artifacts: | | | |
| Name: _____ | _____ | _____ | _____ |
| Name: _____ | _____ | _____ | _____ |
| Optional artifacts: | | | |
| Name: _____ | _____ | _____ | _____ |
| Name: _____ | _____ | _____ | _____ |
| #3. Diverse learners | | | |
| Reflection artifact on standard | _____ | _____ | _____ |
| Reflection cover sheets | _____ | _____ | _____ |
| Required artifacts: | | | |
| Name: _____ | _____ | _____ | _____ |
| Name: _____ | _____ | _____ | _____ |
| Optional artifacts: | | | |
| Name: _____ | _____ | _____ | _____ |
| Name: _____ | _____ | _____ | _____ |

*(continued)*

**Figure 2.6**   Form that can be used to rate the preservice teacher's working and presentation portfolios.

| Standard/Items | Organization | Form and quality | Evidence of understanding |
|---|---|---|---|
| **#4. Management and motivation** | | | |
| Reflection artifact on standard | _____ | _____ | _____ |
| Reflection cover sheets | _____ | _____ | _____ |
| Required artifacts: | | | |
| Name: _____ | _____ | _____ | _____ |
| Name: _____ | _____ | _____ | _____ |
| Optional artifacts: | | | |
| Name: _____ | _____ | _____ | _____ |
| Name: _____ | _____ | _____ | _____ |
| **#5. Communication** | | | |
| Reflection artifact on standard | _____ | _____ | _____ |
| Reflection cover sheets | _____ | _____ | _____ |
| Required artifacts: | | | |
| Name: _____ | _____ | _____ | _____ |
| Name: _____ | _____ | _____ | _____ |
| Optional artifacts: | | | |
| Name: _____ | _____ | _____ | _____ |
| Name: _____ | _____ | _____ | _____ |
| **#6. Planning and instruction** | | | |
| Reflection artifact on standard | _____ | _____ | _____ |
| Reflection cover sheets | _____ | _____ | _____ |
| Required artifacts: | | | |
| Name: _____ | _____ | _____ | _____ |
| Name: _____ | _____ | _____ | _____ |
| Optional artifacts: | | | |
| Name: _____ | _____ | _____ | _____ |
| Name: _____ | _____ | _____ | _____ |
| **#7. Learner assessment** | | | |
| Reflection artifact on standard | _____ | _____ | _____ |
| Reflection cover sheets | _____ | _____ | _____ |
| Required artifacts: | | | |
| Name: _____ | _____ | _____ | _____ |
| Name: _____ | _____ | _____ | _____ |
| Optional artifacts: | | | |
| Name: _____ | _____ | _____ | _____ |
| Name: _____ | _____ | _____ | _____ |

*(continued)*

**Figure 2.6**   *(continued)*

| Standard/Items | Organization | Form and quality | Evidence of understanding |
|---|---|---|---|
| #8. Reflection | | | |
| Reflection artifact on standard | \_\_\_\_\_ | \_\_\_\_\_ | \_\_\_\_\_ |
| Reflection cover sheets | \_\_\_\_\_ | \_\_\_\_\_ | \_\_\_\_\_ |
| Required artifacts: | | | |
| Name: _____ | \_\_\_\_\_ | \_\_\_\_\_ | \_\_\_\_\_ |
| Name: _____ | \_\_\_\_\_ | \_\_\_\_\_ | \_\_\_\_\_ |
| Optional artifacts: | | | |
| Name: _____ | \_\_\_\_\_ | \_\_\_\_\_ | \_\_\_\_\_ |
| Name: _____ | \_\_\_\_\_ | \_\_\_\_\_ | \_\_\_\_\_ |
| #9. Collaboration | | | |
| Reflection artifact on standard | \_\_\_\_\_ | \_\_\_\_\_ | \_\_\_\_\_ |
| Reflection cover sheets | \_\_\_\_\_ | \_\_\_\_\_ | \_\_\_\_\_ |
| Required artifacts: | | | |
| Name: _____ | \_\_\_\_\_ | \_\_\_\_\_ | \_\_\_\_\_ |
| Name: _____ | \_\_\_\_\_ | \_\_\_\_\_ | \_\_\_\_\_ |
| Optional artifacts: | | | |
| Name: _____ | \_\_\_\_\_ | \_\_\_\_\_ | \_\_\_\_\_ |
| Name: _____ | \_\_\_\_\_ | \_\_\_\_\_ | \_\_\_\_\_ |

**Overall evaluation**

\_\_\_\_\_ This portfolio is *exemplary* in documenting the teacher standards at this point in the preservice teacher's program of study; *maintain progress.*

\_\_\_\_\_ This portfolio is *above expectation* in documenting the teacher standards at this point in the preservice teacher's program of study; *minor revisions are advised.*

\_\_\_\_\_ This portfolio is *marginal* in documenting the teacher standards at this point in the preservice teacher's program of study; *several revisions are advised.*

\_\_\_\_\_ This portfolio is *below expectation* in documenting the teacher standards at this point in the preservice teacher's program of study; *major revisions are advised.*

\_\_\_\_\_ This portfolio is *unacceptable* in documenting the teacher standards at this point in the preservice teacher's program of study; *reconsider role as teacher.*

Evaluator signature: _____ Date: _____

**Figure 2.6** *(continued)*

## Employment Portfolio Rating Form

Name: _____ Date: _____

**Portfolio contents**

Components of the employment portfolio should be verified according to the following indicators:

✔ = Fully developed          – = Included but incomplete          0 = Not included

| | | | |
|---|---|---|---|
| _____ | Table of contents | _____ | Letters of recommendation |
| _____ | Cover letter | _____ | List of relevant courses |
| _____ | Biographical sketch | _____ | Student teaching evaluations |
| _____ | Resume | _____ | Reflection artifacts on teacher standards |
| _____ | Philosophy of education statement | _____ | Artifacts representing the teacher standards |
| _____ | Certification/licensing documents | _____ | Evaluations of the working and presentation portfolios |

Comments: _____

_____

_____

_____

**Portfolio quality**

The employment portfolio should evidence an acceptable level of quality. Use the following scale to rate each characteristic and artifact:

2 = High quality; above expectation

1 = Satisfactory quality; meets expectation

0 = Low quality; below expectation

| | | | |
|---|---|---|---|
| _____ | Organization | _____ | Artifact #7: _____ |
| _____ | Layout/visual appeal | _____ | Artifact #8: _____ |
| _____ | Creativity/expressiveness | _____ | Artifact #9: _____ |
| _____ | Spelling, punctuation, grammar | _____ | Artifact #10: _____ |
| _____ | Artifact #1: _____ | _____ | Artifact #11: _____ |
| _____ | Artifact #2: _____ | _____ | Artifact #12: _____ |
| _____ | Artifact #3: _____ | _____ | Artifact #13: _____ |
| _____ | Artifact #4: _____ | _____ | Artifact #14: _____ |
| _____ | Artifact #5: _____ | _____ | Artifact #15: _____ |
| _____ | Artifact #6: _____ | _____ | Artifact #16: _____ |

### Summary evaluation

Portfolio contents: _____ Outstanding   _____ Satisfactory   _____ Unsatisfactory

Portfolio quality:   _____ Outstanding   _____ Satisfactory   _____ Unsatisfactory

Evaluator signature: _____ Date: _____

**Figure 2.7**   Form that can be used to rate the preservice teacher's employment portfolio.

(2) artifacts that represent "holistic" abilities and dispositions toward teaching, (3) how the portfolio verifies that the beginning teacher standards have been met, (4) what teacher standards will likely develop further as a practicing teacher, and (5) teacher standards that need work as revealed by the portfolio.

**Simulation.** The employment portfolio has important practical use. It can be presented to prospective employers as documentation of teaching competence. So far, feedback and evaluation strategies have focused primarily on the "physical" qualities of portfolios. Certainly, the employment portfolio should be assessed in he same manner. But, it would also be beneficial to find out how well it serves the job search process. Through simulation, a job interview could be conducted by a role-playing team of employers. Peers can take on lifelike roles or school personnel could help in creating this real-life situation. Participants and observers (e.g., peers, faculty, advisers) could provide invaluable feedback, not only about the portfolio's contents and quality, but also about its use and effectiveness during a job interview. Feedback could be provided in answer to the following questions: How well does the portfolio portray teaching competence? Which teacher standards are clearly demonstrated? Which teacher standards are not clearly demonstrated? What changes in the portfolio would help the job interview? How could the portfolio be used more effectively during a job interview?

**Performance Rating.** The importance of the employment portfolio cannot be overstated. Because this portfolio is a composite of the beginning physical education teacher, it deserves a more formal rating by advisers, course instructors, and/or committees. Although the teacher standards remain as the foundation, any rating scheme should incorporate explicit content and quality criteria. The rating form in figure 2.7 can be used to evaluate employment portfolios.

# CLOSING STATEMENT

The professional portfolio is an authentic way for preservice physical education teachers to document their competence. Through introductory, working, presentation, and employment types of portfolios, preservice teachers can verify the wide range of knowledge, skills, and dispositions acquired in a teacher education program. Standards for beginning physical education teachers are recommended as the basis for organizing these portfolios. Alternative processes can be used separately or in combination to implement portfolios (i.e., adviser directed, course affiliated, committee oversight, and/or program phases), each of which is characterized by training, presentation, reflection, and self-assessment strategies and by conferences. Also, several storage options and organizational techniques are available for managing and assembling the different types of portfolios. In addition, the selection of required and optional artifacts must consider the teacher standards and the type of portfolio. Finally, the formal and informal feedback and evaluation constructs that should accompany any system of portfolio assessment can serve formative and summative purposes, if properly structured.

# SAMPLE PRESERVICE PROFESSIONAL PORTFOLIO SYSTEM

To synthesize the information presented in this chapter, a sample portfolio system is provided for use in a preservice professional program in physical education. Although the setting for this system is hypothetical, most of the portfolio elements are typical of undergraduate teacher education programs. The system incorporates the concepts and principles advanced in this chapter. It is structured in the form of a practical handbook for preservice physical education teachers.

# HANDBOOK

Preservice Physical Education
Professional Portfolio
(PPEPP)

Wherever State University
College of Education
Department of Physical Education

# PPEPP Handbook

## CONTENTS

# OVERVIEW

The physical education teacher education program at Wherever State University (WSU) develops educators who facilitate student learning in a democratic, pluralistic, and technological society. The program offers comprehensive coursework in general education, professional education, and the major field including clinical activities, field experiences, and student teaching. By successfully completing the program, the preservice physical education teacher is fully competent to assume the role of *beginning physical education teacher* at the inservice level and to qualify for the *multiage teaching license*.

# PROGRAM MODEL AND STANDARDS

Competent beginning physical education teachers can demonstrate certain knowledge and skills within the organizing theme "teacher as reflective, inquiry-oriented practitioner who knows the physical education discipline and applies content and pedagogy that is sensitive to individual learner needs." Successful physical education teachers reflect on their teaching, on their decisions, on their problems and solutions to those problems, on their students, and on the processes of teaching and learning. To operationalize the organizing theme, a set of standards was sought that defines what a beginning physical educator should know and be able to do. Because of their widespread acceptance, NASPE's *National Standards for Beginning Physical Education Teachers* (Tannehill et al., 1995) are targets for the preservice professional physical educator. These standards are as follows:*

*Standard #1:* **CONTENT KNOWLEDGE**

Understands physical education content, disciplinary concepts, and tools of inquiry related to the development of a physically educated person

*Standard #2:* **GROWTH AND DEVELOPMENT**

Understands how individuals learn and develop and can provide opportunities that support their physical, cognitive, social, and emotional development

*Standard #3:* **DIVERSE LEARNERS**

Understands how individuals differ in their approaches to learning and creates appropriate instruction adapted to diverse learners

*Standard #4:* **MANAGEMENT AND MOTIVATION**

Uses an understanding of individual and group motivation and behavior to create a learning environment that encourages positive social interaction, active engagement in learning, and self-motivation

*Standard #5:* **COMMUNICATION**

Uses knowledge of effective verbal, nonverbal, and media communication techniques to foster inquiry, collaboration, and engagement in physical activity settings

*Standard #6:* **PLANNING AND INSTRUCTION**

Plans and implements a variety of developmentally appropriate instructional strategies to develop physically educated individuals

---

*Reprinted from *National Standards for Beginning Physical Education Teachers* (1995) with permission from the National Association for Sport and Physical Education (NASPE), 1900 Association Drive, Reston, VA 20191-1599.

*Standard #7:* **LEARNER ASSESSMENT**

Understands and uses formal and informal assessment strategies to foster physical, cognitive, social, and emotional development of learners in physical activity

*Standard #8:* **REFLECTION**

Is a reflective practitioner who evaluates the effects of his/her actions on others (e.g., learners, parents/guardians, and other professionals in the learning community) and seeks opportunities to grow professionally

*Standard #9:* **COLLABORATION**

Fosters relationships with colleagues, parents/guardians, and community agencies to support learners' growth and well-being

## PURPOSES OF THE PROFESSIONAL PORTFOLIO

The WSU professional portfolio is an organized, goal-oriented documentation of one's professional growth and achieved competence in the complex act of teaching physical education. It illustrates who are you as a teacher. Although the portfolio is a collection of documents, it provides tangible evidence of the wide range of knowledge, dispositions, and skills that one possesses as a growing professional. The portfolio is a personal tool for synthesizing all these aspects. Given a highly competitive job market, you must be able to convey to others the knowledge and skills acquired in a professional teacher education program. The professional portfolio can satisfy this need. Therefore, the primary purpose of the professional portfolio is to verify the knowledge and skills acquired through coursework, clinical and field experiences, student teaching, and community involvements. Secondary purposes are to (1) grow professionally, (2) satisfy licensing requirements, and (3) enhance employment.

## PORTFOLIO MECHANICS

The professional portfolio is a purposeful and systematic collection of work that shows individual effort, progress, and achievement at WSU. More specific information and guidelines are needed regarding the actual mechanics of portfolio development. In this section of the handbook, the following questions are answered: What types of portfolios will be used? How should the PPEPP be organized? What portfolio processes will be employed? How should the PPEPP be managed?

### Types

There are four different types of professional portfolios, all of which are unified by some common work samples and exhibits. They contribute to the primary and secondary purposes of the professional portfolio in their own unique way. Each type of PPEPP is briefly described, and the expected semester in which it is to be completed is identified.

- *Introductory portfolio*—The personal portfolio introduces oneself as a person and as a future teaching professional in physical education. It serves as a catalyst for self-reflection and continual sharing of ideas and insights throughout the teacher education program. The introductory portfolio is completed and evaluated during the fall semester of the sophomore year.

- *Working portfolio*—The ongoing systematic collection of selected work samples is compiled from courses and evidence (exhibits) of school/community activities. The working portfolio is the framework for self-assessment and goal setting. It provides a basis for formative evaluation throughout the teacher education program at planned intervals. Completion date is the spring semester of the junior year.

- *Presentation portfolio*—This includes samples of work that best reflect one's achieved competence, individuality, and creativity as a professional physical educator. The presentation portfolio should be selective and streamlined. It is used during the teacher education program to satisfy different purposes (e.g., field course requirement, clinical experiences, poster-like session) and audiences (e.g., faculty, cooperating teachers, peers). In addition, it provides for formative evaluation, depending on how it is used and when. Completion date is the fall semester of the senior year.

- *Employment portfolio*—This portfolio provides a rich overview of the personality and abilities of the preservice physical education teacher. It focuses on selected artifacts to enhance job placement, and it may be customized to a particular school. The employment portfolio offers a basis for summative evaluation during the spring student teaching semester of the senior year.

## Organization

Regardless of the purpose or type, professional portfolios need an organizational scheme that is clear and meaningful. Because the WSU system uses four types of professional portfolios, the basis for organizing them is also different. For each type of portfolio, required and optional artifacts, as well as suggestions for other kinds of artifacts, are offered later in this handbook in the section on portfolio contents. Specific organizational schemes are presented in this section.

The *introductory portfolio* is meant for you to introduce yourself to the profession as revealed by personal characteristics and reasons for wanting to be a physical education teacher. These aspects serve as the basis for organizing the portfolio. Artifacts should be assembled that are keyed to the following topics: (1) relationships with family, friends, and professionals, (2) personal interests and hobbies, (3) teaching and professional experiences, and (4) reasons for wanting to be a physical education teacher.

The *working portfolio* and the *presentation portfolio* are organized around the nine standards for the beginning physical education teacher that were previously identified and described. These standards provide a core set of expectations for teaching physical education that are written in terms of performance and knowledge. They have wide applicability. Artifacts selected for the presentation portfolio are derived from the ongoing, more quantitative-oriented depository of items found in the working portfolio.

For the *employment portfolio*, "getting a job" should serve as the primary goal around which to organize the portfolio. While the teacher standards should be addressed, it might include artifacts representing more than one standard. Organize artifacts to exemplify the kind of position you are seeking (e.g., elementary, high school).

## Processes

The PPEPP should be a cumulative record of your professional growth and achieved competence. It is the thread running throughout the WSU teacher education program in physical education. Therefore, a systematic process is needed to collect, select, and evaluate appropriate portfolio entries. Various checkpoints and periodic reviews are possible. The system should include some way to introduce the portfolio assessment model and a means for bringing closure to the process.

The WSU system is course affiliated. The four types of professional portfolios are linked to selected key courses. Several processes of the PPEPP are part of individual courses and are graded by the instructor as part of course requirements.

TABLE 1

**Portfolio Processes**

| YEAR | SEMESTER / COURSE / PORTFOLIO TYPE | PROCESSES |
|---|---|---|
| Sophomore | Fall semester<br><br>PED 200—Introduction to the Physical Education Profession<br><br>Introductory portfolio | **Training**—"PPEPP Handbook" is distributed and discussed; illustrative artifacts are exhibited; sample portfolios are inspected; basic skills are developed in self-management, reflection, self-assessment, peer reflection, and conferences.<br>**Presentation**—Introductory portfolio is presented to the entire class; two artifacts should be selected for each of the four topics identified in the previous section on organization. |
| Junior | Spring semester<br><br>PED 310—Adolescent and Young Adult Physical Education<br><br>Working portfolio | **Self-Reflection**—Each artifact should be thoughtfully examined to reveal its meaning and value to the portfolio relative to the nine beginning physical education teacher standards; use the "Reflection Cover Sheet for Working Portfolio Artifacts" in Appendix A.<br>**Self-Assessment**—Collection of artifacts should be reviewed to determine how the working portfolio adheres to the teacher standards; look for ways to document a "missing" artifact or one that has "holes;" set goals and target dates where artifacts are needed; use the "Self-Assessment Checklist of Standards for the Working Portfolio" form in Appendix A.<br>**Peer Conference**—The final working portfolio is shared with other preservice teachers for feedback purposes; use the "Structure for the Working Portfolio Peer Conference" form in Appendix A. |
| Senior | Fall semester<br><br>PED 450—Curriculum Design and Instructional Delivery<br><br>Presentation portfolio | **Self-Reflection**—To enhance the presentation portfolio, more extensive reflections are needed as you contemplate your selections; use the "Bridging Questions for the Presentation Portfolio" form in Appendix A.<br>**Self-Assessment**—The strengths and weaknesses of the presentation portfolio should be assessed relative to the teacher standards; short-term and long-term goals should be set; use the "Self-Assessment of Teacher Standards for the Presentation Portfolio" form in Appendix A.<br>**Presentation**—The final portfolio is presented in a poster-like session that is attended by faculty and peers; portfolio items should be carefully selected and streamlined.<br>**Peer/Faculty Reflection**—Following the poster-like session, peer and faculty feedback will be provided; the "Peer/Faculty Reflection Sheet for the Presentation Portfolio" will be used for this purpose as shown in Appendix A. |

*(continued)*

---TABLE 1---
## *(continued)*

| YEAR | SEMESTER | PROCESSES |
|---|---|---|
| | **COURSE** | |
| | **PORTFOLIO TYPE** | |
| **Senior** | Spring semester | **Peer/Instructor Conferences**—The employment portfolio is shared with other preservice teachers and the instructor for feedback purposes; use the "Structure for the Peer/Instructor Employment Portfolio Conferences" form in Appendix A. |
| | PED 499—Gateway to the Profession | **Presentation**—An interview simulation will be conducted by a role-playing team of employers; portfolio items should be carefully selected to portray teaching competence in a succinct manner. |
| | Employment portfolio | |

Implementation of the PPEPP includes the introduction of the assessment model, periodic reviews (formative), and evaluation of the completed portfolio (summative). The type of portfolio and processes associated with each of the key courses in the system is identified in table 1.

### Management

Ultimately, the preservice teacher assumes responsibility for organizing, maintaining, and storing the types of portfolios throughout the assessment process. Decisions about method of construction, how and where to store portfolios, and how often to "manage" portfolios depend on the type of portfolio. You need to develop a plan to handle the logistics of your professional portfolios. The "container" for collecting artifacts is a matter of personal preference. Possibilities include notebooks, expanding and accordion files, large file box, folders, satchels, pockets for electronic documents, large notebook divided into sections, and cabinet file drawers. The type of portfolio will determine the most practical way to store and manage portfolio items.

The *introductory portfolio* is a scaled-down version of a complete portfolio. Because the number of artifacts is relatively small, an accordion file or cardboard box is all that may be needed. By contrast, the *working portfolio* requires space considerations because the number of artifacts is high. Anything should be collected that relates to a standard, even if not required or eventually selected as an optional piece. You should continually look for ways to document standards, particularly those that may need improvement. The *presentation portfolio* should not be cumbersome or unwieldy. Sample pages from a large project might replace the entire project. A large notebook or accordion file is all that may be needed. Artifacts can represent more than one standard. Each artifact should be labeled with an abbreviated title for the standard so that someone viewing the portfolio will know what it means. Finally, the *employment portfolio* should be a succinct representation of one's teaching competence. Employers do not have a great deal of time to peruse portfolios, so a limited number of carefully selected items should be included in a "professional" container, such as a portfolio satchel. Easy access for employers should be built in. This may be the first impression an employer has of you—spelling, grammar, and neatness should be carefully checked.

You may be good at collecting work samples and exhibits but need help in managing the portfolio. Effective organizational tools that you may want to consider include (1) dividers (separate artifacts according to teaching standards, courses, or incomplete works), (2) color codes (code entries with colored dots, colored files, or markers), (3) artifact registry (record the date, item, and reason for either adding or removing an item), (4) work log (list activities and decisions about the portfolio with dates), (5) index (compile alphabetical index of items), and (6) Post-it™ Notes (attach to each artifact to identify standard and explain why it was collected).

## PORTFOLIO CONTENTS

Now that the standards, purposes, types, organizational schemes, processes, and management options are known, the actual selection of portfolio items can occur. As artifacts are created and selected, ethical factors should be considered. *Confidentiality should be maintained. For journal entries, personal reflections, case studies, etc., do not use actual names of teachers, students, schools, or other identifying information.* The contents of your portfolio must include a combination of both required and optional items. Guidelines are provided for each artifact, followed by a suggestion for how to analyze the scope of your artifacts.

### Required Artifacts

The introductory, working, presentation, and employment portfolios serve different purposes, and they are reviewed by different audiences. Therefore, certain items are required, specific to each type of portfolio.

### Introductory Portfolio

1. Relationships with family, friends, and professionals (e.g., photographs, cards or letters, mementos, keepsakes, meaningful gift)
2. Personal interests or hobbies (e.g., tapes or CDs, ticket stubs, items from a collection, list of favorite books, leisure sport statistics)
3. Teaching and professional experiences (e.g., custom-made materials, coaching handbook, journal entries, note or letter from former student or parent, employer evaluations)
4. Reasons for wanting to be a physical education teacher (e.g., reflections, statement of philosophy, list of professional goals, essay on a controversial topic)

### Working Portfolio

1. Index
2. Artifacts from selected courses representing each teacher standard (see table 2)
3. Reflection cover sheets for each artifact (see Appendix A)
4. Self-assessment checklist of standards (see Appendix A)
5. Artifacts analysis chart (see Appendix A)

### Presentation Portfolio

1. Creative cover
2. Table of contents

—TABLE 2—

## Required Artifacts for the Working Portfolio

| COURSE | PRIMARY STANDARDS | NAME OF ARTIFACTS |
|---|---|---|
| PED 200—Introduction to the Physical Education Profession | 1, 2, 8 | "Contributions of Physical Activity" paper |
| HED 200—First Aid and Emergency Care | 2, 4, 8<br>1, 3, 4, 9 | Case study analyses<br>Emergency response plan |
| DAN 300—Dance for the Physical Educator | 5, 8, 9<br>1, 5, 8, 9 | Self-analysis journal<br>Videotape of movement presentation |
| PED 300—Early and Middle Childhood Physical Education | 1, 2, 3, 6, 7<br>1, 8 | Unit plan including six lessons<br>Article critiques |
| PED 310—Adolescent and Young Adult Physical Education | 2, 3, 4, 5, 6, 7 | Analyses of middle school and high school teachers |
| PED 320—Kinesiology | 1, 6, 7, 8 | Self-selected teaching activity |
| PED 330—Physiology of Exercise | 1, 6, 7, 8 | Self-designed exercise program |
| PED 340—Motor Learning and Development | 1, 3, 6, 9<br>1, 3, 7, 9 | Practice: Design and schedule<br>"Motor Assessment" project |
| PED 350—Legal and Administrative Aspects of Physical Education | 1, 4, 5, 8, 9<br>2, 3, 5, 6<br>2, 3, 4, 5, 8, 9 | "Policy and Procedure" paper<br>Risk assessment and audit<br>Negligence case study analysis |
| DAN 400—Teaching Dance | 1, 2, 3, 4, 5, 6, 7 | Mini-lessons and unit plan |
| PED 410—Psychosocial Aspects of Physical Activity | 2, 3, 4<br>1, 2, 3, 4, 7 | "Gender Reversal" paper<br>Problem-solving report |
| PED 420—Physical Education for Students With Disabilities | 2, 3, 6, 7<br>2, 3, 5, 8<br>1, 2, 3, 5, 6, 7<br>1, 2, 3, 8 | IEP development<br>"Attitude Toward Disabilities" paper<br>Clinical teaching descriptions<br>"Disability Types" project |
| PED 430—Evaluation in Physical Education | 1, 7, 8, 9 | Test construction/administration |
| PED 450—Curriculum Design and Instructional Delivery | 3, 4, 5, 6, 7<br>3, 4, 5, 6, 7 | "Curriculum and Instruction" project<br>Videotape of field teaching |
| PED 499—Gateway to the Profession | 3, 4, 5, 6, 7<br>1, 8, 9 | Videotape of student teaching lesson<br>Standards-based analysis of teaching competence |

3. Artifacts representing each teacher standard selected from the working portfolio

4. Reflection cover sheets for each artifact selected from the working portfolio (see Appendix A)

5. Self-assessment of teacher standards (see Appendix A)

**Employment Portfolio**

1. Table of contents

2. Cover letter (i.e., introduce yourself, tell why you are a good job candidate, describe some pertinent experiences, point out areas of portfolio that are exemplary)

3. Biographical sketch

4. Resume

5. Philosophy of education statement

6. Certification/licensing documents (e.g., copy of certificate, teacher exam scores, transcripts)

7. Letters of recommendation (e.g., adviser, faculty, supervisors, employers)

8. List of relevant courses (i.e., title, credits, grade, teacher standards to which course relates)

9. Student teaching evaluations (i.e., supervisor, cooperating teacher)

10. Artifacts representing the teacher standards selected from the working and presentation portfolios

11. Reflections on each teacher standard relative to selected artifacts

12. Evaluations of working and presentation portfolios by instructors

## Optional Items

A wide variety of optional artifacts can be collected as part of your *working portfolio*. Particular consideration should be given to school and/or community activities. Many of them may ultimately be selected for the *presentation portfolio* and the *employment portfolio* in accordance with previous guidelines. All artifacts must relate to one of the beginning teacher standards. The following artifacts, with examples, show the range of options that exist.

1. Anecdotal records (observation notes on students' skills)

2. Article summaries or critiques (reflect on an article read on your own)

3. Assessments (performance task card you developed)

4. Awards and certificates (volunteer recognition)

5. Bulletin board ideas (photograph)

6. Case studies (show knowledge of an *anonymous* child's development)

7. Classroom management philosophy (written summary including citations)

8. Community resource documents (copies of actual correspondence)

9. Computer programs (programs incorporated into teaching)

10. Cooperative learning strategies (copy of lesson plan)

11. Curriculum plans (thematic units)

12. Essays (writing on a complex social issue)
13. Evaluations (on-the-job performance assessments)
14. Field trip plans (copy of program or brochure)
15. Floor plans (sketch of space/equipment arranged)
16. Goal statements (outline perceived role as a teacher)
17. Individualized plans (show how lessons or units have been adapted for diverse learners)
18. Interviews with students, teachers, parents (copy of questions and answers)
19. Journals (observations during field experiences)
20. Lesson plans (copies of all components)
21. Letters to parents (weekly newsletters)
22. Management and organization strategies (summary of system for grouping students)
23. Media competencies (examples of forms of media used in teaching)
24. Meetings and workshops log (reaction paper with program)
25. Observation reports (results of checklists)
26. Peer critiques (rating sheets from presentations)
27. Philosophy statement (brief position paper)
28. Pictures and photographs (show special projects/learning centers)
29. Portfolio, student (sample artifacts from a student's portfolio)
30. Position papers (scholarly defense of an educational issue)
31. Problem-solving logs (record of solving a professional problem)
32. Professional development plans (list of future workshops or meetings to be attended)
33. Professional organizations and committees list (list memberships and involvements)
34. Professional readings list (list readings and describe reactions)
35. Projects (how teaching materials were developed)
36. References (statements from supervisors)
37. Research papers (highlight knowledge of an academic subject)
38. Rules and procedures descriptions (written guidelines)
39. Schedules (show format for events in a day)
40. Seating arrangement diagrams (reflect on a particular management strategy)
41. Self-assessment instruments (questionnaire results)
42. Simulated experiences (describe role-play experience)
43. Student contracts (samples of agreement with students)
44. Subscriptions (list of journals with address label)
45. Teacher-made materials (games, videotapes, teaching aids)
46. Theme studies (lessons that show integrated curriculum)
47. Transcripts (copy of official transcript with personal analysis)

48. Unit plans (integrated plan covering several weeks)
49. Video scenario critiques (analyses of videotapes of actual teaching episodes)
50. Volunteer experience (list and briefly describe services provided)
51. Work experience (descriptions of work in a nontraditional setting)

### Analysis of Artifacts

In addition to the management and assembly guidelines offered previously in this handbook, preservice teachers need to "manage" the documentation of the teacher standards. Each artifact selected for the working, presentation, and/or employment portfolio should be analyzed to help determine (1) standards that need work, (2) overreliance on some kinds of artifacts, and (3) need to diversify artifacts. The artifacts analysis chart in Appendix A can be used for this purpose. Check marks and/or dates should be entered to record the range of artifacts in support of the nine teacher standards.

## PORTFOLIO EVALUATION

Periodic reviews not only are essential, but they are natural to a system of portfolio assessment and a teacher education program. Because the WSU system is course affiliated, evaluation is an ongoing and cumulative process at each stage of program course requirements. Peer, faculty, and instructor feedback processes are associated with the working, presentation, and employment portfolios (i.e., peer and instructor conferences, peer and faculty reflections). However, more formal evaluation procedures will also be used. Criteria are referenced to the portfolio's *content* and *quality*. Guidelines for the formative and summative evaluation of these professional portfolios are provided.

### Formative

When information is sought to help decide how to adjust or improve performance during a learning process, evaluation serves a formative purpose. The working and presentation portfolios are associated with formative evaluation in the WSU system. Because the teacher standards serve as the basis for organizing these portfolios, they are central to the evaluation instruments. Scoring rubrics for the working and presentation portfolios are in Appendix B.

### Summative

Evaluation of a summative nature is used to decide the extent to which "learners" have been successful in mastering final outcomes (standards). In the WSU system, the employment portfolio is viewed as the final or exit portfolio. It is subject to summative evaluation protocols. However, the evaluation format recognizes the purposes of the employment portfolio—synthesize the knowledge, skills, and dispositions of the preservice teacher and enhance job placement. A scoring rubric for the employment portfolio is in Appendix B.

# Appendix A

Forms

# REFLECTION COVER SHEET

## for Working Portfolio Artifacts

Name: _____ Date: _____

Standard #: _____ Title: _____

Name of artifact: _____

Course/activity: _____

Rationale statement: _____

_____

_____

_____

_____

_____

_____

_____

_____

_____

_____

_____

_____

_____

_____

_____

_____

_____

_____

_____

_____

_____

_____

_____

_____

_____

_____

# SELF-ASSESSMENT CHECKLIST
## of Standards for the Working Portfolio

| Standard | Good | OK | Artifacts needed |
|---|---|---|---|
| #1. Content knowledge | | | Goal:<br><br>Target date: |
| #2. Growth & development | | | Goal:<br><br>Target date: |
| #3. Diverse learners | | | Goal:<br><br>Target date: |
| #4. Management & motivation | | | Goal:<br><br>Target date: |
| #5. Communication | | | Goal:<br><br>Target date: |
| #6. Planning & instruction | | | Goal:<br><br>Target date: |
| #7. Learner assessment | | | Goal:<br><br>Target date: |
| #8. Reflection | | | Goal:<br><br>Target date: |
| #9. Collaboration | | | Goal:<br><br>Target date: |

# STRUCTURE
# FOR THE WORKING PORTFOLIO
## Peer Conference

The following questions should serve as the basis for the conference:

1. What have you learned about yourself by putting your portfolio together?

2. What artifacts are you particularly proud of? Why?

3. If you could publish one thing in your portfolio, what would it be? Why?

4. What areas of your teaching performance need further improvement?

5. How do you feel about your role as a professional physical education teacher?

# BRIDGING QUESTIONS

## for the Presentation Portfolio

As you contemplate your selections, ask yourself the following questions to help "bridge" individual items into the entire portfolio:

1.  Why should I choose this piece?

2.  What are its strengths and weaknesses?

3.  Why is it important?

4.  How does it fit into what I already have?

5.  What if I took it out?

6.  How will others react to it?

# SELF-ASSESSMENT
# OF TEACHER STANDARDS

## for the Presentation Portfolio

Name: _____ Date: _____

Standard #: _____ Title: _____

| | | |
|---|---|---|
| **My strengths** | *Knowledge* | |
| | *Skills* | |
| | *Dispositions* | |
| **My problem areas** | *Knowledge* | |
| | *Skills* | |
| | *Dispositions* | |

# PEER/FACULTY REFLECTION SHEET

## for the Presentation Portfolio

Date: _____

To: _____

From: _____

During the poster-like session, please review my professional portfolio and provide feedback by answering the following questions:

1. What teacher standard is documented the most effectively? Why?

2. What teacher standard is documented least effectively? Why?

3. What artifacts really made an impression on you? Why?

4. What artifact do you feel needs the most work? Why?

5. What is your overall impression of the organization and presentation of artifacts?

Signed: _____  Date: _____

# STRUCTURE FOR THE PEER/INSTRUCTOR

## Employment Portfolio Conferences

Conferences should be structured around a comparison of the preservice teacher's perceptions and the opinion of a peer or the instructor regarding the following:

1. Overall strengths as a physical education teacher

2. Artifacts that represent "holistic" abilities and dispositions toward teaching

3. How the portfolio verifies that the beginning teacher standards have been met

4. What teacher standards will likely develop further as a practicing teacher

5. Teacher standards that need work as revealed by the portfolio

# ARTIFACTS ANALYSIS CHART

## for the Working, Presentation, and Employment Portfolios

| Kind of artifact | Name of artifact | Teacher standard | | | | | | | | |
|---|---|---|---|---|---|---|---|---|---|---|
| | | 1 | 2 | 3 | 4 | 5 | 6 | 7 | 8 | 9 |
| | | | | | | | | | | |
| | | | | | | | | | | |
| | | | | | | | | | | |
| | | | | | | | | | | |
| | | | | | | | | | | |
| | | | | | | | | | | |
| | | | | | | | | | | |
| | | | | | | | | | | |
| | | | | | | | | | | |
| | | | | | | | | | | |
| | | | | | | | | | | |
| | | | | | | | | | | |
| | | | | | | | | | | |
| | | | | | | | | | | |
| | | | | | | | | | | |
| | | | | | | | | | | |
| | | | | | | | | | | |
| | | | | | | | | | | |
| | | | | | | | | | | |
| | | | | | | | | | | |
| | | | | | | | | | | |
| | | | | | | | | | | |
| | | | | | | | | | | |
| | | | | | | | | | | |

# Appendix B

Scoring Rubrics

# WORKING PORTFOLIO

## Scoring Rubric

Name: _____  Semester/year: _____

Course: _____  Instructor: _____

| Elements | Fair | Satisfactory | Good | Outstanding | Weight | Score |
|---|---|---|---|---|---|---|
| **Organization/form** | | | | | | |
| 1. Follows directions | ① | ② | ③ | ④ | ×1 | _____ (4) |
| 2. Clear layout/visual appeal | ① | ② | ③ | ④ | ×1 | _____ (4) |
| 3. Creative cover | ① | ② | ③ | ④ | ×1 | _____ (4) |
| 4. Writing mechanics | ① | ② | ③ | ④ | ×1 | _____ (4) |
| 5. Expressiveness | ① | ② | ③ | ④ | ×1 | _____ (4) |
| **Completeness** | | | | | | |
| 1. Reflection cover sheets | ① | ② | ③ | ④ | ×1 | _____ (4) |
| 2. Self-assessment checklist | ① | ② | ③ | ④ | ×1 | _____ (4) |
| 3. Artifacts analysis chart | ① | ② | ③ | ④ | ×1 | _____ (4) |
| 4. Index | ① | ② | ③ | ④ | ×1 | _____ (4) |
| **Standard #1: Content knowledge** | | | | | | |
| 1. Required artifacts | ① | ② | ③ | ④ | ×2 | _____ (8) |
| 2. Optional artifacts | ① | ② | ③ | ④ | ×2 | _____ (8) |
| **Standard #2: Growth & development** | | | | | | |
| 1. Required artifacts | ① | ② | ③ | ④ | ×2 | _____ (8) |
| 2. Optional artifacts | ① | ② | ③ | ④ | ×2 | _____ (8) |
| **Standard #3: Diverse learners** | | | | | | |
| 1. Required artifacts | ① | ② | ③ | ④ | ×2 | _____ (8) |
| 2. Optional artifacts | ① | ② | ③ | ④ | ×2 | _____ (8) |
| **Standard #4: Management & motivation** | | | | | | |
| 1. Required artifacts | ① | ② | ③ | ④ | ×2 | _____ (8) |
| 2. Optional artifacts | ① | ② | ③ | ④ | ×2 | _____ (8) |

*(continued)*

| Elements | Fair | Satisfactory | Good | Outstanding | Weight | Score |
|---|---|---|---|---|---|---|
| *Standard #5: Communication* | | | | | | |
| 1.  Required artifacts | ① | ② | ③ | ④ | ×2 | _____ (8) |
| 2.  Optional artifacts | ① | ② | ③ | ④ | ×2 | _____ (8) |
| *Standard #6: Planning & instruction* | | | | | | |
| 1.  Required artifacts | ① | ② | ③ | ④ | ×2 | _____ (8) |
| 2.  Optional artifacts | ① | ② | ③ | ④ | ×2 | _____ (8) |
| *Standard #7: Learner assessment* | | | | | | |
| 1.  Required artifacts | ① | ② | ③ | ④ | ×2 | _____ (8) |
| 2.  Optional artifacts | ① | ② | ③ | ④ | ×2 | _____ (8) |
| *Standard #8: Reflection* | | | | | | |
| 1.  Required artifacts | ① | ② | ③ | ④ | ×2 | _____ (8) |
| 2.  Optional artifacts | ① | ② | ③ | ④ | ×2 | _____ (8) |
| *Standard #9: Collaboration* | | | | | | |
| 1.  Required artifacts | ① | ② | ③ | ④ | ×2 | _____ (8) |
| 2.  Optional artifacts | ① | ② | ③ | ④ | ×2 | _____ (8) |

**Grading scale**

A = 162-180
B = 144-161
C = 126-143
D = 108-125
F = Below 108

**Total score:** _____
(180)

**Grade:** _____

Comments: _____

_____

_____

_____

_____

_____

_____

_____

_____

Instructor signature: _____  Date: _____

73

**PPEPP Handbook**

# PRESENTATION PORTFOLIO

## Scoring Rubric

### "POSTER SESSION"

Name: _____   Semester/year: _____

Course: _____   Instructor: _____

1. Required components contained in the presentation portfolio (creative cover, table of contents, reflection cover sheets, self-assessment of teacher standards)

    1 ----------- 2 ----------- 3 ----------- 4 ----------- 5
    Included but incomplete        Some gaps        Fully developed

    Comments: _____

    _____

    _____

2. Presentation portfolio exhibited in a dynamic, creative, and informative manner

    1 ----------- 2 ----------- 3 ----------- 4 ----------- 5
    Poor display        Marginal display        Impressive display

    Comments: _____

    _____

    _____

3. In general, artifacts clearly and convincingly represent each teacher standard

    1 ----------- 2 ----------- 3 ----------- 4 ----------- 5
    Weak evidence        Satisfactorily documented        No doubt

    Comments: _____

    _____

    _____

*(continued)*

4. Connection between artifacts and each teacher standard according to the following rating scale: + = impressive ✔ = acceptable 0 = needs work

———— Standard #1: Content knowledge

———— Standard #2: Growth and development

———— Standard #3: Diverse learners

———— Standard #4: Management and motivation

———— Standard #5: Communication

———— Standard #6: Planning and instruction

———— Standard #7: Learner assessment

———— Standard #8: Reflection

———— Standard #9: Collaboration

5. Overall impression of the presentation portfolio poster session display

1 ------------ 2 ----------- 3 ----------- 4 ----------- 5
Weak quality               Acceptable quality          Exceptional quality

Comments: _____

_____

_____

_____

_____

_____

_____

_____

_____

_____

_____

_____

_____

_____

_____

_____

_____

_____

Instructor signature: _____ Date: _____

# EMPLOYMENT PORTFOLIO
## Scoring Rubric

Name: _____ Date: _____

**Portfolio contents**—components of the employment portfolio are verified and rated according to the following scale:

2 = Fully developed    1 = Included but incomplete    0 = Not included

——— 1. Table of contents

——— 2. Cover letter

——— 3. Biographical sketch

——— 4. Resume

——— 5. Philosophy of education statement

——— 6. Certification/licensing documents

——— 7. Letters of recommendation

——— 8. List of relevant courses

——— 9. Student teaching evaluations

——— 10. Artifacts representing the teacher standards

——— 11. Reflections on each teacher standard relative to selected artifacts

——— 12. Evaluations of working and presentation portfolios by instructors

——— **Total**

Comments: _____

_____

_____

_____

_____

*(continued)*

**Portfolio quality**—the degree of quality is determined by rating each characteristic and artifact according to the following scale:

2 = High quality; above expectation
1 = Satisfactory quality; meets expectations
0 = Low quality; below expectation

| | | | |
|---|---|---|---|
| _____ Organization | | _____ Artifact #5: | _____ |
| _____ Layout/visual appeal | | _____ Artifact #6: | _____ |
| _____ Creativity/expressiveness | | _____ Artifact #7: | _____ |
| _____ Spelling, punctuation, grammar | | _____ Artifact #8: | _____ |
| _____ Artifact #1: _____ | | _____ Artifact #9: | _____ |
| _____ Artifact #2: _____ | | _____ Artifact #10: | _____ |
| _____ Artifact #3: _____ | | _____ Artifact #11: | _____ |
| _____ Artifact #4: _____ | | _____ Artifact #12: | _____ |

_____ **Total** _____ **Average**

**Comments:** _____

_____

_____

_____

_____

_____

_____

_____

_____

_____

## Summary Ratings

**Portfolio contents**

_____ Outstanding (19–24)

_____ Satisfactory (12–18)

_____ Unsatisfactory (0–11)

**Portfolio quality**

_____ Outstanding (ave. 1.6–2.0)

_____ Satisfactory (ave. 1.0–1.5)

_____ Unsatisfactory (ave. 0.0–1.9)

Instructor signature: _____ Date: _____

chapter 3

# Student Portfolios

Student learning needs to be evaluated in a more naturalistic, performance-based manner. Skill tests, multiple-choice exams, and standardized achievement tests do not necessarily tell educators what students really know and are able to do. So, how can a broader, more genuine picture of student learning be presented?

# INTRODUCTION

The search for accountability in student learning has never been more intense. Interest in assessment has also been prompted by these accountability concerns, especially the desire to organize learning data in ways that are credible and comprehensible to all stakeholders—student, teacher, school personnel, parent, and community. This chapter recommends a multifaceted approach for designing student portfolio systems appropriate for K-12 physical education programs. The framework for developing portfolios includes six phases: (1) determine purposes and types, (2) organize and plan logistics, (3) select items, (4) reflect and self-assess, (5) conduct conferences, and (6) evaluate. The chapter provides materials exemplary of established content standards in physical education. To synthesize this information, sample high school, middle school, and elementary school portfolio systems are presented at the end of the chapter.

# PURPOSES AND TYPES

Like other teachers, physical educators think about why they use a particular drill or lead-up game or why they guide a class in a certain direction through skill practice. They also want a clear sense about what they are trying to accomplish when they assess students. Before deciding on student portfolios as the assessment tool of choice, physical educators need only to look at a comparison between what seems to be traditional testing practice and the characteristics of portfolio assessment (Tierney, Carter, & Desai, 1991).

**Testing practices usually**

1. cover a limited content area and may not truly represent what students have learned,
2. rely on teacher-scored or mechanically scored results with little student input,
3. examine all students on the same dimensions,
4. minimize teacher-student and student-student collaboration,
5. address achievement only, and
6. separate assessment, teaching, and learning.

In physical education, testing practices have resulted in end-of-unit skills tests with little relationship to what might have been actually learned. Performance results are determined in artificial or contrived settings (e.g., skill test) rather than in more naturalistic, real situations (e.g., game play). Testing of this nature is not considered authentic.

**Portfolios**

1. represent a wide range of student work in a given content area,
2. engage students in self-assessment and goal setting,
3. allow for student differences,
4. foster collaborative assessment,
5. focus on improvement, effort, and achievement, and
6. link assessment and teaching to learning.

In physical education, these elements have always existed as part of any broad-based assessment process that uses learning data derived from drills, practice, and game settings. Portfolios offer a way to organize and manage these performance results. Assessment of this nature is considered authentic (Melograno,1994).

Although portfolio assessment seems to offer a dynamic, visual presentation of a student's true abilities, strengths, and areas of needed improvement, teachers should look at the "big picture" to determine the primary and secondary uses of portfolios. They need to answer some hard questions: Why involve students in the process of gathering artifacts? In the end, will it make a difference? What are the potential overuses and abuses of portfolios for assessment purposes and beyond? Once these critical decisions are made, a system of portfolio assessment can be initiated with students, assuming the purposes are clear to all. Therefore, the first phase in developing a student portfolio system involves determining the purposes and the types of portfolios that can best achieve these purposes.

## General and Specific Purposes

The reason for creating student portfolios is twofold—to serve students' needs and to serve teacher needs. These two broad categories may seem obvious, but often they are not. For students, it means that they are empowered and motivated to learn and are encouraged to engage in reflection and self-assessment. For teachers, it means that they can examine instructional methodologies and assess teaching performance. As the first step in building a portfolio system, purposes for both students and teachers should be considered. How could artifacts be selected without first deciding for what and for whom the portfolio is intended?

Portfolio purposes can be derived from three primary sources. First, assessments should reflect the content that is important for students to learn (i.e., physical education subject matter). Second, assessments should reflect the processes of learning that promote active, thoughtful, and valuing learners (e.g., skill practice, higher-order thinking, problem solving, acquiring interests, formulating attitudes). And third, assessments should accommodate the diversity that exists among students (e.g., learning styles, multiple intelligences, physical challenges, multicultural differences).

Another question that arises is, How many purposes? Even though the number of possible purposes of portfolios is unlimited, it makes sense to be practical. Teachers are better off setting a manageable number, particularly in the beginning. This is an important decision because the purposes will govern what goes into the portfolio. Given the needs of students and teachers and the sources of purposes, it is useful to think of portfolios as serving both general and specific purposes.

**General Purposes.** These kinds of purposes, gathered from various places, are applicable across subject areas and grade levels. They are global in nature and serve any kind of student portfolio system. Some general purposes include (Murphy & Smith, 1992)

- keeping track of student's progress,
- providing students with an opportunity to assess their own accomplishments,
- assisting the teacher in instructional planning,
- determining the extent to which established learning objectives have been achieved,
- helping parents understand their children's effort and progress,
- serving as a basis for program evaluation, and
- determining student placement within and outside of class.

**Specific Purposes.** These kinds of purposes relate directly to physical education as a teaching discipline. They focus on subject matter, learn-

ing processes, and accommodations represented by the physical education student portfolio system. Some specific purposes include

- helping students practice healthy lifestyles,
- communicating student's strengths and weaknesses in gross and fine motor skills,
- determining degree of personal and social development in an adventure education program,
- developing the student outcomes associated with the definition of the physically educated person, and
- documenting the status of physical education content standards and corresponding grade-level benchmarks.

## Types of Portfolios

The lists of widely varying general and specific purposes suggest that portfolios can go in several directions. A portfolio that emphasizes personal fitness, for example, would look much different from one that documents content standards and benchmarks. Once the purposes for implementing a portfolio system are clear, the type of portfolio should be determined that can best achieve these purposes. The following types of portfolios are not meant to be exhaustive. They can be used alone, in combination, or with other ideas to satisfy established purposes (Batzle, 1992; Burke, Fogarty, & Belgrad, 1994; Kimeldorf, 1994).

**Personal Portfolio.** For other students and the teacher to know more about students and to celebrate their interests, portfolio items from outside school may be included that show hobbies, community activities, musical or artistic talents, sports, family, pets, or travel. To form a more holistic view of students, the portfolio could contain pictures, awards, videos, or other memorabilia. For example, a student might prepare an introductory portfolio that presents himself/herself as a "sports enthusiast." Another possibility is the autobiography portfolio, which traces life events and reflects on the future in terms of school and/or career goals. The personal portfolio can serve as a catalyst for self-reflection and continual sharing of ideas and insights throughout the K-12 experience.

**Working Portfolio.** The ongoing, systematic collection of student work samples and exhibits can be maintained in a working portfolio. This collection of daily, weekly, monthly, or unit work products forms the framework for self-assessment and goal setting, and it provides the basis for selecting items for other types of portfolios (e.g., showcase, thematic, multi-year). The working portfolio is managed and kept by the student.

**Record-Keeping Portfolio.** This maintenance type of portfolio is usually kept by the teacher. It contains necessary assessment and evaluation samples and records that may be required by the school district (e.g., written exams, proficiency tests) and are not chosen by the student. The record-keeping portfolio could also include observational information (e.g., anecdotal notes, frequency index scales, narrative descriptors, behavior checklists), as well as progress reports to supplement traditional report cards.

**Group Portfolio.** Members of a cooperative learning group contribute individual items that show individual strengths. These are included along with group items (e.g., samples, pictures, community projects) to demonstrate the effectiveness of the entire group. The characteristics of cooperative learning are retained, namely, interde-pendence, individual accountability, heterogeneity (i.e., skill level, gender, race, and/or cultural background), cooperative behaviors, and group "score," that is, a collection of individual scores. For example, the sport education curriculum model lends itself to the group portfolio.

**Thematic Portfolio.** This portfolio would relate to a unit of study with a particular focus. The unit would normally last from two to six weeks. For example, with "teamwork" as the theme, entries could reflect an understanding of offensive and defensive strategies (cognitive), sports skills that facilitate team patterns of play (motor), and behavior processes that show working toward a common goal (affective). Other themes in physical education might be socialization through sports, aerobics "away", spatial awareness, or self-expression.

**Integrated Portfolio.** To view the "whole" student, works from all the disciplines showing connections between or among subjects would be included. Selected items, either required or optional, could be drawn from several or all subjects. Students could reflect on the most and least favorite aspects of each subject or discuss what

Cooperative learning can be facilitated by a group portfolio.

concepts and skills transfer across several subjects and outside the school setting. Subjects that could be easily integrated with physical education include health (e.g., fitness, stress), science (e.g., laws of motion, stability), language arts (e.g., nonverbal communication), art (e.g., expression, manipulation), and music (e.g., rhythm, creating).

**Showcase Portfolio.** A limited number of items are selected to exhibit growth over time and to serve a particular purpose. This portfolio usually houses only the student's best work. Because it is streamlined and customized, it can be presented to others in different ways, such as small group, large group, poster-like session, or exhibition. The showcase portfolio, for example, could be focused on growth in a sport, fitness gains, or development of a gymnastics routine.

**Electronic Portfolio.** Technological advances have made electronic portfolios a reality. However, if they are simply software databases—storage for pictures, sound, or words—they are really no different from a hanging file or milk crate. The content of the portfolios and the process for creating it are the most important concerns. Multimedia writing tools, scanners, digital cameras, and recordable CD-ROM drives have all helped in creating true portfolios (Moersch & Fisher, 1995; Mohnsen, 1995). For example, the *Grady Profile* (Aurbach & Associates, Inc.) is a collection of integrated HyperCard stacks that present samples of student work with graphic, text, video, and sound exhibits. Self-reflection, data sharing, and evaluation are built in. Specific to physical education, for example, Project COPE (Computer Organized Physical Education) uses a computer data management system to improve record keeping, planning, and communication (Lambdin, 1997). Information is organized around the definition of the physically educated person (Franck et al., 1992). It serves as an electronic portfolio by allowing teachers to identify individual student needs, determine class performance, communicate with parents about student achievement, and document program effectiveness.

**Multi-year Portfolio.** Students would collect items from a cluster of grade levels over two-, three-, or four-year intervals. The multi-year portfolio would be stored at the school. Reflection on changes over a three-year period, for example, would occur periodically.

**Employment Portfolio.** Students are often required to collect evidence of their employability skills. This portfolio is found mostly at the secondary level, particularly among graduating seniors. Students need to show artifacts that demonstrate the ability to communicate, work cooperatively, and work responsibly. The extent to which work samples and exhibits from physical education might contribute to the employment portfolio depends on the nature of the artifact and the nature of the prospective job. A student will also benefit from compiling a sample portfolio in preparation for a mock job interview.

**Scholarship Portfolio.** Information is compiled to show student eligibility for academic and/or athletic college scholarships. Although transcripts, attendance records, standardized test scores, and recommendations are normally included, other items from physical education might be selected (e.g., physical fitness status, videos, projects). The scholarship portfolio is normally managed by the student and facilitated by a school counselor.

# ORGANIZATION AND LOGISTICS

The second phase in developing a student portfolio system deals with several practical matters. The mechanics of portfolios are decided, and they serve as a guide for the remaining components. Given the complexities of portfolios, these decisions are critical because they affect the ongoing process of assessment and the daily lives of teachers and students.

Regardless of purpose or type of portfolio, a clear and meaningful organizational scheme is needed. Student portfolios can be organized around any number of goals, competencies, concepts, outcomes, and other constructs. The following chapter section discusses some of these alternative organizers. Ultimately, established K-12 physical education content standards and corresponding benchmarks are recommended as the basis for organizing the "academic" types of portfolios.

A successful system of portfolio assessment is also dependent on the role of both teacher and student. Because these roles are likely to be new, expectations should be clear. One of the expectations is to plan a way to handle the logistics of the portfolio process. Decisions are needed about method of construction, how and where to store portfolios, and how often to "manage" portfolios.

## Alternative Organizers

To a large extent, the purpose and type of student portfolio will direct its organizational scheme. For example, perhaps the purpose is to monitor the progress of students' development of locomotor skills, and a showcase portfolio is to be used. The portfolio would likely be organized around the concepts and skills associated with the walk, run, jump, hop, gallop, slide, skip, and leap. Students might be expected to select their best work for each movement (e.g., task sheet, drawing of exercise, matching worksheet) and to demonstrate the movements to a small group of peers who provide feedback using a criteria checklist. To further illustrate, suppose that the purpose is to determine achievement of health-related fitness objectives and that a group portfolio is selected. The predetermined individual and group targets for cardiorespiratory endurance, muscular strength and endurance, flexibility, and body composition could be the basis for organizing the portfolio. These targets would need to be validated with artifacts (e.g., logs, journals, pretest and posttest comparisons, attitude inventory, fitness team project).

Although purposes are the primary means for organizing the portfolio, there are other useful possibilities. For example, existing district goals or outcomes can be translated into criteria and indicators of performance specific to physical education. The result would be portfolios that reflect levels of accomplishment referenced to the performance indicators. Similarly, state-mandated standards are excellent sources for determining the organizational basis for the portfolio. The following additional frameworks for organizing portfolios apply to the "academic" types of portfolios identified previously in this chapter (i.e., working, record-keeping, group, thematic, integrated, showcase, electronic, and multi-year portfolios). They would not be relevant for the other, more private types of portfolios (i.e., personal, employment, and scholarship portfolios).

**Physically Educated Person.** Clearly developed, publicly stated outcomes can provide the basis for organizing portfolios. The five major focus areas and 20 outcome statements of the physically educated person could serve as useful organizing elements. Pages 3-4 identify the five basic parts and the specific outcomes associated with each. A physically educated person (Franck et al., 1992)

**HAS** learned skills necessary to perform a variety of physical activities.

**IS** physically fit.

**DOES** participate regularly in physical activity.

**KNOWS** the implications of and the benefits from involvement in physical activities.

**VALUES** physical activity and its contributions to a healthful lifestyle. (p. 4)

**Mission Statement.** Oftentimes, the school district has a stated mission, which in turn is translated into program mission statements. Elements of such a statement could serve as the focus for organizing portfolios. For example, teachers and students could collect, rationalize, and organize artifacts around the following mission: "Through physical education, students will develop into healthy, physically active, socially adjusted, emotionally stable, and intellectually stimulated persons by attaining the knowledge, skills, and attitudes and values appropriate to these outcomes."

**Learning Dimensions.** Students need to grow and mature physically, intellectually, emotionally, socially, and spiritually (values). Because these individual, developmental needs can be satisfied explicitly through participation in physical activities, they are valuable organizing constructs for the portfolio. Artifacts could be planned for each of the dimensions as represented by the educational domains:

- *Cognitive*—knowledge and intellectual abilities and skills ranging from simple recall tasks to synthesizing and evaluating information (Bloom, 1956).
- *Affective*—likes and dislikes, attitudes, values, and beliefs, ranging from the willingness to receive information and respond to stimuli to the development of an established value system; encompasses the process of socialization (Krathwohl, Bloom, & Masia, 1964).
- *Psychomotor*—all observable voluntary human motion, ranging from reflex movements to the ability to modify and create aesthetic movement patterns (Harrow, 1972).

**Multiple Intelligences.** Although outcomes should be sought by all students, physical educators must respect the diversity among learners. Not all students can achieve outcomes in the same manner. The theory of multiple intelligences (Gardner, 1993) suggests that people possess several capacities for learning and creating products. Artifacts from physical education would be selected for each intelligence depending on content and individual student preferences. The portfolio could be organized around these seven domains of learning:

- *Visual/spatial*—relies on the sense of sight and the ability to visualize an object and create mental images (e.g., chart plays, sketch-out routine).

- *Verbal/linguistic*—relates to written and spoken language (e.g., reactions to videos, written fitness program).

- *Logical/mathematical*—deals with deductive thinking, reasoning, and recognition of abstract patterns (e.g., calculate energy expenditure, biomechanical analysis of sports skills).

- *Bodily/kinesthetic*—involves using the body to solve problems, create products, and convey ideas and emotions (e.g., outdoor education challenges, design free-exercise routine).

- *Musical/rhythmic*—includes recognition of environmental sounds and sensitivity to rhythm and beats (e.g., create a dance step, move to drum beat).

- *Interpersonal*—is the ability to understand and work effectively with others (e.g., plan a cooperative game, role-play sportsmanship).

- *Intrapersonal*—refers to knowledge about and awareness of one's own emotions and self (e.g., reflective fitness journal, describe feeling of being a pro golfer).

**Organizing Centers.** The physical education curriculum often lacks a focus, some frame of reference around which the curriculum is designed. The "organizing center" helps to identify these elements that can serve as focal points (Melograno, 1996). Organizing centers combine those concepts, skills, attitudes, and values underlying physical education goals content. They are global in nature. The resulting program is a series of organizing centers sequentially arranged over various time periods (e.g., single lesson, series of lessons, unit, semester, academic year, four-year high school program, comprehensive K-12 curriculum). In the same manner that organizing

centers provide a curriculum focus, they could provide the basis for organizing portfolios. They go hand in hand. Organizing centers range from comprehensive themes such as "Education for a Global Community," "Worthy Citizenship," or "Meeting the Challenge of a Changing Society" to specific emphases such as "Body Awareness," "Teamwork," or "Solving a Problem." Intermediate ideas can also be used, such as "Growth and Development," "Success," or "Decision Making." Regardless of their complexity, organizing centers offer a rationale for the selection of artifacts.

**Content Standards and Benchmarks.** Although it would be more practical, a universal construct for organizing portfolios does not exist. That should be clear given the options already presented. However, there is some agreement about what students should know and be able to do as a result of their physical education program. These physical education content standards and corresponding benchmarks for four levels (grades K-2, 3-6, 7-8, 9-12) were detailed in table 1.1 (pages 5-8). Because of their widespread acceptance, they are recommended as the basis for organizing student portfolios. They will also be used in subsequent sections of this chapter that deal with the other phases of portfolio development. Recall that the five content standards are as follows:

- Uses a variety of basic and advanced movement forms

- Uses movement concepts and principles in the development of motor skills

- Understands the benefits and costs associated with participation in physical activity

- Understands how to monitor and maintain a health-enhancing level of physical fitness

- Understands the social and personal responsibility associated with participation in physical activity

## Role of Teacher and Students

Implementing portfolio practices requires a profound shift in the responsibilities and roles of teachers and students. Some physical education teachers look at portfolio assessment and say, "I have too many students and not enough time." The reality for most teachers is to manage students first and deliver some kind of instruction second. Assessment may be a distant third priority. However, portfolios demand a high level of student responsibility in terms of reflection, self-management, self-assessment, and peer reflection, conferences, and evaluation. If students gradually learn to use a system of portfolio assessment, restrictions of time and sheer numbers are minimized. Use of partners, small groups, and self-directed tasks can reduce the seemingly high student-teacher ratios. Obviously, the system needs to be well planned and managed. Before going any further with this system, look at the teacher's and students' roles more closely.

**Teacher's Role.** Although elements of current instructional delivery systems could foster alternative assessment strategies, changes are needed to implement portfolios in physical education. Traditional teaching roles, in which teachers inform, direct, and predetermine priorities, will not work. In the portfolio model, the teacher facilitates, guides, and offers choices. Teachers become reflective practitioners. Instead of judging students' work against their own or other mandated standards, they become accomplished facilitators in the process of portfolio self-assessment (Zessoules & Gardner, 1991). Partnerships are established among teacher, students, and parents. More specifically, in the portfolio system, teachers need to address these concepts:

1. Deliberately plan for student involvement. Strategies are needed to ensure student input; involvement cannot be left to chance. Make learning available; do not impose it.

2. Provide time for tasks that encourage decision making and reflection. Do not become overanxious because these tasks look passive. Become an intermediary between student and environment.

3. Demonstrate expected behaviors (e.g., self-management, self-evaluation). Actually show students and model what is being sought. Train students in decision making.

4. Help students manage portfolios. Provide assistance similar to guiding students through a difficult motor skill.

5. Develop positive interactive behaviors. Students need to know where they stand. Feedback and encouragement are needed because of the emphasis on self-management.

6. Actually use interactions to guide instruction. Information derived from portfolios as they are developed could influence what is taught. These kinds of adjustments are formative in nature.

7. Rethink the environment. Try to designate space so that students can become more actively involved in compiling their portfolios (e.g., portfolio storage, project work area, conference area, videotaping station). However, a successful portfolio system can be implemented without any of these considerations.

**Students' Role.** Skills of independence must be learned because portfolios emphasize process as well as product. Acquiring these skills does not come easily to all students, nor does it happen overnight. Students need to observe, practice, and refine the behaviors associated with decision making, self-management, and self-directed learning. Traditional student roles may not work. Students become active rather than passive. Instead of asking the teacher what they need to do or learning only what the teacher wants, students begin to ask themselves what is needed and to learn for themselves. Thus, students develop an increasing capacity to take responsibility for their own learning. More specifically, in the portfolio system, students need to

1. reflect on the value of their own work and engage in metacognition (i.e., manage and assess one's own learning strategies);

2. make critical choices about what work samples and exhibits best represent learning;

3. trace the development of their own learning and make connections between prior knowledge and skills and new learning (i.e., transfer);

4. make decisions and assume responsibility for future learning and set short-term and long-term learning goals;

5. engage in self-monitoring, self-management, and self-evaluation; and

6. collaborate within the physical education class setting (e.g., share best works, peer tutoring, peer reflection, peer conferences).

## Construction and Storage

Perhaps the initial concern with logistics is how to collect and maintain all the possible items that

Physical education teachers need to help students in self-managing the portfolio.

could comprise the portfolio. At least two planning decisions must be made in this regard. First, a method of construction should be chosen. Second, how and where to store portfolios should be determined. Figure 3.1 depicts several options.

Managing portfolios in physical education is different from managing them in a contained classroom. The physical education setting is not like a single room, nor is it usually the "home" base for students, so it is more difficult to centralize the portfolio system. Also, the physical education teacher must accommodate all the students across many different classes, whereas an elementary classroom teacher, for example, may need to manage only 20 to 30 portfolios. Therefore, the physical education teacher may need to establish a common method of construction. It may not be feasible to allow the "container" for collecting artifacts to be a matter of personal preference. Possibilities include file folders, notebooks, hanging files, albums, large envelopes, accordion files, packet folders with spiral bindings, and boxes. Every item should be dated and a cumulative list of items maintained in the front

of the portfolio.

Portfolios should be stored in locations that are accessible to students. Obviously, if students are responsible for storing their own portfolios, then the method of storage is a matter of personal preference. However, the presentation of the portfolio for teacher, peer, and/or parent review may be prescribed. If portfolios are stored in the physical education setting, the primary consideration is space. Depending on space, possibilities include file cabinets, file drawers, milk crates, shelves, large cardboard boxes, cereal boxes cut like a magazine holder, pizza boxes, and large notebooks with jacket folders.

Another storage option is a computer disk, regardless of whether the student and/or teacher assumes responsibility for storage. Written work, logs, scoring rubrics, journals, computer simulations, and digitized video can be kept on computer disks depending on available technology (e.g., personal computers, scanners, camcorders, digital cameras, recordable CD-ROM drives, software). Portfolios can also be stored in a central location (e.g., media center) for easy access and

**Figure 3.1** Selected construction and storage options for student portfolios.

review. However, this storage option requires a great deal of coordination and cooperation among students and school personnel.

Ultimately, construction and storage decisions depend on the types of portfolios. For example, the working portfolio requires sufficient container space because the overall number of artifacts is high (e.g., large notebook divided by sections, expanding and accordion files). By contrast, more selective types of portfolios (e.g., personal, thematic, integrated, showcase) may contain a relatively small number of artifacts because they are drawn from the working portfolio collection. Therefore, file folders or a small notebook may be all that is needed. The construction and storage of other specialized types of portfolios (e.g., record-keeping, group, electronic, multiyear, employment, scholarship) will vary according to purpose, number of artifacts, nature of artifacts, and who is going to review the portfolio.

A final aspect of storing portfolios relates to access. Although students' access to their own portfolios should be as hassle-free as possible, access by others must be established (e.g., peers, parents, other teachers, other school personnel).

*Student confidentiality and privacy must be protected.* Certain portfolio sections and/or items may be designated as public while others are private. Color codes, labels, stickers, or some other means of designation can be used. In any case, guidelines should be established from the beginning and strictly enforced thereafter by teachers and students.

## Management Tools

Students vary in their ability to self-manage all the loose ends associated with assembling and maintaining a portfolio. Some students, regardless of grade level, are natural "organizers." Others struggle at trying to keep things in order. Portfolio management skills should be taught in the same way that a motor skill is taught. Teachers need to demonstrate and model management behaviors, have students practice the behaviors, and reinforce the behaviors repeatedly. In addition, portfolios should be managed regularly by both teachers and students to avoid accumulation of items at the end of a given collection period. Certain management tools are effective in handling the logistics of portfolios. They can be used separately or in combination.

**Dividers.** Whatever kind of container is used, divided notebook folders or divider pages can be used to separate artifacts according to the content standards or by any other category that makes sense (e.g., themes, sport, unit, goal, works in progress, reflections, finished works). A filing system should be created so that the standards or categories are easily identified. Each section could be labeled with a shortened version of the standard.

**Color Codes.** To facilitate easier management, colored dots or colored files could be used to code entries in the portfolio. Artifacts could also be coded using different color markers. A code for the colors needs to be included (e.g., yellow for "not yet" work; blue for reflection; orange for group work; green for self-assessment; red for finished work).

**Table of Contents.** It is generally a good idea to include a list of all the entries and page numbers in the front of the portfolio. Whether required or optional, items other than student work samples should also be listed in the table of contents (e.g., reflection sheets, peer reflections, self-assessment instruments, goal-setting page, teacher's scoring rubrics).

**Artifact Registry.** A sheet could be maintained so that students could record the date, item, and reason for either adding or removing an item. Because the registry is supposed to chronicle when and why items are removed and/or replaced, students engage in a dynamic form of reflection. Figure 3.2 shows an artifact registry form.

**Work Log.** A biography of work could show the evolution of a long-term project like a portfolio and would help in making necessary changes or shifting directions. The log could be as simple as a dated entry that traces all activities and decisions associated with the portfolio. A work log form is also shown in figure 3.2.

**Index.** An alphabetical index of items and related topics could be compiled at the end of the portfolio. Such an organizational tool would help in the cross-referencing of artifacts that show evidence of content standards and benchmarks, organizing centers, multiple intelligences, learning dimensions, mission statement, and/or the physically educated person. An index, because of its complexity, would likely be found at the secondary level only.

**Post-it™ Notes.** Artifacts need to be cataloged so that ideas are not lost over time. A Post-it™ Note or index card could be attached to each artifact to identify the content standard, benchmark, or other appropriate category. A brief statement explaining why the artifact was collected could be included on the card as well. Specific descriptors may help later in connecting the artifact to the standard, benchmark, or category. Also, using a Post-it™ Note or index card protects original works.

**Stickers.** This management tool is similar to Post-it™ Notes except that preprinted stickers could be used to categorize items. For example, stickers could be made representing each content standard. Students could identify the corresponding benchmark and/or explain why it was collected. The standards could be indicated on the stickers with the following phrases: (1) basic/advanced movement form, (2) movement concept/principle, (3) benefits/costs of physical activity, (4) monitor/maintain health-enhancing fitness, and (5) social/personal responsibility. Other standard stickers could be produced with the following phrases:

> I want this in my portfolio because . . .
>
> This was difficult for me because . . .
>
> This item shows that . . .
>
> I think this is one of my best works because . . .

**Stamps.** To save time and to help students reflect on work samples, rubber stamps are a useful tool, particularly at the elementary level. A collection of stamps can facilitate the process of categorizing or labeling pieces. The following is a list of some sample stamp phrases:

> This was fun!
>
> Awesome!
>
> This was easy for me.
>
> Great!
>
> Best yet!
>
> Bravo!
>
> This was hard for me.
>
> 1st try
>
> I could do better.
>
> I need to be neater.
>
> I should take more time.
>
> I worked on _____
>
> I learned how to _____
>
> I need to work on _____

# Portfolio Registry

Name: _____    Topic: _____

| | *Additions* | | |
|---|---|---|
| Date | Item | Reasons |
| | | |
| | | |
| | | |

| | *Deletions* | | |
|---|---|---|
| Date | Item | Reasons |
| | | |
| | | |
| | | |

# Portfolio Work Log

Name: _____    Topic: _____

| Date | Entry |
|---|---|
| | |
| | |
| | |
| | |
| | |
| | |

Comments:

**Figure 3.2**   Artifact registry and work log forms can help in managing portfolios.

**Personalize.** The artwork, design, and layout of the portfolio allow students to interject their personality. By personalizing the portfolio using color, graphics, and shapes, individual portfolios are distinguished from one another. This can help in managing portfolios because individual students and their works will be identifiable. An original, creative cover demonstrates individual personality (collage, photos, patterned and textured designs). Also, children enjoy decorating things like cereal boxes, file folders, or pizza boxes that serve as portfolio containers. Finally, students' personalities can be displayed by the tone of the portfolio. For example, depending on purpose, the appropriate tone could be humorous (e.g., cartoons, jokes, riddles, funny sketches), aesthetic (e.g., artwork, pictures, poems), or serious (e.g., no extras, straightforward design, efficient use of space).

# ITEM SELECTION

Once the purposes and type of portfolio are determined (phase one) and the organizational scheme and logistics are planned (phase two), it is necessary to establish a process for selecting portfolio items. This third phase is related closely to the type of portfolio and the elements around which it is organized. For example, an integrated portfolio organized around the learning dimensions would contain evidence of a student's development of cognitive abilities (e.g., problem solving), affective behaviors (e.g., preferences), and psychomotor abilities (e.g., manipulative skills) across several subjects including physical education. Artifacts selected in physical education might include a problem task sheet, self-report inventory, and rating scale, respectively. Each type of portfolio previously described (pages 81-83) suggests particular kinds of items that would specify what students should know and be able to do.

The process of making selections includes decisions about what, how, who, and when. What to include depends on established criteria and standards. How to select items revolves around performance indicators and quality of work. Who selects items involves decisions about which stakeholders will participate in the selection of portfolio items. When to decide on items will vary significantly depending on portfolio purposes, type, and logistics. These aspects, which are treated separately in the following sections, are not decided in any particular sequence. In fact, they are usually dealt with in conjunction with one another.

## What to Include

Frequently, students' first portfolio items are "baseline" samples. A record-keeping type of portfolio managed by the teacher may be the most practical way to maintain these kinds of artifacts because of their nature and use. Information collected for entry appraisal should be included. For example, behavior sampling through informal techniques (i.e., observations, self-reports) and formal techniques (i.e., criterion-referenced measures) would yield important baseline information to ultimately show student change (learning). Likewise, other sources of entry information such as cumulative record data (e.g., previous test scores, diagnostic reviews, anecdotal records) and performance on a task sequence would also produce invaluable information.

When selecting the contents of a portfolio, two compelling factors should be kept in mind—the students' desires and the purpose for collecting each item. Portfolios should be student centered. When students make decisions about the selection and quality of their work, they begin to establish standards by which their work can be evaluated. However, students must realize that teachers will also decide on portfolio items and that some items may be mandated by school officials (DeFina, 1992). Although portfolios should not be a collection of anything and everything, the range of potential "exhibits of learning" contained in an individual portfolio is unlimited. Various kinds of artifacts include

- preassessment inventories,
- task sheets,
- self-assessment checklists,
- frequency index scales,
- rating scales,
- performance checklists,
- peer reviews,
- attitude surveys,
- self-reports,
- workbook pages,
- logs,
- journals,
- reflections,
- projects,

Videotape of skill performance can be included as a portfolio item.

- independent contracts,
- videotapes,
- anecdotal statements,
- parent observations or comments,
- skill tests,
- quizzes,
- written tests, and
- commercial instruments.

What is ultimately selected for the portfolio depends on its organizational scheme. The focus could be on physical education subject matter, different learning processes, a special project or unit, or the previously identified "organizers" (i.e., physically educated person, mission statement, learning dimensions, spectrum of multiple intelligences, organizing centers, and content standards and benchmarks). The various kinds of artifacts are grouped into three categories: observations, performance samples, and tests and test-like procedures. Illustrative artifacts for these three categories in physical education are identified in table 3.1. Some of the artifacts are partial in nature because they are offered for illustrative purposes.

1. *Observations*—These kinds of behavior cues are seen in everyday class activities. Behaviors that show movement abilities, interests, social conduct, and thinking can be recorded through observational formats (e.g., rating forms, checklists, anecdotes).

2. *Performance samples*—These tangible products or artifacts represent students' accomplishments. These kinds of formats are not as readily available in physical education settings because learning is usually centered on movement forms rather than on "documents." However, there are many samples of performance that should be considered (e.g., projects, videotapes).

3. *Tests and test-like procedures*—These include the full range of instruments (e.g., teacher-designed, commercial). "Test" does not necessarily imply formal, teacher-directed procedures. Informal inventories and end-of-unit tasks are valuable in documenting student learning.

## How to Select

In connection with what can be included, some decisions are needed as to how items are selected.

TABLE 3.1

## Portfolio Artifacts Possibilities

| CATEGORY | KIND OF ARTIFACT | ILLUSTRATIVE ARTIFACT (PARTIAL) |
|---|---|---|
| Observations | Rating scale | **Tennis Forehand** <br> • Contacts ball when even with front foot <br> • Keeps wrist firm; swings with whole arm from shoulder <br> • Rotates trunk so hips and shoulders face net on follow through <br><br> Not yet (1) □ (2) □ (3) □ (4) □ (5) Awesome □ <br> (repeated for each of the 3 items) |
| | Frequency index scale | See behavior trends table below |
| | Performance checklist | **Forward Roll** <br> • Tucks head with chin to chest <br> • Shifts body weight forward until off balance <br> • Accepts body weight with arms <br><br> Trial 1 □  Trial 2 □  Trial 3 □ (for each item) |
| | Peer review | Partner checks performance according to the criteria <br> **Cartwheel Criteria** <br> • Faces mat with preferred foot forward; same-side arm vertical <br> • Throws weight upon preferred foot; leans forward, placing same-side hand on mat <br> • Throws opposite leg up at the same time, placing same-side hand on mat <br><br> Perfect □  Acceptable □  Needs improvement □ (for each item) |

Frequency index scale:

| Behavior trends | 1st observation | | | | | 2nd observation | | | | | Rating average |
|---|---|---|---|---|---|---|---|---|---|---|---|
| | Never | Seldom | Fairly often | Frequently | Regularly | Never | Seldom | Fairly often | Frequently | Regularly | |
| 1. Limits interactions to friends | 5 | 4 | 3 | 2 | 1 | 5 | 4 | 3 | 2 | 1 | |
| 2. Shares equipment | 1 | 2 | 3 | 4 | 5 | 1 | 2 | 3 | 4 | 5 | |
| 3. Takes turn at circuit stations | 1 | 2 | 3 | 4 | 5 | 1 | 2 | 3 | 4 | 5 | |

*(continued)*

## TABLE 3.1
### (continued)

| CATEGORY | KIND OF ARTIFACT | ILLUSTRATIVE ARTIFACT (PARTIAL) |
|---|---|---|
| | Log | Fitness calendar showing aerobic training workout schedule: |

| Day | Time | Program | Level | Training description |
|---|---|---|---|---|
| Monday | 7:30 a.m. | Jogging | 3 | 220 yards; 110 yard relief; 4 repeats |
| Wednesday | 6:00 p.m. | Swimming | 5 | 50 yards; 90 second relief; 8 repeats |
| Friday | 7:30 a.m. | Jogging | 4 | 330 yards; 110 yard walk relief; 3 repeats |

| CATEGORY | KIND OF ARTIFACT | ILLUSTRATIVE ARTIFACT (PARTIAL) |
|---|---|---|
| | Anecdotal statement | Notes about a student's abilities during movement exploration activities: |

"In games of tag and dodging, Craig has difficulty moving his entire body rapidly in different directions and in response to unexpected situations; needs to improve his ability to change direction and make sudden stops and starts. He also had problems putting a hula hoop at different levels in relation to his body."

| CATEGORY | KIND OF ARTIFACT | ILLUSTRATIVE ARTIFACT (PARTIAL) |
|---|---|---|
| Performance samples | Task sheet | Draw a line from the locomotor movement in the picture to the word (Hopple, 1995). |

JUMP     WALK     HOP     RUN

*(continued)*

TABLE 3.1

*(continued)*

## ILLUSTRATIVE ARTIFACT (PARTIAL)

| CATEGORY | KIND OF ARTIFACT | |
|---|---|---|
| | **Self-assessment checklist** | Evaluate your own ability according to the criteria |

**Golf Grip** *(bottom hand)*

| | I have achieved | Working to achieve |
|---|---|---|
| • Place on club first, fingers as close together as possible | ☐ | ☐ |
| • Thumb close to hand at the first joint | ☐ | ☐ |
| • Wrist is directly above shaft | ☐ | ☐ |
| • Thumb forms "V"; forefinger points over opposite shoulder | ☐ | ☐ |

**Journal**

## DOUBLE-ENTRY JOURNAL

| Starting my tennis program | One month after my tennis program |
|---|---|
| 1. My goals are: | 1. |
| 2. My fears are: | 2. |
| 3. I feel good about: | 3. |

**Reflection**

*For secondary students:*

Circle the words that describe how you feel (mostly) about gymnastics:

Interesting   Too easy   Useless   Dull   Helpful   Worthless   Fun   Important   Boring   Too hard

Super   Others: _____

*For elementary students:*

Check (✔) the face you wear when you look at this picture:

☐ :)     ☐ :|     ☐ :(

*(continued)*

TABLE 3.1

*(continued)*

| CATEGORY | KIND OF ARTIFACT | ILLUSTRATIVE ARTIFACT (PARTIAL) |
|---|---|---|
| | Project | **Personalized fitness program** <br><br> • Plot a personal physical fitness profile based on ratings for cardiorespiratory endurance, muscular strength and endurance, flexibility, and body composition. <br> • Generate fitness goals based on ratings for health-related components. <br> • Select exercise and/or leisure activities in terms of contribution to fitness goals. <br> • Design a program based on goals, activity selection, and activity schedule. |
| | Independent contract | **Badminton contract:** <br><br> • Improve performance in 6 of 8 skills by at least one ability rating. <br> • Use mechanical principles, points of contact, and possible uses of criteria to compare and contrast: (1) overhead clear vs. forehand drive, (2) smash vs. overhead drop, and (3) long serve vs. short serve. <br> • Write a brief report (4–5 pages) on the history of badminton. <br> • Create a test on badminton terms, rules, and strategies; test and grade three classmates. |
| | Videotape | Free exercise routine; swimming stroke; game play |
| **Tests and test-like procedures** | Pre-assessment inventory | On the diagram, draw diagonal lines to show the area that is used during a singles game in tennis. Place an "X" where the server stands to begin a game, and an "O" where the server stands when the score is 30–15. <br><br> |

*(continued)*

TABLE 3.1
*(continued)*

| CATEGORY | KIND OF ARTIFACT | ILLUSTRATIVE ARTIFACT (PARTIAL) |
|---|---|---|
| | **Self-report** | Check the space that shows how you feel most of the time. Coed volleyball is:<br><br><table><tr><td>Exciting</td><td></td><td></td><td></td><td></td><td>Dull</td></tr><tr><td>Boring</td><td></td><td></td><td></td><td></td><td>Fun</td></tr><tr><td>Worth the time</td><td></td><td></td><td></td><td></td><td>Waste of time</td></tr><tr><td>Stupid</td><td></td><td></td><td></td><td></td><td>Great</td></tr><tr><td>Interesting</td><td></td><td></td><td></td><td></td><td>Uninteresting</td></tr></table><br>**Scoring:**  Exciting — 5  4  3  2  1 — Dull<br>Boring — 1  2  3  4  5 — Fun |
| | **Skill test** | ***Balance***<br>1. Stand on line; one foot; eyes open; hands on hips<br>2. Stand on line; one foot; eyes closed; hands on hips<br>3. Repeat #1; jump and turn 180°; land on line; hold momentarily<br><br>　　　　　　Pre　　　Post　　% Change<br>　　　___ sec.　___ sec.　___<br>　　　___ sec.　___ sec.　___<br>　　　___ sec.　___ sec.　___ |
| | **Quiz** | For each pair of descriptions, indicate the associated component<br><br>Strength　　　　　　Endurance<br>☐ ☐ ☐ ☐ ☐　　☐ ☐ ☐ ☐ ☐<br>1. (a) One maximal contraction<br>　 (b) Sustained contraction<br>2. (a) Light weights, many reps<br>　 (b) Heavy weights, few reps<br>3. (a) Greater hypertrophy<br>　 (b) Greater capillarization |
| | **Commercial instrument** | *Bruininks-Oseretsky Test of Motor Proficiency* (Bruininks, 1978); sports skills tests (Strand & Wilson, 1993) |

The criteria established for evaluation, developed later in this chapter, could be used for this purpose. Other criteria, however, should be considered. For example, an item might be selected that represents "something that was hard for you to do," "something that makes you feel really good," or "something that you would like to work on again." Some additional suggestions for selecting items are a "best" or "most representative" skill (e.g., gymnastic stunt); work in progress with written plans for revision (e.g., dance routine); and samples organized chronologically according to a theme (e.g., personalized physical fitness program).

Teachers and students can also create their own criteria for selection. In this manner, there is greater assurance that the portfolio contains representative work but gives students some choice. Some selection categories include media such as cassettes, slides, videos, photos, and computer programs; group work items such as projects, performances, and group feedback; individual work items such as worksheets, logs, journals, task cards, and tests; processes such as work biography, rough and final drafts, and beginning and final attempts; and reflections such as self-assessments, short-term goals, and artifact registry (Burke, Fogarty, & Belgrad, 1994).

Finally, in deciding how to select items, attention should be given to whether or not they demonstrate established standards. The recommended physical education content standards and benchmarks for four levels (grades K-2, 3-6, 7-8, 9-12) detailed in table 1.1 (pages 5-8) should be analyzed relative to artifacts selection. The artifact selection planning matrix in figure 3.3 can be used to "manage" the documentation of the content standards and corresponding benchmarks. The matrix should help avoid having standards and benchmarks that are covered poorly and avoid an overreliance on some kinds of artifacts. The need to diversify artifacts can be satisfied. In figure 3.3, the name of the artifact is entered to show its support of the benchmark. The number of artifacts for each benchmark is a matter of priority. Also, some kinds of artifacts are ongoing and may, therefore, appear across all benchmarks (e.g., log, journal).

## Who Will Select

Deciding who selects portfolio artifacts is dictated by the purposes and type of portfolio. If the purpose is to provide students with an opportunity to assess their own accomplishments through a showcase portfolio, then students should have a major voice in selection. The teacher's role may be to establish selection categories and criteria and to assist students in making selections. If the purpose is to determine students' status relative to district standards, other local mandates and the teacher are essential to artifact selection.

Physical educators need only look at the "players" in the portfolio assessment system to know who may select artifacts. For the most part, consideration needs to be given to the following stakeholders: students, peers, parents/others, teachers, and local and/or state mandates. These potential stakeholders can make selections separately or in combination.

**Student.** Selection can range from all the entries in the portfolio to a limited few. If students are to be truly responsible for their own learning, then they should be involved in selecting "best works," "works in progress," and "work that needs work." However, students and teacher can combine efforts. For example, the student might select two of five exhibits while the teacher selects one of the remaining three. Or, the teacher could provide the selection category (e.g., peer review of swimming strokes) and the student selects two criteria checklists.

**Peer.** Students should be able to review other students' work, provide helpful feedback, and offer an opinion about what artifacts should be selected for the portfolio. After all, other students are part of the same portfolio assessment system and should, therefore, be able to provide an objective assessment in accordance with established criteria and indicators. Techniques such as peer reflection and peer conferences are discussed later in this chapter. Involving peers in the selection process also promotes cooperation, team building, and a community atmosphere.

**Parent/Others.** One way to include parents and significant others (e.g., brother, grandparent, counselor, baby-sitter) is to ask them to select items. It has the benefit of bringing others into the learning process. Teachers can help guide the selections by providing guidelines and criteria. Techniques such as reflection and conferences by parents and/or others are also discussed later in this chapter.

**Teacher.** Because of the need to satisfy subject matter and learning process goals, the teacher is critical in selecting artifacts. Even when students are given a great deal of liberty in selec-

# Artifact Selection Planning Matrix

Content standard: *Uses movement concepts and principles in the development of motor skills*

Level: *Middle school/junior high (grades 7–8)*

| Kind of portfolio artifact | Benchmarks | | | |
|---|---|---|---|---|
| | Understands principles of training and conditioning for specific physical activities | Understands the critical elements of advanced movement skills | Uses basic offensive and defensive strategies in a modified version of a team and individual sport | Understands movement forms associated with highly skilled physical activities |
| Preassessment inventory | | | | |
| Task sheet | | | | |
| Self-assessment checklist | | | | |
| Frequency index scale | | | | |
| Rating Scale | | | | |
| Performance checklist | | | | |
| Peer review | | | | |
| Attitude survey | | | | |
| Self-report | | | | |
| Workbook page | | | | |
| Log | | | | |
| Journal | | | | |
| Reflection | | | | |
| Project | | | | |
| Independent contract | | | | |
| Videotape | | | | |
| Anecdotal statement | | | | |
| Parent observation or comments | | | | |
| Skill test | | | | |
| Quiz | | | | |
| Written test | | | | |
| Commercial instrument | | | | |
| Other: | | | | |
| Other: | | | | |
| Other: | | | | |

**Figure 3.3** Portfolio artifacts can be linked to physical education content standards and specific grade-level benchmarks.

tion, teachers may reserve some selections for progress reports, teacher-made tests, and evaluation rubrics. The teacher can provide the overall framework through selection categories such as reflections, projects, performance checklists, and journals.

**Local and/or State Mandates.** To monitor student achievement, some school districts and/or state education departments require certain kinds of work samples or exhibits. It is common, for example, that health-related fitness status be documented. Artifacts may then be placed in multi-year portfolios. Other mandates might relate to agreed upon state-level content standards and benchmarks appropriate for K-12 grade levels. Physical education would also have an obligation to produce certain kinds of artifacts for integrated portfolios with other subject areas.

### When to Decide

The collection of artifacts can be an ongoing, cumulative process, usually stored in a working portfolio. Selection for the final portfolio is a different matter. Unless the artifacts to be contained in the final portfolio are predetermined, selection decisions are needed at some point during the assessment process. Assuming that aspects of what, how, and who are known, the remaining decision revolves around when to make the selections. Once again, the purposes and type of portfolio may suggest the checkpoints or occasions at which time final selections are made. Although the actual timing can vary widely, there are some natural times when artifact selections may occur.

- *Weekly/monthly*—To help manage portfolios, making regular selections may be advisable. Also, entries in logs, journals, and registries can be facilitated as a way to monitor selections.

- *End of unit*—Selection can coincide with the completion of a sport unit, learning sequence, or thematic topic.

- *Scheduled conference/exhibition*—In preparation for teacher and parent conferences or displays (e.g., portfolio poster session, "Portfolio Night"), key selections are necessary to show learning progress.

- *End of grading period*—Presenting portfolios along with traditional reporting procedures offers more concrete information about student accomplishments than do report card grades.

- *End of year*—Selections at the end of a school year should represent key learning outcomes. It is possible that these selections would be made from a series of portfolios maintained throughout the year.

- *K-12 intervals*—If cumulative, multi-year portfolios are maintained, then selections are needed as the interval is completed (e.g., every three years, end of elementary school).

# REFLECTION AND SELF-ASSESSMENT

Inherent to portfolios is the chance for students to think about why certain items are included and to gain personal insights throughout the entire process. In other words, students can reflect on individual pieces and their value to the whole portfolio, and they can reflect on how they learn and why they fail to learn. Students can also engage in a self-assessment of their portfolios relative to growth in targeted areas, strengths and weaknesses, and short-term and long-term goals. Thus, the fourth phase of portfolio assessment involves these essential processes.

### Strategies for Reflection

Students should thoughtfully examine each item involved in the portfolio, whether required or optional, teacher selected, peer selected, or student selected. By carefully reflecting on its meaning and value, students discover that each item becomes a "mirror" of self. Reflection can occur at various stages of the portfolio process. For example, before the start of a sport unit, students might think ahead about portfolio content and design relative to the strategies and skills of the sport. During the process, students need to monitor their portfolios as they take shape. Another stage is for students to critically evaluate their work in terms of quality. Several reflection strategies can be used across these stages.

**Visualization.** A powerful strategy in developing sports skills is to visualize the successful performance of the skill. In the same manner, students can visualize how the portfolio will take shape and what it will look like. They can also envision a particular task sheet or project in its final form and the final portfolio itself.

**Tag, Label, or Stamp.** An easy way to reflect on portfolio items is to tag, label, or stamp each piece. Premade tag lines, Post-it™ Notes, printed stick-

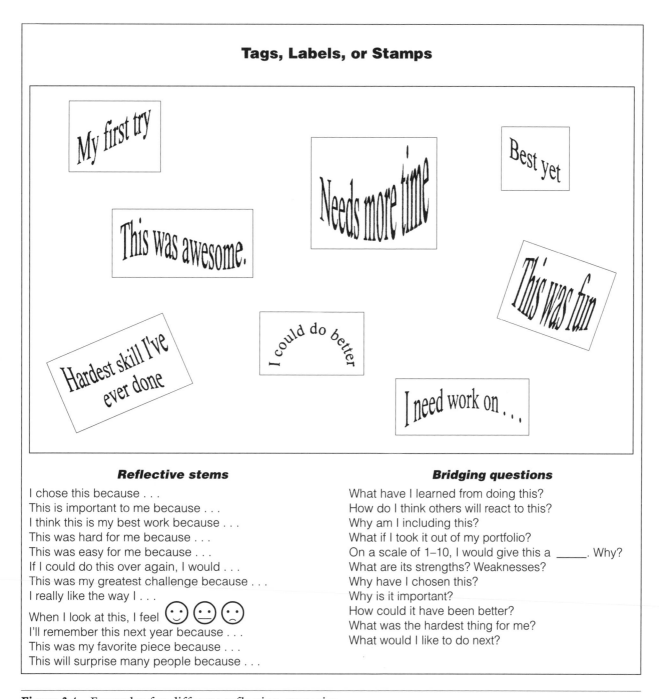

**Figure 3.4** Examples for different reflection strategies.

ers, and/or rubber stamps can include a key phrase or comment. They may explain the value of the item and/or why the item has significance. They also provide an initial inventory of what is included and why it is valued. Some examples of tags, labels, or stamps are shown in figure 3.4.

**Reflective Stems.** To help students get started in reflection, some phrases can be used to stimulate their "inner voice." These phrases are referred to as reflective stems, examples of which are listed in figure 3.4. Although some of these stems could be used by elementary students, others could be read to students using simpler words to guide reflection.

**Bridging Questions.** Students can respond to key questions that help them clarify their purposes and selections. Most of these questions should solicit how and why responses. Examples are identified in figure 3.4. Many of these questions can be read to younger students using simpler words as necessary.

**Benchmarking.** Because portfolio development is usually a long process, students could reflect on any established benchmarks along the way that support the end result (i.e., content standards). The recommended physical education content standards and benchmarks for four levels (grades K-2, 3-6, 7-8, 9-12) detailed in table 1.1 (pages 5-8) could be used for this purpose. Each artifact could be labeled to reveal its meaning and value to the entire portfolio relative to the benchmarks. Students get to know why an artifact was chosen for a particular benchmark in support of the corresponding content standard. Students can ask themselves, Why is the artifact filed under this benchmark? What does it say about my growing knowledge and skills? A reflection cover sheet that includes name, date, benchmark, name of artifact, and rationale could be required for each artifact.

**Artifact Registry.** If this management tool is used properly, the artifact registry is a form of reflection. Students would be required to state a reason when they add or delete items. These statements are a useful, reflective record of portfolio management over time. The artifact registry form presented in figure 3.2 can be used for this purpose.

## Self-Assessment Techniques

Reflection is directed toward individual portfolio items. In self-assessment, a broadened view is taken by looking at the overall direction of the portfolio. This informal, self-evaluation means that students themselves are the center of the learning process. As active participants, they become more autonomous, independent, and self-monitoring. Students assume responsibility for inspecting their own performance. "They should not depend on a teacher to follow them around throughout life giving them stickers, happy faces, or A's and B's. Too many students become dependent upon authority figures with red pens to provide feedback on how they are doing" (Burke, Fogarty, & Belgrad, 1994, p. 71).

Physical education teachers can choose from a large array of self-assessment techniques that allow students to monitor their own behavior and set goals. Teachers need to accept certain realities—they are not the only ones who can carry out evaluation and they need to empower students to become self-regulating. Several self-assessment techniques foster student ownership and responsibility.

**Checklists.** Probably the most fundamental way to carry out self-assessment is through behavioral checklists. Task checklists are commonly used in physical education to analyze the component parts of movement skills and social behaviors. Because it is difficult to observe one's own performance, except through videotape or digitized video, checklists are often used in a peer-assessment arrangement. Examples of self-assessment and peer-assessment checklists appear in table 3.1 for two sports skills. An example of a self-assessment checklist for a social skill is shown in figure 3.5.

**Learning Logs.** To keep track of learning goals and outcomes, students can maintain a daily record of activities and performance. Short, objective entries about in-class tasks and out-of-class experiences help students monitor their own progress. Logs can be used to record key ideas, make predictions, identify questions, connect ideas to other subjects, brainstorm ideas, and identify problems (Burke, 1994). Look back to the example of a log in table 3.1. Entries can also be made in response to a variety of stem statements.

Something new I learned today was . . .

I hate it when . . .

One thing I'm excited about is . . .

I'm having trouble with . . .

My skill is getting better in . . .

I was surprised today at . . .

**Journals.** Student goals can be monitored and reflected upon using a journal. Unlike logs, journals are used to record more subjective feelings about learning experiences. Over time, students can trace how their feelings change as a result of new learning experiences. An example of a double-entry journal appears in table 3.1 in which students reveal some initial impressions about some topic and then wait until they have learned more about the topic to reflect a second time. Students can see their change in feelings. Journal stem statements can also be used to facilitate self-analysis reflections.

The best part of this movement is . . .

I wonder why . . .

I predict that . . .

---

## Self-Assessment Checklist

Name: _____ Date: _____

| Social behavior: Interpersonal relations in a fitness group | Frequently | Sometimes | Seldom |
| --- | --- | --- | --- |
| 1. I help others in my group. | ❑ | ❑ | ❑ |
| 2. I isolate myself from my group. | ❑ | ❑ | ❑ |
| 3. I interact consistently with both males and females in my group. | ❑ | ❑ | ❑ |
| 4. I criticize others in my group. | ❑ | ❑ | ❑ |
| 5. I show favoritism to those who are more physically fit in my group. | ❑ | ❑ | ❑ |
| 6. I accept feedback from others in my group. | ❑ | ❑ | ❑ |

---

**Figure 3.5** *Self-assessment checklists can be used to reflect on social skills.*

One of the interesting things about this is . . .

How could I . . .

**Strengths and Weaknesses Chart.** Every now and then, students can take a look at their strengths and problem areas or "not yet" areas. It is useful for students to analyze their behaviors and abilities in all learning domains (i.e., cognitive, affective, and psychomotor). Two formats are shown in figure 3.6 for conducting this kind of self-assessment (Burke, Fogarty, & Belgrad, 1994).

**Goal-Setting Sheet.** As a result of reflection and other forms of self-assessment (e.g., checklists, logs, journals), students should establish goals. It is helpful to think of short-term and long-term goals that cover all learning domains. Sometimes, students will not engage in goal setting until after a portfolio conference has been held (phase five) or after the final portfolio has been evaluated (phase six). However, this technique can also be used by students before the final portfolio evaluation by applying the same criteria used by the teacher, possibly in the form of a scoring rubric. This aspect is covered later in the chapter section on evaluation. A sample goal-setting sheet is shown in figure 3.7.

# CONFERENCES

In some portfolio systems, student conferences involving the physical education teacher, parents, and/or other students are held at the end of a portfolio cycle after the final portfolio evaluation. Conferences are treated as a culminating event. This certainly makes sense, and the idea should not be abandoned if that sequence is practical. However, portfolio-related conferences are also recommended during the artifact selection, reflection, and self-assessment phases. Such conferences can range from simple, informal dialogue between student and teacher, peer, and/or parent to more involved, formal meetings among the same parties. Because conferences are viewed as an ongoing process of portfolio development, they are presented as phase five, before the evaluation phase. It may still be desirable to conduct portfolio conferences after portfolio evaluation (phase six).

Regardless of decisions about participants or timing, conferences should be consciously planned and implemented. Although some "conferences" may occur spontaneously and last only a few minutes (i.e., mini-conferences), more substantive ones depend on some careful decision making around purposes and procedures. The following framework for conducting portfolio conferences describes the purposes and types of conferences, the varied conference audiences, and the strategies for carrying out conferences in the physical education setting.

## Purposes and Types

Conferences offer another kind of self-reflection and a chance for students to demonstrate their

## My Strengths and Problem Areas: *Physical Education*

Name: _____    Grade: _____

| My strengths | Performing sports skills |
| | Understanding game strategies |
| | Showing teamwork and cooperation |
| My problem areas | Performing sports skills |
| | Understanding game strategies |
| | Showing teamwork and cooperation |

Signed: _____    Date: _____

**Analysis of My Strengths and Problem Areas: *Physical Education***

Old me (weaknesses)
_____
_____
_____
_____

I still need improvement in
_____
_____
_____

New me (strengths)
_____
_____
_____
_____

Signed: _____    Date: _____

**Figure 3.6**  Analyzing strengths and weaknesses is a useful self-assessment technique.

autonomy as learners. The contents of individual portfolios can be shared at a deeper level of inspection. The general purposes of conferences—be they informal or formal, simple or complex—can be placed in these three categories:

- *Foster goal setting*—Personal goals serve as a basis for artifact selection, and they are an important aspect of reflection and self-assessment. It follows that, through conferences, progress toward goals is reinforced once again.

- *Promote communication*—In portfolio development, the most common mode of communication is through paper artifacts (e.g., logs, checklists, written reflections, task cards, projects, tests, inventories). Dialogue adds another dimension to the quest for authentic assessment, particularly in cognitive and affective learning. The opportunity

to verbally express one's accomplishments enhances self-responsibility.

- *Satisfy standards* —Because of the emphasis on teacher and school accountability, multiple measures of learning are desirable. The conference provides another vehicle for matching student products with content standards and benchmarks.

Given these general purposes, the specific focus of the conference should also be decided. There are several directions that can be taken (Burke, Fogarty, & Belgrad, 1994). These types of conferences, which can be used separately or in combination, can help orient students as they further narrow their artifact selections for the conference:

- *Achievement*—Significant achievements are given primary attention, as shown, for ex-

---

## Physical Education Goal Setting

Name: _____  Date: _____

Topic: _____  Time period: _____

| Short-term goals | Target date |
|---|---|
| 1. | |
| 2. | |
| 3. | |

| Long-term goals | Target date |
|---|---|
| 1. | |
| 2. | |
| 3. | |

---

**Figure 3.7**  Setting short-term and long-term goals is a valuable self-assessment technique.

ample, by a learning log, performance video-tape, project, or improvement in skill tests.

- *Goals*—The status of goals is presented, based on portfolio items that show how goals have been met or surpassed. For example, health-related fitness goals could be documented through selected artifacts.

- *Learning process*—Artifacts would be selected and discussed around a particular process. In physical education, the focus might be on solving movement problems, becoming an effective "dancer," or being a team player.

- *Personal satisfaction*—Students select items for the conference that have the greatest meaning to them. Preferably, the items represent achievements that the student feels best about.

- *Group accomplishment*—Students as a group present their cooperative efforts and successes as a community of learners. The results of adventure/risk activities, cooperative games, or sport education would be applicable to physical education.

- *Total portfolio*—This holistic conference should survey the student's strengths and successes versus weaknesses and failures. Overall performance is assessed and discussed.

## Audiences

Depending on the purpose and type of conference, decisions are needed about who will participate in conferences. These decisions can be made by the student alone, by the teacher alone, or by the student and teacher together. The student whose portfolio is under review could be involved at different conference levels. The range is from one-on-one dialogues with the teacher, parents, or peers to presentation and discussion at a portfolio display with numerous people.

**Teacher.** Naturally, the teacher is primarily involved either alone or with others (e.g., parents, other students). If the conference is teacher led, questions can be prepared in advance to help guide the student. For example, if the conference focuses on goals, some questions might be, How do you want to grow as a tennis player? What do you need to do to improve? What are your goals for the rest of the year?

**Parents.** While parent-teacher conferences are still common, the nature of such conferences can be changed. The portfolio offers a full view of student learning not represented by grades and report cards. Therefore, parent conferences can celebrate a child's accomplishments and provide a more personally satisfying experience. Child-parent portfolio conferences are also possible to promote family involvement. The physical education teacher could provide parents with a portfolio conference guide that suggests questions to ask, such as, What have you found out about yourself by completing the "wellness" portfolio? What part of your "wellness" portfolio do you like the most? What are you going to do now that you have completed the "wellness" portfolio?

**Peers.** Several options exist for student-student conferences. Conferences with a peer can be helpful because peers are involved in their own portfolio development. Therefore, they are qualified to review others' work. The conference can center on answers to questions like, What items are you proud of and why? If you could publish one thing in your portfolio, what would it be? What areas of fitness need improvement? What items should be taken out of your portfolio and why? Conferences could also be held by a group of peers to solicit more dialogue and diverse opinions. Group-based conferences are particularly relevant if the physical education setting promotes cooperative learning or the concept of a community of learners. Another form of peer conference is for the student to hold a conference with a pen pal via electronic mail. Obviously, artifacts would need to be exchanged in advance in written form or on computer disks. Finally, the student could hold conferences with students of various ages who have experience in the portfolio process.

**Significant Others.** For individual students, conferences with other family members (e.g., grandparents, brother, sister) and other persons in their lives (e.g., baby-sitter, coach) may be particularly meaningful. Also, an exhibition of portfolios (e.g., "Portfolio Night") would afford another chance for conversation about the portfolio with a potentially varied audience.

## Strategies

Unlike classrooms, the physical education setting is unique for conducting portfolio conferences during the regular instructional routine. Devoting time for conferences may also be more difficult than in classrooms because the conference activity itself is not as easily integrated into typical physical education learning experiences. Sitting down with the teacher or others is more like the setup in classrooms. Obviously, out-of-class conferences could be held in an office or a classroom. Because of these limitations, some ideas for conducting portfolio conferences in physical education are mini-conferences, conference stations, and student-directed conferences.

**Mini-conferences.** Teachers can create conference time within the organizational flow of the physical education teaching-learning process. For example, while students are engaged in self-directed tasks, practice activities, or game play, individual students can be taken aside for mini-conferences. The teacher could even post a conference schedule so that students can prepare in advance. Selected aspects of the portfolio could then be available for the conference, as necessary. Peer conferences could also be organized in this format.

**Conference Stations.** Learning stations are commonly used in physical education. Circuit training and rotated self-directed tasks are examples of stations arranged in a gymnasium or outdoor facility to foster variety and independent learning. On selected occasions, one of these stations could be devoted to portfolio conferences in which students could engage in group-based discussions or in one-on-one dialogues with peers or with the teacher.

**Student-Directed Conferences.** Portfolio conferences with the teacher, peers, parents, and others can be planned by students themselves. If students are responsible for handling the date and time, as well as the conference protocol, then student autonomy and ownership are reinforced once again. Students are capable of establishing their own conference goals. For example, the elementary school student might want to tell how he learned to be a gymnast, the middle school student might want to show how she improved her volleyball skills, and the high school student might want to present an analysis of the effects of a personal weight-training program.

# EVALUATION

Given the nature of portfolio assessment, is it really necessary to evaluate portfolios? The answer is yes! Simply collecting items for the sake of collection serves no meaningful teaching or learning function without some measure of worth. Phase six, therefore, is the development of criteria and procedures for evaluating portfolios. It is a challenging task. However, the portfolio's purpose should help define the nature of evaluation as well as determine the persons who will do the evaluating. Physical education teachers should collaborate with students so that expectations are clearly communicated.

To complete this phase, teachers and/or students must decide among several grading options. In addition, scoring rubrics have emerged as a popular evaluation method in conjunction with portfolio assessment. A rubric is a scoring guide designed to evaluate a student's performance.

## Grading Options

It should be clear that evaluating portfolios is not the same as grading portfolios. For example, evaluative feedback can be given to students in an informal manner about their improvement in a sport as evidenced by the portfolio. A grade may not be assigned even though the portfolio is evaluated to provide information feedback. No doubt, one of the most controversial and difficult portfolio issues is whether to grade or not to grade the portfolio, and some options are available for each side of this issue.

**Not Graded.** If the basis for the portfolio is growth and development over time, the portfolio itself may not be graded, even though individual pieces in the portfolio may have been graded. In this case, the portfolio is designed to showcase the student's artifacts, including reflections and self-assessments. It is still a valuable synthesis of learning for review by the teacher and parents. The final, nongraded portfolio could also be integrated to represent a student's work across a certain time period (e.g., semester, school year). Items would be selected from several subject areas as a way to profile students' accomplishments. By removing the stigmas attached to grades, students are more likely to take learning risks, be more honest about their true learning, feel less constrained, and focus on "Look what I learned" instead of "What is my grade?" Self-esteem usually improves because portfolios can accommodate a greater variety of learning styles.

Traditional grading systems and report cards are a reality within the educational establishment. Translating portfolio contents into report card grades can be difficult because grades typically rate students on a curve and portfolios place students on a developmental continuum. Also, portfolios are normally skewed because students' "best" work is presented. Therefore, a full representative sample of students' actual learning should be assured. Report cards can be redesigned to include narrative statements and/or descriptive labels, but it may be more practical to supplement report cards with anecdotal progress reports. Learners' accomplishments, their strengths and difficulties, and their development can be more clearly communicated with progress reports. The example shown in figure 3.8 is based on performance indicators rather than on grades. Progress is judged "achieved," "needs improvement," or "working to achieve." Space is provided for general comments about strengths and weakness in each component. Plans for supporting learner growth can also be included.

**Graded.** If the basis for the portfolio is performance, the portfolio should be graded in some manner. The evaluation should be tied to established content standards and corresponding benchmarks. Consideration should be given to different grading options. Physical education teachers can use these options in combination, can alternate them at various times during the year, or can alternate them for various purposes and types of portfolios.

- *Whole portfolio*—One grade is given for the whole portfolio, which considers the entire body of artifacts. The grade is based on criteria that have been predetermined by both students and teacher, such as organization, completeness, creativity, reflectiveness, understanding of subject matter, and quality of products.

- *Separate items*—Each piece of work in the portfolio is graded separately either before or after the portfolio is submitted. Grades are based on predetermined criteria for each artifact or task. The portfolio as a whole could still be graded using the criteria mentioned earlier. This option can be very time-consuming for the teacher, particularly if items are not graded until after the portfolio is submitted. The advantage is that students know that each item is important because each is graded.

- *Selected key items*—A number of possibilities exist with this option. For example, the

A station can be established for conducting in-class teacher and peer miniconferences.

teacher might predetermine and announce the two items that will be evaluated, and the student must identify the two that he or she wants graded. Another option is not to tell students which three items will be graded. Thus, students should be motivated to seek quality on all items. Key items could also be selected from predetermined categories (e.g., learning dimensions, content standards, multiple intelligences).

- *Continual tracking*—Several items from the portfolio are graded and passed on to the next physical education teacher. Each year, some items are removed and others added that are representative of the student's performance. The portfolio can be compiled and graded at key intervals (i.e., after elementary school, middle school, and high school).

## Use of Rubrics

Rating scales and checklists are relatively easy-to-use, efficient evaluation tools. Some ex-

amples were provided in table 3.1, figure 3.5, and figure 3.8. Responses to performance tasks and open-ended questions can be evaluated with two kinds of rating scales. Bipolar scales are used to respond to statements about students' responses or performance, such as, "The overload smash was executed correctly." The scale for rating it might be strongly disagree (-2), disagree (-1), not sure (0), agree (1), strongly agree (2). Hierarchical scales can be used to evaluate student abilities along a continuum of levels of quality or proficiency. A commonly used scale is poor (1), fair (2), good (3), excellent (4). Checklists contain categories for evaluation and rating options for each category. The rating options could be "yes" or "no" or be presented as a narrow scale such as "never," "seldom," "sometimes," "frequently," "always." Although rating scales and checklists are simple to apply, they do not offer the detailed, explicit criteria found in scoring rubrics (McTighe & Ferrara, 1994).

A scoring rubric consists of a measurement scale of criteria that explains the possible levels of performance for a learning task. Usually, the

# Physical Education Progress Report: *Grades 3–4*

Student: _____  Date: _____

Teacher: _____

_____ 1st qtr. (Nov.)  _____ 2nd qtr. (Feb.)  _____ 3rd qtr. (April)  _____ 4th qtr. (June)

| | Working to achieve | Needs improvement | Achieved |
|---|:---:|:---:|:---:|
| **Intellectual** | | | |
| 1. Knows rules and procedures governing movement activities and games | ❑ | ❑ | ❑ |
| 2. Recognizes the effects of space, time, force, and flow on the quality of movement | ❑ | ❑ | ❑ |
| 3. Applies basic mechanical principles that affect and control human movement | ❑ | ❑ | ❑ |
| Comments: _____ | | | |
| **Social** | | | |
| 1. Respects rights, opinions, and abilities of others | ❑ | ❑ | ❑ |
| 2. Shares, takes turns, and provides mutual assistance | ❑ | ❑ | ❑ |
| 3. Participates cooperatively in student-led activities | ❑ | ❑ | ❑ |
| Comments: _____ | | | |
| **Emotional** | | | |
| 1. Assumes responsibility for giving and following directions | ❑ | ❑ | ❑ |
| 2. Makes decisions on an individual basis | ❑ | ❑ | ❑ |
| 3. Responds freely and confidently through expressive bodily movement | ❑ | ❑ | ❑ |
| Comments: _____ | | | |
| **Values** | | | |
| 1. Carries out tasks to completion | ❑ | ❑ | ❑ |
| 2. Displays preferences for various forms of movement | ❑ | ❑ | ❑ |
| 3. Engages in movement activities voluntarily | ❑ | ❑ | ❑ |
| Comments: _____ | | | |
| **Physical** | | | |
| 1. Executes all locomotor movements in response to rhythmic accompaniments | ❑ | ❑ | ❑ |
| 2. Controls body while balancing, rolling, climbing, and hanging | ❑ | ❑ | ❑ |
| 3. Shows body control in manipulating playground ball while stationary and moving | ❑ | ❑ | ❑ |
| Comments: _____ | | | |

**Figure 3.8**  Progress report that includes physical education goals for cognitive, affective, and psychomotor learning.

rubric has three to five levels. For example, a three-point scale might include criteria for the following levels: needs improvement, acceptable, and exemplary. On a four-point scale, criteria could be determined for descriptive levels such as novice, apprentice, proficient, and distinguishable. Performance on a task is compared to the criteria at each level (Hopple, 1995; Ryan, 1995).

In the previous section, a distinction was made between grading portfolio artifacts and grading the portfolio itself. Similarly, scoring rubrics can be designed for and applied to specific performance tasks, and they can provide general criteria for evaluating the overall portfolio. For illustrative purposes, several rubrics are provided that represent the range of learning dimensions. In figure 3.9, two examples are shown for the elementary school level; the rubric in figure 3.10 could be used at the middle school level, and figure 3.11 offers a rubric appropriate for use at the high school level. Finally, a sample scoring rubric is presented in figure 3.12 for evaluating the whole portfolio.

# CLOSING STATEMENT

Student portfolios offer a more naturalistic, genuine assessment of student learning. Designing portfolio systems appropriate for K-12 physical education programs requires a multifaceted approach that includes six phases: (1) determine purposes and types, (2) organize and plan logistics, (3) select items, (4) reflect and self-assess, (5) conduct conferences, and (6) evaluate. Depending on the purpose, various types of portfolios can be used (i.e., personal, working, record-keeping, group, thematic, integrated, showcase, electronic, multi-year, employment, scholarship). Alternatives exist around which these portfolios can be organized, including the physically educated person, mission statements, learning dimensions, multiple intelligences, organizing centers, and content standards and benchmarks. For logistics, numerous options for construction and storage as well as various management tools should be considered. The process of selecting portfolio artifacts includes decisions about what, how, who, and when. The range of possible artifacts in physical education is unlimited. Once selected, reflection strategies (i.e., visualization, tag, label, or stamp, reflective stems, bridging questions, benchmarking, artifact registry) and self-assess-

ment techniques (i.e., checklists, learning logs, journals, strengths and weaknesses charts, goal-setting sheet) should be applied. In addition, portfolio conferences offer another kind of self-reflection, be they informal or formal, simple or complex. Conferences should consider various audiences (i.e., teacher, parents, peers, significant others) and strategies such as mini-conferences, stations, and student-directed formats. Finally, evaluation of portfolios involves decisions about grading (i.e., whole portfolio, separate items, selected key items, continual tracking) and the use of scoring rubrics.

# SAMPLE K–12 PORTFOLIO SYSTEMS

To synthesize the information presented in this chapter, sample portfolio systems are provided for use at the high school, middle school, and elementary school levels. Although the settings for these systems are hypothetical, the portfolio elements are applicable to actual K-12 physical education programs.

## Sample High School Portfolio System

The type of portfolio described for the high school level is thematic in nature. The theme is "Fitness for Life." The portfolio is designed for a one-semester course in physical education. It is structured in the form of guidelines for personal growth.

## Sample Middle School Portfolio System

A showcase type of portfolio is described for the middle school level. The portfolio focuses on the development of knowledge, skills, and attitudes in volleyball. The unit in volleyball is one of several sports offered across the middle school curriculum in which students maintain a continual "Sportfolio" (Marmo, 1994). It is structured in the form of directions for the volleyball sport unit.

## Sample Elementary School Portfolio System

In an attempt to develop students' responsibility and self-management skills early in the educational process, a thematic, working portfolio

**Theme:** Space awareness
**Task:** Design, refine, and perform a movement sequence with a partner
**Learning dimensions:** Physical, intellectual, social
**Level:** Grades 3–4
**Criteria:** Use at least two directions and two levels with a definite beginning and ending shape

| 3. Achieved | Sequence clearly shows<br>• two (different) directions and two levels,<br>• a definite beginning and ending, and<br>• excellent refinement (no visible breaks in continuity and smooth transitions between movements). |
|---|---|
| 2. Needs improvement | Sequence shows<br>• one or two different directions or levels,<br>• a beginning and ending shape, although they may not be held long enough, and<br>• an attempt at refining the sequence (breaks in continuity and smoothness may appear by one or both partners). |
| 1. Working to achieve | Sequence<br>• lacks any planned directions, levels, or a beginning and ending shape, and<br>• shows that no or few attempts have been made to refine it (one or both partners have repeated losses of execution, smoothness, or memory). |

**Theme:** Kicking
**Task:** Design and play a game with a small group (2-on-2, 3-on-3) of students of similar skill level
**Learning dimensions:** Physical, intellectual, social
**Level:** Grades 5–6
**Criteria:** Use the skills of kicking and punting toward a goal area

| 2 = Outstanding | Student clearly and consistently demonstrates the ability to<br>• cooperate with others and help create the rules and boundaries for the game,<br>• work with others in a (physically and verbally) positive manner,<br>• abide by group decisions when playing,<br>• use the offensive strategies of keeping the body between the ball and the defender and of creating space by moving to get open, and<br>• use the defensive strategy of keeping the body between the opponent and goal. |
|---|---|
| 1 = Acceptable | Student usually shows the ability overall to<br>• cooperate with others and help create the rules and boundaries for the game,<br>• abide by and accept decisions of the group (any challenging is done in a nonthreatening manner),<br>• keep the body between the ball and the defender and to move to pass and receive the ball, and<br>• keep the body between the opponent and goal. |
| 0 = Deficient | Student<br>• does not cooperate with others in a positive way,<br>• contributes barely or not at all to developing the rules and boundaries for the game,<br>• has difficulty in abiding by and accepting decisions made by the group and may interact with others in a nonpositive manner,<br>• is consistently unable to (or doesn't try to) use the offensive strategies of keeping the body between the ball and the opponent or of moving to open spaces, and<br>• is consistently unable to keep the body between the opponent and goal when on defense. |

**Figure 3.9**   Rubrics for performance assessment at the elementary school level. *Note.* Adapted, by permission, from C.J. Hopple, 1995, *Teaching for Outcomes in Elementary Physical Education* (Champaign, IL: Human Kinetics), 22-23.

**Theme:** Leisure pursuits
**Sport:** Tennis
**Task:** Execute the forehand drive in returning a real serve
**Learning dimensions:** Physical, emotional
**Level:** Grades 7–8
**Type of assessment:**     ❑ Teacher     ❑ Peer     ❑ Self (videotape)

| *Criteria/Elements* *(circle letter of elements that need work)* | Scale | | | |
|---|---|---|---|---|
| | ① All silence | ② Scattered applause | ③ Round of applause | ④ Standing ovation |
| 1. Criterion: **Grip** <br> a. Base knuckle of thumb centered on top of grip <br> b. Palm is behind handle <br> c. Thumb overlaps and is next to middle finger with index finger spread <br> d. Fingers evenly spread <br> e. Butt end just protrudes from hand | ① <br> Comments: | ② | ③ | ④ |
| 2. Criterion: **Backswing** <br> a. Move as quickly as possible into position after opponent hits ball <br> b. Turn both shoulders and pivot hips so forward shoulder points in direction of ball flight <br> c. Racket drawn back approximately parallel to body between waist and knee height (below intended point of contact) <br> d. Straight-back technique with racket <br> e. Racket at comfortable length from body; grip hand hidden from opponent | ① <br> Comments: | ② | ③ | ④ |
| 3. Criterion: **Forward swing** <br> a. Dictate body and racket position at impact by "going after" ball <br> b. As forward foot hits the ground, front knee is bent so that eyes are closer to line of flight of ball <br> c. Arm and racket move forward as a unit with racket head trailing wrist during early stage; racket head catches up with wrist before contact; racket moves forward and upward <br> d. At impact, racket is laid back (hyperextended); ball struck in line with or slightly in front of lead foot <br> e. Wrist kept firm; not changed from original position during forward swing; vertical racket head in line with wrist at impact | ① <br> Comments: | ② | ③ | ④ |
| 4. Criterion: **Follow-through** <br> a. Wrist and racket stay together as a unit for short time during early follow-through <br> b. Watch spot where contact was made to avoid pulling eyes off ball <br> c. Head remains in precisely the same position as when ball was contacted <br> d. Stroke completed with full sweep of arm close to chin with body balanced to move to next shot | ① <br> Comments: | ② | ③ | ④ |

**Figure 3.10**   Rubric that can be used at the middle school level for assessing the tennis forehand drive.

**Theme:** Expressive movement
**Task:** Choreograph and perform own dance routine
**Learning dimensions:** Intellectual, physical
**Level:** Grades 9–12

| Criteria | Elements | Scale 1 | Scale 2 | Scale 3 | Score |
|----------|----------|---------|---------|---------|-------|
| **Creativity** | (a) Shows innovative patterns | Little | Partial | Complete | |
| | (b) Includes original moves | None | A few | Many | |
| | (c) Contrasts speed | Same pace | Some change | Varied pace | |
| **Fluidity** | (a) Coincides with rhythm of music | Off-beat | Off-&-on beat | Right on beat | |
| | (b) Connects moves to patterns | No fit | Some fit | Fits together | |
| | (c) Brings together beginning, body, and ending | Can't tell | Somewhat | Clearly evident | |
| | | | | **TOTAL:** | |

**Figure 3.11** A rubric for assessing a choreographed dance routine can be used at the high school level.

is described for the elementary school level, appropriate for grade two or three. The P.E.P. (Physical Education Portfolio) system includes a series of units. The sample presented focuses on the development of locomotor skills. It is structured in the form of a workbook for students. Because many of the terms associated with portfolios are beyond the language levels of primary-aged students, they are not used explicitly in the workbook. Although not labeled as such, the worksheets integrate many of the portfolio concepts and principles, such as reflection, self-assessment, goal setting, and conferences.

# Physical Education Portfolio: *Weighted Scoring Rubric*

Name: _____    Date: _____

Title: _____    Teacher: _____

| Criteria | 1 | 2 | 3 | Wt. | Score |
|---|---|---|---|---|---|
| **Appearance** | ❏ Messy<br>No attempt<br>to individualize | ❏ Neat<br>Some attempts<br>to individualize | ❏ Creative<br>Individual<br>touches added | ×1 | (3) |
| **Organization** | ❏ Poor layout<br>Can't follow<br>Many missing items | ❏ Layout OK<br>Hard to follow<br>Some missing items | ❏ Clear layout<br>Follows all directions<br>All items complete | ×3 | (9) |
| **Form/Style** | ❏ No variety<br>Weak sentences<br>Many mechanical errors | ❏ Some variety<br>Good sentences<br>Some mechanical errors | ❏ Wide variety<br>Variety of sentences<br>No mechanical errors | ×3 | (9) |
| **Understanding of subject matter** | ❏ Inaccurate<br>Basic information<br>No originality | ❏ Some inaccuracies<br>Limited use of ideas<br>Some originality | ❏ Very accurate<br>Applies new ideas<br>Shows much originality | ×4 | (12) |
| **Quality of items** | ❏ No depth to reflections<br>Lacks thoroughness<br>Not very expressive | ❏ Some vague reflections<br>Several gaps<br>Limited expressiveness | ❏ Thoughtful reflections<br>Very thorough<br>Highly expressive | ×5 | (15) |

**Comments:** _____

_____

_____

_____

_____

_____

_____

**Scale**

A = 43–48

B = 38–42

C = 33–37

D = 28–32

**Total:** _____
(48)

**Grade:** _____

**Figure 3.12**   Weighted scoring rubric for evaluating the whole portfolio.

# FITNESS FOR LIFE

## Guidelines for the

# PERSONAL GROWTH PORTFOLIO

# PERSONAL GROWTH PORTFOLIO

Over the next four months, you will learn why it is important to adopt a physically active lifestyle *now* and in later *adulthood*. You will discover the benefits of physical activity and physical fitness in preventing cardiovascular disease and how they improve your sleep, increase your capacity to perform daily functions, improve your mental health, and help you to maintain a desirable weight. You may also find that physical activity and physical fitness help reduce your stress, offer chances for social contacts, and even help with your academics.

You will learn about the concepts and principles of what is called "health-related fitness." This means that you will participate in learning experiences designed to improve fitness, promote health, and prevent future disease. The goal of the "Fitness for Life" course is to make sure you have the chance to engage in physical activity during physical education class and to encourage you to obtain physical activity outside of school and throughout life.

Because physical fitness is a personal matter, you need a way to develop, maintain, and monitor your own program of fitness. That is what the personal growth portfolio is all about. A *portfolio* is a collection of work samples and exhibits that shows your effort, progress, and achievement. In this case, the portfolio will present a picture of your physical fitness. You probably have many questions about the portfolio process. These guidelines will help answer them.

## QUESTION #1

What are the *PURPOSES* of the personal growth portfolio?

- Keep track of your own fitness progress
- Assess your own accomplishments
- Help your family members understand your effort and achievement
- Motivate you to practice a healthy lifestyle
- Determine your degree of personal satisfaction and social development
- Meet health-related fitness standards
- Know how to monitor and adjust activity levels to meet personal fitness needs
- Understand how to maintain an active lifestyle throughout life
- Design a personal fitness program that is based on sound concepts and principles of training that include all fitness components

## QUESTION #2

How should the portfolio be *ORGANIZED* and *MANAGED*?

Your personal growth portfolio should be organized in a way that is clear and meaningful. Because it is designed for the "Fitness for Life" course, it should be organized around aspects of fitness. The one broad *standard* that should be kept in mind as you develop the portfolio is supported by eight *benchmarks*. They define what you should know and be able to do, which indicates progress toward the standard. Your portfolio should be organized around the standard and benchmarks.

## STANDARD

Understands how to monitor and maintain a health-enhancing level of physical fitness; achieves and maintains a health-enhancing level of physical fitness; exhibits a physically active lifestyle

## BENCHMARKS

1. Knows personal status of cardiorespiratory endurance
2. Knows personal status of muscular strength and endurance of the arms, shoulders, abdomen, back, and legs
3. Knows personal status of flexibility of the joints of the arms, legs, and trunk
4. Knows personal status of body composition
5. Meets health-related fitness standards for appropriate level of a physical fitness test (e.g., aerobic capacity, body composition, muscle strength and endurance, flexibility)
6. Knows how to monitor and adjust activity levels to meet personal fitness needs
7. Understands how to maintain an active lifestyle throughout life (e.g., participate regularly in physical activities that reflect personal interests)
8. Designs a personal fitness program that is based on the basic principles of training and encompasses all components of fitness (e.g., cardiorespiratory efficiency, body composition, muscular strength and endurance, flexibility)

You will need to "manage" the collection of items as your portfolio is developed throughout the "Fitness for Life" course. This is called your *working portfolio*. It will evolve over time and serves as the repository for your work samples and exhibits. Eventually, your *final personal growth portfolio* will be made up of items selected from your working portfolio, some of which are required, others of which involve your making choices. The question of what to include in your portfolio is answered later. The following guidelines will help you assemble and maintain your portfolio.

## CONSTRUCTION AND STORAGE

You will have access to your *own* portfolio on a daily basis. *You are not allowed to look into or use someone else's portfolio for any reason without permission. Likewise, your portfolio is private. Access to it is strictly forbidden without your permission.* Storage options for the working and final personal growth portfolio are described.

*WORKING PORTFOLIO:* Individual hanging files will be maintained alphabetically in milk crates on rollers. File folders will be available to help separate and organize your portfolio items by fitness topics, by the eight benchmarks, and/or by works in progress and finished works. Working portfolios will be stored in the physical education office until the last three weeks of the course.

*FINAL PORTFOLIO:* You are responsible for storing and maintaining the personal growth portfolio during the last three weeks of the course. Your final portfolio must be placed in a softcover notebook binder. Required elements are identified later.

## MANAGEMENT TOOLS

You should manage your portfolio on a regular basis. The following management tools can be used separately or in combination. They should be particularly helpful with the working portfolio.

*TABLE OF CONTENTS:* A list of *all* entries and file/page numbers must be maintained on a sheet placed at the front of your hanging file or attached to the inside cover of the hanging file.

*COLOR CODES:* Use color stick-on dots and/or different color markers to organize items. Make sure a code for the colors is indicated, probably as part of the table of contents.

*REGISTRY:* Record the date, item, and reason for either adding or removing an item. Use the "Portfolio Item Registry" form (FFL-A) that appears at the end of these guidelines.

*POST-IT™ NOTES:* So that your ideas are not forgotten and to protect original items, use Post-it™ Notes (or attach index cards) to *briefly* explain why the item was collected. You may want to connect it to one or more of the benchmarks.

*PERSONALIZE:* Do not hesitate to inject your personality into the portfolio through colors, graphics, and shapes.

## QUESTION #3

What *ITEMS* should be included and how are they *SELECTED*?

As you should know by now, you are really developing two portfolios. The working portfolio is the regular, day-to-day collection and management of items. The final personal growth portfolio is more streamlined and includes items selected from the working portfolio. The expected contents for each are outlined.

### WORKING PORTFOLIO

*Everything* related to the "Fitness for Life" course should be kept in the working portfolio, including such things as handouts, class notes, journals, logs, workout sheets, project drafts, item registry, conference forms, reflections, peer assessments, copies of articles, etc. The items should be linked primarily to the eight benchmarks. However, certain key items are required for each of the benchmarks.

### FINAL PERSONAL GROWTH PORTFOLIO

While the working portfolio focuses on the eight benchmarks, the final personal growth portfolio is linked to the broad standard established for the "Fitness for Life" course:

*Understands how to monitor and maintain a health-enhancing level of physical fitness; achieves and maintains a health-enhancing level of physical fitness; exhibits a physically active lifestyle*

The final personal growth portfolio is made up of several items, some of which include choices. In addition, some of the items are described later (e.g., reflections, conference records). The following items are required:

1. Creative cover
2. Table of contents

| Benchmarks | Required items for the working portfolio |
|---|---|
| Personal status of:<br>1. Cardiorespiratory endurance<br>2. Muscular strength and endurance<br><br><br>3. Flexibility of the joints<br><br>4. Body composition | "Physical Fitness Profile" chart (FFL-B)<br>1. 1-mile walk/run (min./sec.)<br>2. 1-RM tests (lbs.): bench press, standing press, curl, leg press; push-ups (#); curl-ups (#); modified pull-ups (#)<br>3. Shoulder lift (inches); trunk extension (inches); sit-and-reach (inches)<br>4. Sum of triceps and calf skinfolds (mm); "Food Log" (FFL-C) for five days |
| 5. Health-related fitness standards | "Physical Fitness Goals" sheet (FFL-D)<br><br>Compare pretest results and FitnessGram standards for age and gender (Cooper Institute for Aerobics Research, 1992); establish short-term and long-term goals for each fitness component |
| 6. Monitor and adjust activity levels to meet fitness needs | "Physical Fitness Journal" form (FFL-E)<br>"Fitness Workout Schedule" form (FFL-F) |
| 7. Maintain active lifestyle | "Physical Activity and Leisure Questionnaire" (FFL-G)<br>"Physical Activity Log" (FFL-H) for same five days as the food log |
| 8. Personal fitness program | Project: "Fitness for Life" program |

3. Reflections:
    a. Health style self-test inventory
    b. Article reviews for four different benchmarks
    c. Food/activity logs
    d. Dietary guidelines/food guide pyramid
4. Conference records:
    a. Peer
    b. Family
5. Project (select ONE):
    a. *New Activities:* Identify three activities available to you that you have not experienced but think you might like; observe and participate in the activity; submit a report about the activity, its equipment, cost, where it is available, etc.
    b. *Concepts Scrapbook:* Describe the components of physical fitness and related principles; collect drawings, illustrations, and/or pictures that depict various exercises and activities to improve the components.
    c. *Interviews:* Conduct interviews of a male and female for three age groups (15-30, 31-50, 51-65 years); determine their activity patterns and evaluate them in terms of gender and age trends.

6. "Fitness for Life" program criteria:
   a. Plot a personal physical fitness profile based on ratings for cardiorespiratory endurance, muscular strength and endurance, flexibility, and body composition.
   b. Generate fitness goals based on ratings for health-related components.
   c. Select exercise and/or leisure activities in terms of contribution to fitness goals.
   d. Design a program based on goals, activity selection, and activity schedule.
   e. Satisfy principles of exercise, including heart rate training zone, specificity, overload, progression, and regularity (frequency, intensity, time).
7. Fitness contract: As a result of the "Fitness for Life" course, it is hoped that you are interested in changing some habits so that new "fitness" behaviors become a normal part of your lifestyle; complete all parts of the change contract.
   a. Behaviors I want to change
   b. Reasons for wanting to change
   c. Specific outcomes
   d. Goals for four consecutive weeks
   e. Plan of action (actual activities)
   f. Plan to monitor success (diary, log, graph, or chart)
   g. Barriers and strategies to overcome barriers
   h. People who will be on my support team
   i. When successful, how I will reward myself
   j. When I will start and how long I will stay with it
   k. My estimated chance of success (0 to 100%)
   l. Sources to refer to about my behavior change
   m. Plan for motivational strategies to enhance my success

## QUESTION #4

How should *REFLECTION* and *SELF-ASSESSMENT* be carried out?

To gain insights throughout the portfolio process, you are expected to reflect on your work. Reflection means that you thoughtfully examine your work samples. You think and/or write about their meaning and value. Through reflection, you will get to think about what you have learned and how you have learned it. You should also get to know yourself better, particularly about your physical fitness status.

The "Portfolio Item Registry" form (FFL-A) that you need to keep in the working portfolio is one kind of reflection. As you add and/or delete items, a reason must be stated. In addition, you need to reflect on four items that are required for the final personal growth portfolio.

1. *Health style self-test inventory:* You will complete an inventory that covers different categories of healthy behavior. Reflect on your scores for each of the following categories: tobacco use, alcohol and other drugs, nutrition,

exercise and fitness, emotional health, safety, and stress. The following questions could help your reflections: What scores surprised me? Why? What changes can be made to improve my health? How would others react to my scores?

2. *Article reviews:* Select four of the eight benchmarks and find magazine articles for each that relate to the benchmark. Do not simply summarize the article. Instead, reflect on its meaning and significance in developing fitness. Questions to ask are, Why does the article relate to the benchmark? What aspects about the article could I use in my fitness program? What is the most important thing I learned from the article?

3. *Food and activity logs:* Use the results of your food and activity logs to reflect on your caloric intake versus caloric expenditure. Use these reflective stems: The thing I'll remember is . . .; I was really surprised about . . .; I really like the way I . . .; My biggest challenge now is . . .

4. *Dietary guidelines/food guide pyramid:* Review the seven "dietary guidelines" for Americans. How does your diet measure up to *each* guideline? Look at the "food guide pyramid." Do you meet the daily criteria for recommended servings in each food group? Explain! What are two dietary changes you could make that would enhance your nutrition?

Reflection is mostly directed toward individual portfolio items. You should also look at the overall direction of your portfolio. That is the purpose of self-assessment. The "Fitness for Life" course provides many opportunities to become self-monitoring and to assume responsibility for inspecting your own performance. Self-assessment is built into several items required for the working and final personal growth portfolios, as follows:

1. Food log (FFL-C)
2. Physical fitness goals (FFL-D)
3. Physical fitness journal (FFL-E)
4. Fitness workout schedule (FFL-F)
5. Physical activity log (FFL-H)
6. Fitness contract

# QUESTION #5

What kinds of *CONFERENCES* are to be held?

Holding conferences with others is an important aspect of the portfolio process. Conferences offer another kind of self-reflection. They will allow you to discuss your fitness progress, look at the status of your fitness goals, and receive feedback about your efforts and achievements. It is expected that you will engage in conferences with peers and family members, records of which are required for the final personal growth portfolio.

## PEER CONFERENCES

During the "Fitness for Life" course, you should hold conferences with two other students, one after the second month and the other after the third month. You should focus on the benchmarks and the items required for the working portfolio. A "conference station" will be available in the gymnasium for you to conduct the conference. To verify the conferences, ask the person you hold conferences with to complete the "Peer Portfolio Conference" form (FFL-I) that appears at the end of these guidelines.

## FAMILY CONFERENCES

You are expected to share your final personal growth portfolio with two family members, one of which must be a parent or guardian. This will give you a chance to show off and celebrate your achievements. The "Family Portfolio Conference Guide" (FFL-J) should be given to the family member. It will help structure the conference. These forms should be submitted along with your final personal growth portfolio.

## QUESTION #6

How will the portfolio be *EVALUATED*?

The working portfolio is reviewed periodically by your teacher. Feedback is provided using Post-it™ Notes so that your original materials are protected. These reviews focus on the eight benchmarks and whether or not they are complete.

Your final personal growth portfolio is evaluated using the "Portfolio Scoring Rubric" (FFL-K). Criteria are used for evaluating both the *contents* and *quality* of your portfolio. The rating (score) is converted to a letter grade for the whole portfolio. Individual items do not receive separate grades. The grading scale is also shown on the rubric.

# FITNESS FOR LIFE

## Portfolio Item Registry

| Additions | | | Deletions | | |
|---|---|---|---|---|---|
| Date | Item | Reason | Date | Item | Reason |
| | | | | | |
| | | | | | |
| | | | | | |
| | | | | | |
| | | | | | |
| | | | | | |
| | | | | | |
| | | | | | |
| | | | | | |
| | | | | | |
| | | | | | |
| | | | | | |
| | | | | | |
| | | | | | |
| | | | | | |
| | | | | | |
| | | | | | |
| | | | | | |
| | | | | | |

# FITNESS FOR LIFE

## Physical Fitness Profile

Name: _____

| Component/Test | Pre | Mid | Post |
|---|---|---|---|
| Cardiorespiratory endurance | | | |
| 1-mile walk / run (min. / sec.) | _____ | _____ | _____ |
| Muscular strength and endurance | | | |
| 1-RM bench press (lbs.) | _____ | _____ | _____ |
| 1-RM standing press (lbs.) | _____ | _____ | _____ |
| 1-RM curl (lbs.) | _____ | _____ | _____ |
| 1-RM leg press (lbs.) | _____ | _____ | _____ |
| Push-ups (#) | _____ | _____ | _____ |
| Curl-ups (#) | _____ | _____ | _____ |
| Modified pull-ups (#) | _____ | _____ | _____ |
| Flexibility | | | |
| Shoulder lift (inches) | _____ | _____ | _____ |
| Trunk extension (inches) | _____ | _____ | _____ |
| Sit-and-reach (inches) | _____ | _____ | _____ |
| Body composition | | | |
| Sum of triceps and calf skinfolds (mm) | _____ | _____ | _____ |

# FITNESS FOR LIFE

## Food Log

Name: _____   Date: _____
(12:00 a.m.–midnight)

| Time of day | Food item | Amount | Calories consumed |
|---|---|---|---|
|  |  |  |  |

# FITNESS FOR LIFE

## Physical Fitness Goals

Name: _____  Date: _____

| Component | Pre-test | FitnessGram standard | Reason for goal (check one) | |
| --- | --- | --- | --- | --- |
| | | | Needs improvement | Desire to maintain |
| Cardiorespiratory endurance (1-mile walk/run) | | | | |
| | Short-Term Goal: | | Long-Term Goal: | |
| | Target Date: | | Target Date: | |
| Muscular strength and endurance (curl-up) | | | | |
| | Short-Term Goal: | | Long-Term Goal: | |
| | Target Date: | | Target Date: | |
| Flexibility (sit-and-reach) | | | | |
| | Short-Term Goal: | | Long-Term Goal: | |
| | Target Date: | | Target Date: | |
| Body composition (sum of skin-folds/% fat) | | | | |
| | Short-Term Goal: | | Long-Term Goal: | |
| | Target Date: | | Target Date: | |

# FITNESS FOR LIFE

## Physical Fitness Journal

Name: _____

|  | I wish I could . . . | I predict that . . . | I feel good about . . . | My fears are . . . |
|---|---|---|---|---|
| Before my fitness pre-tests<br><br>Date: _____ |  |  |  |  |
| After my fitness pre-tests<br><br>Date: _____ |  |  |  |  |
| One month after my fitness program<br><br>Date: _____ |  |  |  |  |
| Two months after my fitness program<br><br>Date: _____ |  |  |  |  |
| Three months after my fitness program<br><br>Date: _____ |  |  |  |  |

# FITNESS FOR LIFE

## Fitness Workout Schedule

| Day | Activity | Location | Time of day | Duration | Description of tasks |
|---|---|---|---|---|---|
| *Example* | *Warm-up Jogging Cool-down* | *School track* | *7:30 a.m.* | *20 minutes* | *Jogging program; training level #5; 440-yard distance; 220 yard walk relief; 3 repeats; walk 220 yards.* |
| Monday | | | | | |
| Tuesday | | | | | |
| Wednesday | | | | | |
| Thursday | | | | | |
| Friday | | | | | |
| Saturday | | | | | |
| Sunday | | | | | |

# FITNESS FOR LIFE

## Physical Activity and Leisure Questionnaire

Name: _____    Date: _____

1. Which leisure activities do you engage in on a regular basis? (check all that apply)

| | | | |
|---|---|---|---|
| ❑ Playing cards | ❑ Swimming | ❑ Racket sports | ❑ Board games |
| ❑ Fishing | ❑ Snow skiing | ❑ Video games | ❑ Camping |
| ❑ Water skiing | ❑ Watching TV | ❑ Canoeing | ❑ Hiking |
| ❑ Reading | ❑ Horse riding | ❑ Climbing | ❑ Painting |
| ❑ Shooting sports | ❑ Rappelling | ❑ Sewing | ❑ Crafts |
| ❑ Basketball | ❑ Volleyball | ❑ _____ | ❑ _____ |
| ❑ _____ | ❑ _____ | ❑ _____ | ❑ _____ |

2. How do you rate the amount of physical activity you perform daily?

   ❑ Very little   ❑ Slightly active   ❑ Moderately active   ❑ Very active

3. On the average (over the past year), how many hours a day have you spent performing the following activities?

   _____ Sitting   _____ Walking   _____ Moderate physical work

   _____ Standing   _____ Light physical work   _____ Heavy physical work

4. Which sports do you engage in on a regular basis?  (check all that apply)

| | | | |
|---|---|---|---|
| ❑ Golf | ❑ Tennis | ❑ Cycling | ❑ Bowling |
| ❑ Soccer | ❑ Basketball | ❑ Archery | ❑ Skiing |
| ❑ Hiking | ❑ Volleyball | ❑ Swimming | ❑ Skating |
| ❑ Racquetball | ❑ Jog/run | ❑ Weight training | ❑ _____ |
| ❑ _____ | ❑ _____ | ❑ _____ | ❑ _____ |

5. How often do you exercise for fitness?

   ❑ Daily   ❑ 3-6 times weekly   ❑ Occasionally   ❑ Seldom   ❑ Never

6. How do you rate your cardiorespiratory endurance compared with others of your age and sex?

   ❑ Excellent   ❑ Good   ❑ Average   ❑ Fair   ❑ Poor

7. What can you conclude about your leisure patterns?

8. What can you conclude about your fitness/exercise patterns?

# FITNESS FOR LIFE

## Physical Activity Log

Name: _____ Date: _____
(12:00 a.m.-midnight)

| Time of day | Activity | Location | How long | Calories expended |
|---|---|---|---|---|
| | | | | |

# FITNESS FOR LIFE

## Peer Portfolio Conference

Portfolio Owner: _____

*Conference focus:* "Fitness for Life" benchmarks
*Directions to peer:* Jot down your impressions and/or comments from your discussion about the following questions:

1. What aspects of fitness are you proud of? Why?

2. What areas of fitness need your attention? What are you doing about it?

3. What areas of fitness are your biggest challenges?

4. How do you feel about your portfolio?

Peer Signature: _____   Date: _____

# FITNESS FOR LIFE

## Family Portfolio Conference Guide

Dear Family Member:

Please review _____ personal growth portfolio that was completed for the "Fitness for Life" course. Ask him/her questions about his/her portfolio items and accomplishments. The following questions might help start the discussion. Thank you for your help and cooperation!

1. What did you find out about yourself by developing the "Fitness for Life" portfolio?

2. What part of your portfolio do you like the most?

3. What surprised you the most in putting your portfolio together?

4. What are you going to do now that you have completed the portfolio?

Please include any comments about the "Fitness for Life" portfolio and/or the conference:

_____

_____

_____

_____

Signed: _____ Date: _____

# FITNESS FOR LIFE

## Portfolio Scoring Rubric

Name: _____  Date: _____

| Elements | Content | | Quality | | | | Sub-total | Wt. | Score |
|---|---|---|---|---|---|---|---|---|---|
| | Components of the portfolio system should be verified; required items should be present | | *Organization:* Follows directions; clear layout *Form/Style:* Visual appeal, writing mechanics; expressiveness *Understanding:* Shows knowledge of fitness components; application of ideas; realistic | | | | | | |
| | ① Included, but incomplete | ② Fully developed | ① Fair | ② Satisfactory | ③ Good | ④ Outstanding | | | |
| Creative cover; table of contents | ① | ② | ① | ② | ③ | ④ | | ×1 | (6) |
| *Reflection:* Health style self-test inventory | ① | ② | ① | ② | ③ | ④ | | ×2 | (12) |
| *Reflection:* Article reviews (4) for different benchmarks | ① | ② | ① | ② | ③ | ④ | | ×2 | (12) |
| *Reflection:* Food and activity logs | ① | ② | ① | ② | ③ | ④ | | ×2 | (12) |
| *Reflection:* Dietary guidelines and food guide pyramid | ① | ② | ① | ② | ③ | ④ | | ×2 | (12) |
| *Conference records:* Peers (2), Family members (2) | ① | ② | ① | ② | ③ | ④ | | ×2 | (12) |
| *Project:* New activities ☐ Interviews ☐ Concepts scrapbook ☐ | ① | ② | ① | ② | ③ | ④ | | ×5 | (30) |
| "Fitness for Life" program | ① | ② | ① | ② | ③ | ④ | | ×6 | (36) |
| Fitness contract | ① | ② | ① | ② | ③ | ④ | | ×3 | (18) |
| | | | | | | | | | (150) |

Comments: _____

Scale: A = 135-150, B = 120-134, C = 105-119, D = 90-104, F = below 89

TOTAL: _____

GRADE: _____

# SPORTFOLIO

## Volleyball

### Directions for the
# SHOWCASE PORTFOLIO

# SPORTFOLIO FRAMEWORK

The "Sportfolio" is a series of showcase portfolios that are maintained all year throughout the physical education program. It is a way for you to continually keep track of your accomplishments in each sport.

## Goal

Develop knowledge, skills, and values in a variety of individual and team sports: soccer, flag football, basketball, volleyball, team handball, softball, tennis, and golf.

## Standards

    A. Uses a variety of basic and advanced movement forms

    B. Uses movement concepts and principles in the development of motor skills

    C. Understands and practices social and personal responsibility associated with participation in physical activity

## Outcomes

    A1. Uses intermediate sport-specific skills for individual and team sports

    B1. Understands the critical elements of advanced movement skills

    B2. Uses basic offensive and defensive strategies in a modified version of a team and individual sport

    B3. Understands movement forms associated with highly skilled physical activities

    C1. Works in a group to accomplish a set goal in both cooperative and competitive activities

    C2. Knows the difference between inclusive and exclusionary behaviors in sports

    C3. Understands that sports are a vehicle for self-expression

## Showcase Portfolio

*Purpose:* Display your *best* work in a particular individual or team sport

*Description:* The portfolio should be streamlined. You are *not* expected to collect and store all the day-to-day items (e.g., checklists, worksheets, task cards) that are part of the physical education program. You are expected, however, to complete certain tasks and projects for each sport that will be part of your showcase portfolio. You will be given directions for each sport. Eventually, you will have a series of showcase portfolios that, together, make up your personal "Sportfolio."

*Management:* The showcase portfolio will be self-managed. You are responsible for collecting, organizing, storing, and maintaining any items or materials that are needed for any given showcase portfolio. Even though some items will be developed in physical education class, it is still your responsibility to manage what you need. Most items are developed out of physical education class. *Be very careful with and protect your work samples.* A due date will be announced for each of the showcase portfolios as the different sports are covered during the school year.

# VOLLEYBALL
## Showcase Portfolio

## TASKS

The showcase portfolio for volleyball includes several tasks that must be completed. The common set of "Sportfolio" categories is used to organize these tasks. Some choices are built into certain categories.

### A. Tracking Growth

*Description:* To record your experiences, results, feelings, and perceptions, a volleyball journal will be maintained. You will be able to track your growth in volleyball. Entries to the journal will be made at the end of the 2nd, 4th, and 6th weeks. Use the form that is attached to these directions.

*Task:* Maintain a journal during the volleyball sport unit

### B. Personal Skill Analysis

*Description:* You will be videotaped during game play. Time will be provided for you to view the videotape and to analyze each of the major skills of volleyball: overhand or underhand serve, overhead pass/front set, bump pass, spike, and block. Use the self-analysis rating sheet for these skills that is attached to these directions.

*Task:* Write a description of your *two best* skills, based on your self-analyses

### C. Sport Insight

*Description:* Through different kinds of projects, you can learn more about the game of volleyball. You would gain greater insights into volleyball. The following projects could be used for this purpose.

1. *Scouting report*—A class volleyball tournament will be held at the end of the unit. Once teams are selected, write a scouting report for each team, including your own team. Include an analysis of the teams' strengths and weaknesses and their offensive and defensive strategies. Predict the outcome of the tournament and the reasons for your predictions.

2. *Interview*—Conduct an interview with one of the varsity volleyball players at the high school. The interview should focus on how he/she became a volleyball player, how to develop skills, and what practice routines and training techniques are used. Develop questions in advance. Write a script of the questions and answers.

3. *Essay*—Write an essay about the origins, history, and future of the sport of volleyball. You should also include how volleyball was introduced into the United States and background of volleyball as an Olympic and NCAA sport.

4. *Article summaries*—Read and analyze *three* articles in sports magazines or journals about volleyball skills, practice techniques, and training and conditioning tips. Each written summary should be at least one page per article.

*Task:* Select and complete one of the "sport insight" projects

## D. Game Analysis

The skills, rules, and strategies of volleyball all come together when a game is played. To show your understanding of the sport, you will have a chance to analyze a class volleyball tournament game or a high school volleyball game and to communicate your analysis in one of three ways.

1. *Newspaper sports reporter*—Observe one of the class volleyball tournament games or a high school volleyball game. Write a newspaper article about the game. The article should include a complete analysis of individual and team performances as well as game statistics. Design a volleyball "box score" as part of the article. Include action photos if possible.

2. *Radio sports announcer*—Observe one of the class volleyball tournament games or a high school volleyball game. Record, on a tape recorder, your play-by-play commentary of the game as though you were a radio sports announcer. Select a player of the game and conduct a postgame interview on the audio tape.

3. *TV sports broadcaster*—Observe one of the class volleyball tournament games or a high school volleyball game. Record, on videotape, your play-by-play commentary of the game as though you were a TV sports broadcaster. Select a player of the game and conduct a postgame interview on the videotape.

*Task:* Select and complete one of the "game analysis" projects

## E. Goal Setting

*Description:* You will be able to look at what you know about volleyball, what your skills are in volleyball, and how much you like volleyball. After the unit, you should be well aware of your strengths and problem areas. By looking at yourself, you should be able to establish some volleyball goals for yourself. Use the strengths and problem areas and goal-setting chart that is attached to these directions.

*Task:* Set goals for volleyball based on strengths and problem areas

## F. Communicating Achievement

*Description:* It is hoped that you will want to show others how you developed your volleyball abilities. You should be proud of your accomplishments in volleyball. Therefore, you are expected to share your showcase portfolio with your parents or guardians. Use the parent/guardian conference guide attached to these directions.

*Task:* Arrange and conduct a "portfolio conference" with your parents/guardians

## CONTENTS

It is suggested that you use either an accordion file with dividers or a softcover notebook with pockets as your portfolio container. To help you organize the portfolio, a list of required items follows.

1. *Informational cover*—Make sure your name and class are included. Your cover design is a matter of personal choice and creativity.

2. *Table of contents*—All items should be listed with page numbers. Clearly indicate your choice of projects for the "sport insight" and "game analysis" tasks.

3. *Journal*—The volleyball journal should include complete entries following the 2nd, 4th, and 6th weeks.

4. *Description of two best skills*—Using your personal skills self-analyses, decide your two best skills and describe them in detail.

5. *Sport insight project*—Include one of the following: (a) scouting report, (b) interview script, (c) essay, or (d) article summaries

6. *Game analysis project*—Include one of the following: (a) newspaper article as sports reporter, (b) audiotape as radio sports announcer, or (c) videotape as TV sports broadcaster.

7. *Goals for volleyball*—Using your identified strengths and problem areas, indicate the volleyball goals you have set for yourself.

8. *Conference results*—Include any notes from your conference with your parents or guardians and their written comments and sign-off.

## ASSESSMENT

The showcase portfolio will be assessed in different ways. A simple rating scale (+, ✔, 0) will be used for the basic required items: informational cover, table of contents, journal, skill descriptions, goals, and parent conference. A letter grade will be assigned to the special required items: sport insight project and game analysis project. Then, the whole showcase portfolio will be assessed considering the ratings for the basic items and the grades for the special items. The criteria for the overall grade are detailed in the assessment form that is attached to these directions.

# VOLLEYBALL

Journal

Name: _____

| Questions | End of 2nd week ( / / ) | End of 4th week ( / / ) | End of 6th week ( / / ) |
|---|---|---|---|
| 1. *What volleyball activities were really good?* | | | |
| 2. *Which of my volleyball skills are pretty good or better?* | | | |
| 3. *Which of my volleyball skills could use more work?* | | | |
| 4. *The things I like best about volleyball are . . .* | | | |
| 5. *The things I like least about volleyball are . . .* | | | |
| 6. *My overall impressions of volleyball are . . .* | | | |

# VOLLEYBALL

## Self-Analysis Skills Rating Sheet

Name: _____

| | Not yet | OK | Good |
|---|---|---|---|
| **Overhand serve:** | | | |
| 1. Faces net in a stride position with foot opposite striking arm forward | ❏ | ❏ | ❏ |
| 2. Ball tossed 2-3 feet above net and in front of hitting shoulder | ❏ | ❏ | ❏ |
| 3. Striking arm moves rearward at approximately shoulder height | ❏ | ❏ | ❏ |
| 4. Elbow flexes, permitting forearm and hand to drop behind the head | ❏ | ❏ | ❏ |
| 5. Arm rotated forward at shoulder | ❏ | ❏ | ❏ |
| 6. Forearm lags behind upper arm and hand behind forearm | ❏ | ❏ | ❏ |
| 7. Upper palm/heel of hand used to contact ball | ❏ | ❏ | ❏ |
| 8. Ball contacted momentarily at its midpoint with little follow-through | ❏ | ❏ | ❏ |
| **Underhand serve:** | | | |
| 1. Faces net with foot opposite the striking arm in front | ❏ | ❏ | ❏ |
| 2. Rest ball in nonstriking hand at about knee to waist height | ❏ | ❏ | ❏ |
| 3. Striking arm moved rearward to shoulder height in a swinging action | ❏ | ❏ | ❏ |
| 4. Body weight shifted rearward onto back foot at same time | ❏ | ❏ | ❏ |
| 5. Hit ball off the holding hand with striking hand in an open and cupped position, a half fist for striking with heel of hand, or a fist | ❏ | ❏ | ❏ |
| 6. Hitting arm swings forward and upward during hit (as in bowling a ball) | ❏ | ❏ | ❏ |
| 7. Hand follows ball straight through in the direction of the flight of the ball | ❏ | ❏ | ❏ |
| **Overhead pass/Front set:** | | | |
| 1. Perform "ready position" (stance of shoulder-width with body weight equally distributed over both feet) | ❏ | ❏ | ❏ |

|  | Not yet | OK | Good |
|---|---|---|---|
| 2. Knees flexed, head tilted back to focus on ball | ❏ | ❏ | ❏ |
| 3. Arms move forward and upward until upper arms are parallel with floor; elbows flexed and pointing out to sides | ❏ | ❏ | ❏ |
| 4. Hands bent backward at wrist; fingers spread; hands slightly cupped | ❏ | ❏ | ❏ |
| 5. Thumbs and index fingers form a triangle | ❏ | ❏ | ❏ |
| 6. Extend legs and arms at same time into ball | ❏ | ❏ | ❏ |
| 7. Fingers (not palms) contact ball above and in front of forehead | ❏ | ❏ | ❏ |
| 8. Fingers close in a grabbing action once contact is made | ❏ | ❏ | ❏ |
| 9. Follow-through with continuous upward extension of body in direction of hit | ❏ | ❏ | ❏ |

**Bump pass:**

|  | Not yet | OK | Good |
|---|---|---|---|
| 1. Clasp hands together (clenched fist, curled fingers, or thumb over palm) | ❏ | ❏ | ❏ |
| 2. Move quickly to a position behind ball | ❏ | ❏ | ❏ |
| 3. Knees bent, feet shoulder-width apart in forward-stride position, trunk slightly forward | ❏ | ❏ | ❏ |
| 4. Hands and arms extended, together and parallel with elbows locked during contact | ❏ | ❏ | ❏ |
| 5. Hands point toward floor | ❏ | ❏ | ❏ |
| 6. Ball contacted on the forearms above wrists | ❏ | ❏ | ❏ |
| 7. Arm movement in an arc from shoulders with legs involved | ❏ | ❏ | ❏ |

**Spike:**

|  | Not yet | OK | Good |
|---|---|---|---|
| 1. Use step-hop, three-step, or four-step approach | ❏ | ❏ | ❏ |
| 2. On last step or hop, body drives downward by flexing at ankles; knees and hips with shoulders face net | ❏ | ❏ | ❏ |
| 3. Immediately, extension at knees and hips propels body upward into jump | ❏ | ❏ | ❏ |
| 4. Arms held close to body in the forward and upward swinging action | ❏ | ❏ | ❏ |
| 5. Striking arm moves in a straight horizontal path rearward as in the overarm throwing pattern | ❏ | ❏ | ❏ |
| 6. After hips begin to rotate, striking arm starts forward at the shoulder | ❏ | ❏ | ❏ |
| 7. Elbow begins extension while the wrist is bent backward | ❏ | ❏ | ❏ |
| 8. Upper arm lags behind shoulder, forearm behind upper arm, and hand behind forearm | ❏ | ❏ | ❏ |

|  | Not yet | OK | Good |
|---|---|---|---|
| 9. Arm fully extended at contact, made in front of body above shoulder at height equal to length of fully extended arm | ❏ | ❏ | ❏ |
| 10. Ball contacted slightly above its center with entire hand | ❏ | ❏ | ❏ |
| 11. Trunk flexes forward with snapping of wrist as part of follow-through | ❏ | ❏ | ❏ |

**Block:**

|  | Not yet | OK | Good |
|---|---|---|---|
| 1. Ready position established after reaching position of 1-2 feet from net | ❏ | ❏ | ❏ |
| 2. Stance is parallel with feet shoulder-width apart and knees flexed | ❏ | ❏ | ❏ |
| 3. Hands held at shoulder height, elbows flexed, fore-arms parallel with net | ❏ | ❏ | ❏ |
| 4. Jump preparation consists of flexion at ankles, knees, and hips with trunk slightly flexed forward to assume half-squat position | ❏ | ❏ | ❏ |
| 5. Jump begins immediately after spiker jumps | ❏ | ❏ | ❏ |
| 6. With extension of ankles, knees, and hips, arms are extended vertically over top of net on vertical jump | ❏ | ❏ | ❏ |
| 7. Fingers spread and arms held firm for ball contact | ❏ | ❏ | ❏ |
| 8. Reach is sustained for as long as possible | ❏ | ❏ | ❏ |

# VOLLEYBALL

## Setting Goals Based on Strengths and Problem Areas

Name: _____

| | | |
|---|---|---|
| **My volleyball strengths** | Performing volleyball skills | |
| | Understanding the rules of volleyball | |
| | Applying offensive strategies in volleyball | |
| | Applying defensive strategies in volleyball | |
| | Working with others on volleyball team | |
| **My volleyball problem areas** | Performing volleyball skills | |
| | Understanding the rules of volleyball | |
| | Applying offensive strategies in volleyball | |
| | Applying defensive strategies in volleyball | |
| | Working with others on volleyball team | |

| Volleyball goals | Target date |
|---|---|
| | |
| | |
| | |
| | |
| | |
| | |

# VOLLEYBALL

## Parent/Guardian Conference Guide

Name: _____

## TO THE STUDENT

You are expected to direct the conference with your parent/guardian. Some of the things you could focus on are answers to the following questions:

- How did you improve your volleyball skills?
- If you could publish one portfolio item, what would it be?
- What are you most proud of?
- What aspects of volleyball need more work?
- What surprised you most about the volleyball unit?
- What do you think about the showcase portfolio? About the "Sportfolio" process?
- What would you change if you could?
- What was your biggest challenge?

## TO THE PARENT/GUARDIAN

Your child would like to share his/her showcase portfolio with you. Please look it over and discuss it with your child, who will direct the conference. You may also be interested in answers to some of the questions above. After the conference, please offer your reactions below and verify the conference with your signature.

**Comments:**

_____

_____

_____

_____

_____

_____

_____

**Parent/guardian signature:** _____ **Date:** _____

# VOLLEYBALL

## Assessment Form

Name: _____

| Basic items | 0<br>Does not meet<br>expectations | ✓<br>Meets<br>expectations | +<br>Exceeds<br>expectations |
|---|:---:|:---:|:---:|
| Informational cover | _____ | _____ | _____ |
| Table of contents | _____ | _____ | _____ |
| Journal | _____ | _____ | _____ |
| Descriptions of best skills | _____ | _____ | _____ |
| Goals | _____ | _____ | _____ |
| Conference | _____ | _____ | _____ |

**Comments:** _____

_____

_____

| Special items | F<br>Poor | D<br>Fair | C<br>Satisfactory | B<br>Good | A<br>Excellent |
|---|:---:|:---:|:---:|:---:|:---:|
| Sport insight project | _____ | _____ | _____ | _____ | _____ |
| ❏ Scouting report  ❏ Interview  ❏ Essay  ❏ Article summaries | | | | | |
| Game analysis project | _____ | _____ | _____ | _____ | _____ |
| ❏ Newspaper article  ❏ Radio commentary  ❏ TV commentary | | | | | |

**Comments:** _____

_____

_____

_____

**Overall grade**

_____ A = Portfolio is exemplary in terms of contents and quality

_____ B = Portfolio is fully developed; there is room for improved quality

_____ C = Portfolio includes all required items; meets all minimum expectations

_____ D = Portfolio is not fully developed in some aspects; quality is below
expectations

_____ F = Portfolio items are incomplete and/or missing; quality is lacking

Signed: _____ Date: _____

# PHYSICAL
# EDUCATION
# PORTFOLIO

## Locomotor Skills
## Workbook

WALK    RUN    JUMP

HOP    LEAP

SLIDE    GALLOP    SKIP

# PHYSICAL EDUCATION PORTFOLIO

## How to Make Your Container

1. Get a regular size cereal box.

2. Cut the cereal box.

3. Cover your portfolio.

4. Put your name on the portfolio.

5. Decorate the sides of your portfolio.

# PHYSICAL EDUCATION PORTFOLIO

## Locomotor Skills Journal

Name: _____

*Directions:* During the next 3 weeks, write down different exercises, activities, or sports that use each locomotor skill.

| Locomotor skill | Exercise, activity, or sport |
|---|---|
| Walk | 1. |
|  | 2. |
|  | 3. |
| Run | 1. |
|  | 2. |
|  | 3. |
| Jump | 1. |
|  | 2. |
|  | 3. |
| Hop | 1. |
|  | 2. |
|  | 3. |
| Leap | 1. |
|  | 2. |
|  | 3. |
| Slide | 1. |
|  | 2. |
|  | 3. |
| Gallop | 1. |
|  | 2. |
|  | 3. |
| Skip | 1. |
|  | 2. |
|  | 3. |

# PHYSICAL EDUCATION PORTFOLIO

## Locomotor Skills Partner Activity

Name: _____

Partner's name: _____

*Directions:* With a partner, design a *movement* sequence using 4 different locomotor patterns (skills). Each pattern (skill) should last for 8 counts. You should repeat the sequence 4 times to 4/4 beat music which will be provided. Use the chart below to design your sequence. Practice the sequence together!

| Sequence | Description |
|---|---|
| *1st pattern/skill* | |
| *2nd pattern/skill* | |
| *3rd pattern/skill* | |
| *4th pattern/skill* | |

# PHYSICAL EDUCATION PORTFOLIO

## Locomotor Skills Group Project

Name: _____

Group member's name: _____

Group member's name: _____

*Directions:* In a group of 3, write a rhyme that you can jump to with a long jump rope. The rhyme should last at least 12 jumps or more. Include at least 3 different types of jumps (e.g., one-foot, skip-step, turns). Write out each line of your rhyme below. Show what type of jump is used for each line of the rhyme.

| Rhyme | Type of jump |
|-------|--------------|
| *Line 1:* | |
| *Line 2:* | |
| *Line 3:* | |
| *Line 4:* | |
| *Line 5:* | |
| *Line 6:* | |

# PHYSICAL EDUCATION PORTFOLIO

## Rate Your Locomotor Skills

Name: _____

*Directions:* Think about the correct way to do each locomotor skill. At the end of each week, check (✔) the face that shows how well you think you can do each locomotor skill.

| Locomotor skill | Week 1 Friday ( / / ) | | | Week 2 Friday ( / / ) | | | Week 3 Friday ( / / ) | | |
|---|---|---|---|---|---|---|---|---|---|
| *Walk* | ☹ ☐ | 😐 ☐ | 🙂 ☐ | ☹ ☐ | 😐 ☐ | 🙂 ☐ | ☹ ☐ | 😐 ☐ | 🙂 ☐ |
| *Run* | ☹ ☐ | 😐 ☐ | 🙂 ☐ | ☹ ☐ | 😐 ☐ | 🙂 ☐ | ☹ ☐ | 😐 ☐ | 🙂 ☐ |
| *Jump* | ☹ ☐ | 😐 ☐ | 🙂 ☐ | ☹ ☐ | 😐 ☐ | 🙂 ☐ | ☹ ☐ | 😐 ☐ | 🙂 ☐ |
| *Hop* | ☹ ☐ | 😐 ☐ | 🙂 ☐ | ☹ ☐ | 😐 ☐ | 🙂 ☐ | ☹ ☐ | 😐 ☐ | 🙂 ☐ |
| *Leap* | ☹ ☐ | 😐 ☐ | 🙂 ☐ | ☹ ☐ | 😐 ☐ | 🙂 ☐ | ☹ ☐ | 😐 ☐ | 🙂 ☐ |
| *Slide* | ☹ ☐ | 😐 ☐ | 🙂 ☐ | ☹ ☐ | 😐 ☐ | 🙂 ☐ | ☹ ☐ | 😐 ☐ | 🙂 ☐ |
| *Gallop* | ☹ ☐ | 😐 ☐ | 🙂 ☐ | ☹ ☐ | 😐 ☐ | 🙂 ☐ | ☹ ☐ | 😐 ☐ | 🙂 ☐ |
| *Skip* | ☹ ☐ | 😐 ☐ | 🙂 ☐ | ☹ ☐ | 😐 ☐ | 🙂 ☐ | ☹ ☐ | 😐 ☐ | 🙂 ☐ |

# PHYSICAL EDUCATION PORTFOLIO

## Locomotor Skills Checklist

Name: _____

*Directions:* Keep this checklist in your portfolio. It shows your progress in each of the locomotor skills. Your physical education teacher will observe you and fill it out.

| Locomotor skill/criteria | 1st observation | | 2nd observation | |
|---|---|---|---|---|
| | Working to achieve | Have achieved | Working to achieve | Have achieved |
| **Walk:** | | | | |
| • Head is up, body erect | ____ | ____ | ____ | ____ |
| • Leg swings forward | ____ | ____ | ____ | ____ |
| • Diagonal push-off backward against ground with ball of one foot | | | | |
| • Arms swing in opposition to legs | ____ | ____ | ____ | ____ |
| • Heel-to-toe placement of foot | ____ | ____ | ____ | ____ |
| • Toes point straight ahead | ____ | ____ | ____ | ____ |
| **Run:** | | | | |
| • Head is up, body leans forward | ____ | ____ | ____ | ____ |
| • Support foot contacts ground close to body's center of gravity | ____ | ____ | ____ | ____ |
| • Knee swings forward and upward | ____ | ____ | ____ | ____ |
| • Lower leg flexes, bringing heel close to buttocks | ____ | ____ | ____ | ____ |
| • Push-off sends body momentarily into air | ____ | ____ | ____ | ____ |
| • Arms drive in opposition to legs | ____ | ____ | ____ | ____ |
| • Toes point forward | ____ | ____ | ____ | ____ |
| **Jump:** | | | | |
| • Crouch is taken by flexing hips, knees, and ankles | ____ | ____ | ____ | ____ |
| • Forceful extension of legs depending on need | ____ | ____ | ____ | ____ |
| • Use arms, timing them with the leg action; arms out to sides for stability | ____ | ____ | ____ | ____ |
| • Land softly by bending ankles, knees, and hips | ____ | ____ | ____ | ____ |

| Locomotor skill/criteria | 1st observation | | 2nd observation | |
|---|---|---|---|---|
| | Working to achieve | Have achieved | Working to achieve | Have achieved |
| **Hop:** | | | | |
| • Body is erect | ____ | ____ | ____ | ____ |
| • Push-off from one foot and land on same foot | ____ | ____ | ____ | ____ |
| • Flex hip, knee, and ankle for greater force | ____ | ____ | ____ | ____ |
| • Non-support leg is held up with knee bent, usually with foot held back | ____ | ____ | ____ | ____ |
| • Arms bent at elbow, slightly out from body to aid balance | ____ | ____ | ____ | ____ |
| • Land softly, with flexion in ankle, knee, and hip to absorb force | ____ | ____ | ____ | ____ |
| • Contact with ground begins with forward part of foot, shifting gradually to ball of foot, then heel | ____ | ____ | ____ | ____ |
| **Leap:** | | | | |
| • Head is up, body leans forward | ____ | ____ | ____ | ____ |
| • Take-off from one foot landing on the other foot | ____ | ____ | ____ | ____ |
| • Flexion in hip, knee, and ankle for thrust | ____ | ____ | ____ | ____ |
| • Body remains airborne to cover greater distance | ____ | ____ | ____ | ____ |
| • Body is more fully extended, including legs | ____ | ____ | ____ | ____ |
| • Arms move in opposition to legs but move upward | ____ | ____ | ____ | ____ |
| • Land softly by flexing hip, knee, and ankle | ____ | ____ | ____ | ____ |
| **Slide:** | | | | |
| • Body is erect, head is up | ____ | ____ | ____ | ____ |
| • Step (leap) to side | ____ | ____ | ____ | ____ |
| • Transfer weight with drawing/closing step with other foot | ____ | ____ | ____ | ____ |
| • As weight transfers to trailing foot, lead leg reaches to side again | ____ | ____ | ____ | ____ |
| • Same foot leads each step | ____ | ____ | ____ | ____ |
| • Step is longer than draw phase of slide | ____ | ____ | ____ | ____ |

| Locomotor skill/criteria | 1st observation | | 2nd observation | |
|---|---|---|---|---|
| | Working to achieve | Have achieved | Working to achieve | Have achieved |
| **Gallop:** | | | | |
| • Slide performed in a forward direction | —— | —— | —— | —— |
| • Step forward (short leap) | —— | —— | —— | —— |
| • Transfer weight with drawing/ closing step with other foot | —— | —— | —— | —— |
| • As weight transfers to trailing foot, lead leg reaches forward again | —— | —— | —— | —— |
| • Same foot leads each step | —— | —— | —— | —— |
| • Step is longer than draw phase of slide | —— | —— | —— | —— |
| **Skip:** | | | | |
| • Body erect, head is up | —— | —— | —— | —— |
| • Initiated by taking a step forward on one foot | —— | —— | —— | —— |
| • Followed by a hop on the same foot; opposite foot brought forward to begin next step, lead leg lifts | —— | —— | —— | —— |
| • Arms move in opposition to legs; may be brought upward and forward | —— | —— | —— | —— |
| • Step forward performed on first beat in rhythm | —— | —— | —— | —— |
| • Skip is repeated with a step on the opposite foot | —— | —— | —— | —— |

# PHYSICAL EDUCATION PORTFOLIO

## Locomotor Skills Letter/Conference

Name: _____

*Directions:* Write a letter to your parents/guardians telling them about your loco-motor skills. Use the space below. Try to answer these questions in your letter:

- What locomotor skills am I good at?
- What was fun about learning locomotor skills?
- What locomotor skills still need more work?
- What are my physical education goals?

Then, sit down and talk to your parents/guardians about your portfolio. Ask them to write their comments below and sign this sheet.

Dear _____ :

_____
_____
_____
_____
_____
_____
_____
_____
_____
_____
_____
_____
_____
_____

Parent's/guardian's comments: _____
_____
_____
_____
_____

Signed: _____  Date: _____

chapter 4

# Inservice
# Professional Portfolios

Practicing teachers who effectively enhance student learning and demonstrate high levels of knowledge, skills, and commitment need a "symbol" of professional competence. Their outstanding work often goes unrecognized and unrewarded. So, how can teaching excellence be best represented in the real world?

# INTRODUCTION

Pursuing teaching goals and charting one's own professional growth are worthy endeavors. Accomplished teachers continually look for ways to improve and bring distinction to their successful practices. This chapter presents a process for organizing an inservice professional portfolio, specific to physical education, around a set of advanced standards for experienced teachers. First, various primary and secondary purposes for documenting professional accomplishments are identified. Then, working and showcase portfolios are described, followed by suggestions for organizing and managing these types of portfolios. Guidelines are also provided for collecting and selecting items. Lastly, some ideas are offered for how teachers can evaluate their portfolios. To synthesize this information, a sample inservice professional portfolio system is presented at the end of the chapter.

# DEFINITION AND PURPOSES

Preservice teachers are primarily focused on satisfying program requirements and certification or licensing standards. Inservice teachers with limited experience are usually focused on achieving tenure and meeting more advanced certification or licensing standards. Experienced inservice teachers, however, must operate under a different incentive for maintaining effectiveness—professional success and personal satisfaction. Therefore, like any other professional occupation, a systematic way is needed to determine and recognize teaching excellence in physical education.

Professional physical educators possess expert knowledge of the subject field, cope with unique problems and act wisely, and pursue the interests of their students. These dimensions of professionalism also suggest an ethical standard—the ongoing obligation and commitment to conduct oneself as a model of an educated person. Although the knowledge, skills, dispositions, beliefs, and practices that characterize professional physical education teachers are substantial, they need to be documented.

The inservice professional portfolio is an organized, goal-driven documentation of growth and achieved competence in the complex act of teaching. In deciding whether to engage in such a demanding demonstration of knowledge and skills, some difficult questions emerge. Why should practicing teachers involve themselves in the ongoing process of gathering information about their work? How will the portfolios be used? What is the actual intent of this assessment tool? What are the potential uses, overuses, and abuses of portfolios for assessment purposes and beyond? The first step in answering these questions is to determine the primary and secondary purposes of the inservice professional portfolio.

## Primary Purpose

Selecting items for a portfolio with no sense of what the portfolio represents is unimaginable. Given the real-world demands on physical education teachers, there need to be some solid reasons for spending time and energy on portfolios. To help make this task easier, the professional portfolio should be an adaptable yet incisive tool that serves multiple purposes. The primary purpose of the portfolio developed by inservice teachers is to verify the wide range of knowledge, skills, and dispositions acquired through teaching experience, professional development, advanced training, and reflection. Together, these competencies define excellence in teaching, or what is often called the "master teacher."

## Secondary Purposes

The specific, day-to-day purposes of portfolio engagement will vary according to personal preference, nature of school setting, school governance, and/or bargaining agreement policies. These secondary purposes will likely depend on whether a portfolio review process is voluntary or mandatory. Regardless, the following purposes could be served by a system of portfolio assessment, either separately or in combination.

**Help Teachers Grow Professionally.** Inservice teachers are fully capable of assessing their own progress as teachers. When they review and reflect on their accomplishments, they are involved in a process that fosters lifelong professional advancement. Strengths and weaknesses are revealed so that teachers can monitor their own growth. They should know from their experience as preservice and inservice teachers that this cumulative process is just as valuable as the product (e.g., student work samples, student performance scores, instructional videos).

**Monitor Goals.** By compiling their own professional portfolio, teachers model how to use portfolios. Completed short- and long-term goals can be validated with artifacts. For example, sport education could be a goal for the next semester. Unit plans, lesson plans, performance records, partner checklists, student notebooks, and tournament schedules could be collected to show goal achievement.

**Satisfy Evaluation Procedures.** Teachers may be required to engage in preconferences and postconferences with their supervisors for evaluative purposes. The professional portfolio could be structured around preestablished criteria (e.g., positive learning environment, accommodate diversity) as well as those agreed upon by the teacher and supervisor during the preconference.

**Show Contribution to Educational Mission.** It is reasonable to expect teachers to seek to fulfill their school's and program's stated mission. The extent to which a teacher has contributed to this mission can be documented through the portfolio. For example, teachers could collect and rationalize artifacts in support of the following mission: "Through physical education, students will develop into healthy, physically active, socially adjusted, emotionally stable, and intellectually stimulated persons by attaining the knowledge, skills, and attitudes and values appropriate to these outcomes."

**Track Action Research.** Physical educators often engage in site-based "research" in an attempt to systematically and objectively evaluate the outcome of educational activities. For example, a teacher might, following pretests, teach tennis skills using method "A" in one class and method "B" in another. The combined test results would then be compared to determine whether there was a significant difference in performance under the two instructional conditions. The portfolio could be the vehicle to organize, assemble, reflect, and evaluate this kind of endeavor.

**Guide Career Path.** Many school districts have implemented "career ladders" or "local professional growth plans" to facilitate advancement within the system. A multiyear portfolio would be a natural way to organize progress along a career path at appropriate intervals.

**Enhance New Job Opportunities.** The prospects of increased job mobility, new career opportunities, and higher salary are attractive to most teachers. Although the professional portfolio offers no guarantees, it can go a long way in helping teachers build a case for themselves when seeking alternative job placements.

# TYPES OF PORTFOLIOS

Unlike the different types of preservice professional and student portfolios, a wide variety of portfolios is not necessary for the inservice teacher. The two types of portfolios recommended here seem adequate. They will be covered again in subsequent sections of this chapter that deal with organization and management, collecting and selecting items, and evaluation.

## Working Portfolio

The ongoing, systematic collection of teacher artifacts, and related student work samples, should occur on a weekly basis or, preferably, as part of one's daily routine. The overall collection forms the framework for goal setting and reflection. It also provides a basis for review by colleagues and self-appraisal at planned intervals during a given school year and/or teaching career. As a result, evaluation of a formative nature is facilitated.

## Showcase Portfolio

A limited number of items are selected to exhibit growth over time and to serve a particular purpose. This type of portfolio can be customized to provide a professional overview of the personality and abilities of the inservice physical education teacher. For example, while showcase portfolios used for supervisor evaluation, professional growth, goal monitoring, or job enhancement would be different in content, they would all, nonetheless, "showcase" particular aspects of the teacher's competence. They would also offer a basis for summative evaluation.

# ORGANIZATION AND MANAGEMENT

Once inservice teachers decide on the purposes of their professional portfolios, an organizational

The showcase portfolio is useful for the evaluation conference.

scheme is needed, one that is clear and meaningful to other professionals. In addition, a plan should be developed for handling the logistics of the portfolio process. The following section describes a set of teaching standards that can be used as the basis for organizing the inservice professional portfolio. Some management techniques are provided that might help in constructing, storing, and maintaining the portfolio.

## Focus on Standards

In many instances, the purpose of the professional portfolio will dictate its organizational scheme. For example, if the purpose is to monitor goals, then the actual short- and long-term goals become the organizing center. To satisfy evaluation procedures, the portfolio would be organized around preestablished criteria. The portfolio would be organized around the elements of a mission statement if teachers were showing their contributions to that mission.

In addition to organizing the portfolio around specific purposes, it would be more practical if a universal set of knowledge, skills, and dispositions could be used across disciplines and grade levels. Fortunately, some relatively clear requirements for proficient teaching do exist, which means that everything collected for the inservice professional portfolio could be organized around such performance categories. Because they have widespread acceptance and general applicability, the standards of the National Board for Professional Teaching Standards (1994) are recommended for this purpose.

The five core propositions advanced by the board were identified in chapter 1 (pages 9-10). The artifacts selected should provide tangible evidence that each proposition has been met. Collectively, these propositions cover (1) knowledge of the subject to be taught, skills to be developed, and curricular materials that organize the content, (2) knowledge of general and content-specific strategies for teaching and evaluating, (3) knowledge of human development, (4) skills in effectively teaching students from diverse backgrounds, and (5) dispositions to use such knowledge and skills in the best interest of students. The standards that support each core proposition follow. They will also be used in subsequent sections of this chapter that deal with item selection and evaluation.

### National Board for Professional Teaching Standards*

*Core Proposition 1: Teachers are committed to students and their learning.*

(a) Teachers recognize individual differences in their students and adjust their practice accordingly.

(b) Teachers have an understanding of how students develop and learn.

(c) Teachers treat students equitably.

(d) Teachers' mission extends beyond developing the [psychomotor] capacity of their students.

*Core Proposition 2: Teachers know the subjects they teach and how to teach those subjects to students.*

(a) Teachers appreciate how knowledge in their subjects is created, organized, and linked to other disciplines.

(b) Teachers command specialized knowledge of how to convey a subject to students.

(c) Teachers generate multiple paths to [learning].

*Core Proposition 3: Teachers are responsible for managing and monitoring student learning.*

(a) Teachers call on multiple methods to meet their goals.

(b) Teachers orchestrate learning in group settings.

(c) Teachers place a premium on student engagement.

(d) Teachers regularly assess student progress.

(e) Teachers are mindful of their principal objectives.

*Core Proposition 4: Teachers think systematically about their practice and learn from experience.*

(a) Teachers are continually making difficult choices that test their judgment.

(b) Teachers seek the advice of others and draw on education research and scholarship to improve their practice.

*Core Proposition 5: Teachers are members of learning communities.*

(a) Teachers contribute to school effectiveness by collaborating with other professionals.

(b) Teachers work collaboratively with parents.

(c) Teachers take advantage of community resources.

## Techniques

The inservice teacher must assume responsibility for storing, maintaining, and updating the professional portfolio throughout the process. Decisions about the method of construction, how and where to store portfolios, when to "manage" portfolios, and how to get feedback depend on the purpose and type of portfolio. Although there are many ways to assemble portfolios, the following suggestions are among the most useful for handling these logistics. Consideration is given to both working and showcase portfolios.

**Storage.** The actual container for collecting artifacts is a matter of personal preference. Some options include notebooks, expanding and accordion files, hanging files, large file box, folders, satchels, pockets for electronic documents, large notebook divided into sections, and file drawers in a cabinet. The working portfolio may require considerable space because it serves as an artifacts repository. Items for the different showcase portfolios would be drawn from this collection. Because the showcase portfolio is a more concise representation of accomplishments (e.g., goals achieved, criteria met, professional standards), the number of items is limited. Thus, an accordion file or satchel is all that may be needed, depending on who is going to review the portfolio (e.g., supervisor, prospective employer).

**Tools.** Even experienced teachers may not be good at organizing what they collect. They may have a good collection of artifacts but could use some of the following tools to help manage the loose ends:

- Dividers—Whatever kind of container is used, divided notebook folders or divider pages can be used to separate artifacts according to the professional standards or by any other category that makes sense (e.g., goals, criteria, program mission statements). A filing system should be created so that the standards are easily identified. Each section could be labeled with a shortened version of the standard.

---

*Note. Summary of core propositions is reprinted by permission of the National Board for Professional Teaching Standards, 1994, all rights reserved. Full document is available from the National Board, 26555 Evergreen Road, Suite 400, Southfield, MI 48076.

- Color codes—To facilitate easier management, colored dots or colored files could be used to code entries in the portfolio. Artifacts could also be coded using different color markers. A code for the colors needs to be included.

- Artifact registry—A sheet could be maintained for each standard on which inservice teachers could record the date, item, and reason for either adding or deleting an item. Because the registry is supposed to chronicle when and why items are removed and/or replaced, inservice teachers engage in a dynamic form of reflection. An artifact registry form is shown in figure 4.1.

- Work log—A biography of work could show the evolution of a long-term project like a portfolio. This would help in making necessary changes or shifting directions. The log could be as simple as a dated entry that traces all activities and decisions associated with the portfolio.

- Index—An alphabetical index of items could be compiled as the portfolio evolves. Such an organizational tool would help in the cross-referencing of artifacts that represent more than one standard and vice versa. The index could be placed in the front of the portfolio like a table of contents.

- Post-it™ Notes—Artifacts need to be cataloged so that ideas are not lost over time. A Post-it™ Note or index card could be attached to each artifact to identify the standard. The card could contain a brief statement explaining why the artifact was collected. Specific descriptors from the standard statement may help later in connecting the artifact to the standard. Using a Post-it™ Note or index card protects original works.

**Reflection.** Artifacts collected for the working portfolio should be thoughtfully examined and labeled to reveal their meaning and value to the entire portfolio. At the very least, the inservice teacher will avoid having to determine later why a particular item was collected. By reflecting on the artifact, inservice teachers get to know why an artifact was collected for a particular standard, goal, and/or purpose. The reflection, which can be brief, should not summarize the artifact. It should state what the artifact is, why it fits the standard, goal, and/or purpose, and what it says about one's competence. A sample reflection cover sheet appears in figure 4.2. These reflection sheets can remain with those items selected for the showcase portfolio.

**Self-Assessment.** In addition to item-by-item reflection, the entire collection of artifacts should be reviewed with reference to short- and long-term goals and/or how the portfolio covers the professional standards. The process of self-assessment is usually an informal self-check to determine what is not well documented by artifacts. The teacher should become a "pack rat" in looking for ways to help a goal and/or standard that is incomplete. These missing areas should be kept in mind as professional activities are completed (e.g., school or community projects, student exhibits, teacher-made materials, seminars, personal growth conferences, unit plans). The artifacts self-assessment checklist shown in figure 4.3 can be used to identify professional standards that are well documented ("Good"), standards that are satisfactorily evidenced ("OK"), and standards for which goals and artifacts are needed along with a target completion date ("Artifacts needed"). Review of the showcase portfolio will be covered in the subsequent section of this chapter that deals with evaluation.

**Conferences With Colleagues.** An independent, neutral review of one's portfolio is almost always worthwhile. Receiving feedback while the portfolio is being organized and managed can be invaluable. It is reasonable to assume that more and more experienced physical educators and other school personnel will be involved in professional portfolios. As a result, opportunities for meaningful dialogue are expanded. Holding conferences with colleagues offers an excellent chance for feedback about the portfolio. In addition, these professional connections should foster relationships with colleagues and a collaborative environment. When planning a conference, the following questions should be answered: What are the goals of the conference? What reflections are needed? What questions should be prepared for the conference? When will it be held? At the conference, some basic questions are, What have you learned about yourself? What aspects of the portfolio are you particularly proud of? If you could publish one thing in your portfolio, what would it be and why? What aspects of your teaching need some attention? How do you plan to deal with these needs?

# Artifact Registry

Standard/goal/purpose: _____

| A | D | Date | Item | Reasons |
|---|---|------|------|---------|
|   |   |      |      |         |
|   |   |      |      |         |
|   |   |      |      |         |
|   |   |      |      |         |
|   |   |      |      |         |
|   |   |      |      |         |
|   |   |      |      |         |
|   |   |      |      |         |
|   |   |      |      |         |
|   |   |      |      |         |
|   |   |      |      |         |
|   |   |      |      |         |
|   |   |      |      |         |
|   |   |      |      |         |
|   |   |      |      |         |
|   |   |      |      |         |
|   |   |      |      |         |
|   |   |      |      |         |
|   |   |      |      |         |
|   |   |      |      |         |
|   |   |      |      |         |
|   |   |      |      |         |
|   |   |      |      |         |
|   |   |      |      |         |
|   |   |      |      |         |
|   |   |      |      |         |
|   |   |      |      |         |
|   |   |      |      |         |
|   |   |      |      |         |
|   |   |      |      |         |
|   |   |      |      |         |

**Figure 4.1** Form that can be used to chronicle when and why artifacts are added (A) or deleted (D).

```
┌─────────────────────────────────────────────┐
│            Reflection Cover Sheet             │
│                                               │
│   Name: _____  Date: _____    │
│                                               │
│   Standard/goal/purpose: _____    │
│                                               │
│   Name of artifact: _____    │
│                                               │
│   Source: _____    │
│                                               │
│   Rationale statement: _____    │
│                                               │
│   _____    │
│                                               │
│   _____    │
│                                               │
│   _____    │
│                                               │
│   _____    │
│                                               │
│   _____    │
│                                               │
│   _____    │
│                                               │
│   _____    │
│                                               │
│   _____    │
│                                               │
│   _____    │
└─────────────────────────────────────────────┘
```

**Figure 4.2**   Format for reflecting on individual pieces collected for the inservice working portfolio.

# SELECTING ITEMS

Ultimately, decisions must be made about what is included in the professional portfolio and what is excluded from it. The selection process is related closely to the type of portfolio. Even for the working portfolio, criteria should be predetermined or formalized to avoid an overabundance of artifacts. The purposes of the showcase portfolio dictate the selection of specific items. The process of selection answers several important questions: What items should be included? How will the items be selected? Who will select these items? When will these items be selected?

Most artifacts will be derived from school and community activities, professional development experiences, teacher-made materials, and curriculum plans that include units and lesson plans. The inservice teacher must decide what is essential to the types of professional portfolios in accordance with their purposes. Consideration should always be given to the professional teaching standards as a factor in making selection decisions.

## Artifacts Possibilities

A wide range of artifacts can be selected for the working portfolio. Many artifacts may be selected for one or more of the different kinds of showcase portfolios. The artifacts possibilities briefly explained here show the range of options that exists, but this list does not include all the possibilities. In fact, experienced physical educators will probably have available numerous alternative artifacts from which to select.

1. Philosophy statement—position paper or statement of philosophy about teaching and/or physical education; includes underlying beliefs about practices in physical education that enhance student learning.

2. Goals statement—perception of role as a physical education teacher; provides information about the direction one wants to take professionally and the means for getting there; includes list of accomplishments in relation to goals.

3. Videotapes of teaching—recording of actual teaching episodes; documents management and motivation techniques, communication modes,

## Artifacts Self-Assessment Checklist

Name: _____ Date: _____

| Core proposition | Standard | Good | OK | Artifacts needed |
|---|---|---|---|---|
| #1—Teachers are committed to students and their learning. | (a) Recognize individual differences in students and adjust practice accordingly | | | Goal:<br><br>Target date: |
| | (b) Understand how students develop and learn | | | Goal:<br><br>Target date: |
| | (c) Treat students equitably | | | Goal:<br><br>Target date: |
| | (d) Extend mission beyond developing the [psycho-motor] capacity of students | | | Goal:<br><br>Target date: |
| #2—Teachers know the subjects they teach and how to teach those subjects to students. | (a) Appreciate how knowledge in subjects is created, organized, and linked to other disciplines | | | Goal:<br><br>Target date: |
| | (b) Command specialized knowledge of how to convey subject to students | | | Goal:<br><br>Target date: |
| | (c) Generate multiple paths to [learning] | | | Goal:<br><br>Target date: |

*(continued)*

**Figure 4.3** The artifacts self-assessment checklist can help inservice teachers determine overall status of the working portfolio.

| Core proposition | Standard | Good | OK | Artifacts needed |
|---|---|---|---|---|
| #3—Teachers are responsible for managing and monitoring student learning. | (a) Call on multiple methods to meet goals | | | Goal:<br><br>Target date: |
| | (b) Orchestrate learning in group settings | | | Goal:<br><br>Target date: |
| | (c) Place a premium on student engagement | | | Goal:<br><br>Target date: |
| | (d) Regularly assess student progress | | | Goal:<br><br>Target date: |
| | (e) Are mindful of principal objectives | | | Goal:<br><br>Target date: |
| #4—Teachers think systematically about their practice and learn from experience. | (a) Are continually making difficult choices that test judgment | | | Goal:<br><br>Target date: |
| | (b) Seek advice of others and draw on education research and scholarship to improve practice | | | Goal:<br><br>Target date: |
| #5—Teachers are members of learning communities. | (a) Contribute to school effectiveness by collaborating with other professionals | | | Goal:<br><br>Target date: |
| | (b) Work collaboratively with parents | | | Goal:<br><br>Target date: |
| | (c) Take advantage of community resources | | | Goal:<br><br>Target date: |

**Figure 4.3** *(continued)*

accommodation of diverse learners, alternative teaching strategies, and learner assessment procedures.

4. Teacher-made instructional materials—custom-made teaching aids; includes transparencies, charts, posters, videotapes, games, and equipment; shows creativity in planning and teaching; photographs of materials may be necessary.

5. Lesson plans—instructional planning and use of multiple methods; components include goals, objectives, student activities, teaching strategies, resources, time schedule, and evaluation standards and procedures.

6. Unit plans—comprehensive plan for instruction on a content area covering several days or weeks; includes organizing centers, content goals, learning objectives, content outlines, learning activities, evaluation methods, and resources.

7. Integrated units—physical education is integrated with other subjects, which might include health, art, music, science, math, social studies, and language arts; lesson plans or resource materials that fit a central theme (e.g., science of movement, Greek mythology, measuring human performance); shows how physical education contributes to overall theme.

8. Technology resources—samples of materials representing how state-of-the-art technology is incorporated into physical education (e.g., electronic mail, electronic bulletin boards, information databases, interactive video); includes computer software used or incorporated into teaching (e.g., computer-assisted instruction, HyperCard, digitized video).

9. Student works—samples of student products and/or exhibits generated in physical education, including individual and class portfolios, learning contracts, projects, and performance evaluations; shows a range of learning experiences based on diagnostic review.

10. Case studies—in-depth analysis of an anonymous student's development in physical education over a certain time period; shows understanding of growth and development and ability to maintain student learning.

11. Community and extracurricular involvement—interactions with students, parents, school

Computer-assisted instruction can be documented in the professional portfolio.

personnel, and community members that maintain positive school-community collaboration; includes volunteer experiences and services and responsibilities with clubs, intramurals, and interscholastic athletics.

12. Professional growth activities—list and description of seminars, inservice training, and/or personal conferences attended, participation in professional organizations and committees, and coursework completed.

13. Professional readings—identify reactions to issues and concepts covered in list of professional readings; includes article summaries and critiques and subscriptions to professional publications.

14. Awards, honors, and commendations—documents (e.g., letters, certificates) that verify outstanding contributions to the field of education and/or physical education; includes community, professional, and/or volunteer recognition.

15. Letters—written statements from students, parents, school personnel, and/or community members in support of teaching practices; reference should be made to professional commitment and responsibility, along with comments about professional practice.

16. Photographs—represents teacher competence and accomplishments that cannot be physically included in a portfolio; shows active learning, special events and projects, bulletin boards, learning centers, and movement exhibitions.

17. Logs and journals—highlight professional activities and/or record of identifying professional problems, dealing with a problem, choosing a strategy to solve the problem, and showing results of implementing the problem-solving strategy; documents instructional strategies, management and motivation skills, and collaboration with family and community.

18. Reflections and self-assessments—thoughtful examination of artifacts contained in the professional portfolio (reflection) and review of the entire collection of artifacts in reference to short- and long-term goals (self-assessment).

Although the working portfolio is an all-inclusive documentation of teaching competence, it is assembled primarily for personal use as a repository of artifacts. The showcase portfolio,

however, should be streamlined and targeted. Depending on purpose, other kinds of items may be essential, such as the following:

1. Cover letter (i.e., introduce self, describe some pertinent experiences, point out areas of portfolio that are exemplary, justify job candidacy, if appropriate)
2. Creative cover
3. Table of contents and/or index
4. Biographical sketch
5. Resume
6. Certification/licensing documents (e.g., copy of certificate, transcripts)
7. Letters of recommendation
8. List of relevant courses (i.e., title, credits, grade, professional standard to which course relates)

## Link to Professional Standards

Emphasis has been placed on the established teaching standards for experienced and accomplished teachers. The applicability of these general standards to physical educators can be established through the professional portfolio. Therefore, strong consideration should be given to the link between the standards and the artifacts selected to represent these standards. A broad array of artifacts should be selected for the working portfolio so that the task of selecting a more limited number of items for the different showcase portfolios is made easier. The greater the variety of representative artifacts, the easier it should be to serve the purpose of a given showcase portfolio (e.g., show professional growth, satisfy goals, meet evaluation criteria, qualify for a new job). In table 4.1, the link between the professional standards and artifacts in physical education is established. Possible artifacts are indicated for each standard.

# PORTFOLIO EVALUATION

If inservice teachers are thorough in evaluating their competence, then they need to communicate their accomplishments to others and receive evaluative feedback. The contents of the showcase portfolio should undergo continual review. This does not include the built-in review by a supervisor for evaluation purposes or by a

---TABLE 4.1---

# Teaching Standards and Physical Education Artifacts

| | SUPPORTING STANDARDS | POSSIBLE ARTIFACTS |
|---|---|---|
| **Core Proposition 1:** Teachers are committed to students and their learning | (a) Teachers recognize individual differences in their students and adjust their practice accordingly. | Reflective journal describing accommodations and response to self-control strategies for five students with mild behavior disabilities in a sport education teaching unit. |
| | (b) Teachers have an understanding of how students develop and learn. | Project for a graduate course titled "How Children Learn Motor Skills" showing how principles and concepts are applied to an elementary physical education program. |
| | (c) Teachers treat students equitably. | Case studies showing development in physical education for a student of cultural origin different from most members of a class, a student at-risk, and a student who is gifted and talented. |
| | (d) Teachers' mission extends beyond developing the [psychomotor] capacity of their students. | Observational checklists for determining students' tendencies toward self-responsibility, respect for others, sense of fair play, and higher-order thinking in movement awareness activities. |
| **Core Proposition 2:** Teachers know the subjects they teach and how to teach those subjects to students | (a) Teachers appreciate how knowledge in their subjects is created, organized, and linked to other disciplines. | Integrated unit plan with language arts and speech titled "Communicating Through Movement." |
| | (b) Teachers command specialized knowledge of how to convey a subject to students. | Self-appraisal worksheets and inventories for health-related components of fitness (i.e., cardiorespiratory endurance, muscular strength and endurance, flexibility, body composition). |
| | (c) Teachers generate multiple paths to [learning]. | Videotape of series of teaching episodes in which a variety of instructional strategies is used (e.g., problem solving, simulations, self-check, reciprocal). |
| **Core Proposition 3:** Teachers are responsible for managing and monitoring student learning | (a) Teachers call on multiple methods to meet their goals. | Student portfolio work samples representing different intelligences (e.g., linguistic, mathematical, kinesthetic, spatial, personal, musical) for a six-week unit on "Creative Use of Leisure Time." |
| | (b) Teachers orchestrate learning in group settings. | Guidelines for group work at fitness stations, participation in team drills, and role playing a sensitive problem (e.g., mocking others' ability, respecting officiating calls of opponent). |
| | (c) Teachers place a premium on student engagement. | Floor plans and setups for gymnasium and outdoor space showing arrangement of equipment and materials and locations of students that maximize active learning. |
| | (d) Teachers regularly assess student progress. | Scoring rubrics for a set of sequential lessons on manipulative skills (e.g., dribbling, kicking, throwing, catching, volleying, striking). |
| | (e) Teachers are mindful of their principal objectives. | Lesson plans that link explicit learning objectives with specific student activities and performance standards. |
| **Core Proposition 4:** Teachers think systematically about their practice and learn from experience | (a) Teachers are continually making difficult choices that test their judgment. | Descriptions of how the rules and strategies of traditional games (e.g., soccer, volleyball, basketball) are modified to encourage greater participation and teamwork. |
| | (b) Teachers seek the advice of others and draw on education research and scholarship to improve their practice. | Annotated bibliography of the principles and applications of "cooperative learning" specific to physical education instruction at the middle school level. |

*(continued)*

TABLE 4.1

*(continued)*

| | SUPPORTING STANDARDS | POSSIBLE ARTIFACTS |
|---|---|---|
| **Core Proposition 5:** Teachers are members of learning communities | (a) Teachers contribute to school effectiveness by collaborating with other professionals. | Individualized Education Plans (IEP) showing the motor development component for a group of students with learning disabilities. |
| | (b) Teachers work collaboratively with parents. | Reflection sheet for use by parents to review and comment on a videotape of a choreographed dance routine. |
| | (c) Teachers take advantage of community resources. | Photographs from an elective course conducted at a local state park titled "Outdoor Pursuits" (e.g., camping, backpacking, hiking, orienteering, cross-country skiing). |

*Note.* Outlines of core propositions and supporting standards are reprinted by permission of the National Board for Professional Teaching Standards, 1994, all rights reserved. Full document is available from the National Board, 26555 Evergreen Road, Suite 400, Southfield, MI 48076.

prospective employer when seeking a new job. Rather, review in this context refers to feedback during the progressive stages of portfolio development and refinement. Periodic reviews not only are essential, but they are natural to a system of portfolio assessment and a career development plan.

The professional portfolio is an evaluative tool itself. The individual artifacts and/or the entire portfolio should be reviewed according to established purposes. Criteria should focus on the portfolio's content and quality. There appears to be at least two primary sources of evaluative feedback—colleagues and self.

## Colleague Feedback

A common practice among professional educators is to share ideas or materials and to solicit an informal opinion about them. This approach would likely be the most practical way to handle individual artifacts for the working portfolio. For the showcase portfolio, however, a more structured approach is recommended.

Several feedback and evaluation constructs can be used, including reflection, conferences, and performance rating. Each is described here with techniques for providing feedback and evaluation data to inservice teachers. Colleagues who provide such reviews should be experienced, trustworthy, and willing to offer objective, constructive feedback. In addition, for illustrative purposes, the teaching standards outlined in the previous chapter section serve as the basis for these reviews.

**Reflection.** Because other practicing teachers may be involved in their own professional growth

plan and/or portfolio development, they are qualified to review the work of the inservice physical education teacher and provide feedback. Self-reflection was described previously as a technique to help manage the portfolio (figure 4.2, page 166). In a similar manner, reflection by colleagues serves as a cross-check. Colleagues should be asked to (1) offer constructive or encouraging words, (2) disagree with an idea rather than with the teacher, and (3) assess the quality of work based on the established standards. The sample colleague reflection sheet that appears in figure 4.4 could be used for this purpose.

**Conferences.** As mentioned previously (page 164), another way to "connect" with professional colleagues is a conference using the portfolio as the basis for discussion. The conference could be planned as a general process that answers questions such as, What have you learned about yourself by putting together a professional portfolio? What artifacts are particularly meaningful and why? What areas of your teaching performance need further improvement? However, conferences at this level are meant to be more evaluative. The focus should be on the teaching standards and how they document accomplishments and professional competence. Direct personal communication is a legitimate form of evaluation if structured properly. Conferences could compare the inservice teacher's perceptions and the colleague's opinion regarding (1) overall strength as a physical education teacher, (2) artifacts that represent "holistic" abilities and dispositions toward teaching, (3) how the portfolio verifies that the professional teaching standards have been met, and (4) what standards need further justifi-

## Colleague Reflection Sheet

Date: _____

To: _____

From: _____

Please review the items contained in my professional portfolio and provide feedback. Thanks!

1. What teaching standard is documented the most effectively? Why?

2. What teaching standard is documented the least effectively? Why?

3. What artifacts really made an impression on you? Why?

4. What artifacts do you feel need the most work? Why?

5. What is your overall impression of the organization and presentation of artifacts?

Signed: _____ Date: _____

**Figure 4.4** Format for colleague reflection on the showcase portfolio.

cation as revealed by the portfolio. Colleagues could focus their feedback around answers to the following statements:

The part of the portfolio I like best is _____ because . . .

The part I'm not really clear about is _____ because . . .

The part you need to tell me more about is . . .

You could improve your portfolio by . . .

My overall impression is . . .

**Performance Rating.** Some physical educators may not feel comfortable asking colleagues to render a more formal rating of their portfolios.

Likewise, some colleagues may feel uncomfortable in giving one. However, a truly professional relationship should allow such an activity without any repercussions. The showcase portfolio represents the broadest view of the inservice teacher's professional competence. Its evaluation should consider the generic teaching standards and general criteria such as organization, form and quality, and evidence of understanding. The rubric rating form in figure 4.5 can be used by colleagues.

## Self-Analysis

The sample checklist in figure 4.3 (pages 167-168) for reviewing the teaching standards represents

## Portfolio Rating Form

Name: _____ Date: _____

**Directions:** Use the following scale to rate each portfolio item according to the criteria below.

4 = Outstanding    3 = Good    2 = Satisfactory    1 = Fair    0 = Poor

**Organization:** Follows guidelines; completeness of items; clear layout; overall creativity
**Form and quality:** Writing mechanics; expressiveness; visual appeal; spelling, punctuation, and grammar
**Evidence of understanding:** Explicit demonstration of standard's knowledge, skills, and dispositions; application of ideas

| Core proposition, supporting standards, and items | Organization | Form and quality | Evidence of understanding |
|---|---|---|---|
| #1. Commitment to students and their learning | | | |
| (a) Recognize individual differences in students; adjust practice accordingly | | | |
| Artifacts: | | | |
| Name: _____ | _____ | _____ | _____ |
| Name: _____ | _____ | _____ | _____ |
| (b) Understand how students develop and learn | | | |
| Artifacts: | | | |
| Name: _____ | _____ | _____ | _____ |
| Name: _____ | _____ | _____ | _____ |
| (c) Treat student equitably | | | |
| Artifacts: | | | |
| Name: _____ | _____ | _____ | _____ |
| Name: _____ | _____ | _____ | _____ |
| (d) Extend mission beyond developing the [psychomotor] capacity of students | | | |
| Artifacts: | | | |
| Name: _____ | _____ | _____ | _____ |
| Name: _____ | _____ | _____ | _____ |
| #2. Knowledge of subjects taught and how to teach those subjects to students | | | |
| (a) Appreciate how knowledge in subjects is created, organized, and linked to other disciplines | | | |
| Artifacts: | | | |
| Name: _____ | _____ | _____ | _____ |
| Name: _____ | _____ | _____ | _____ |

*(continued)*

**Figure 4.5** Form that can be used by colleagues to rate the inservice teacher's showcase portfolio.

| Core proposition, supporting standards, and items | Organization | Form and quality | Evidence of understanding |
|---|---|---|---|
| (b) Command specialized knowledge of how to convey subject to students | | | |
| Artifacts: | | | |
| Name: _____ | _____ | _____ | _____ |
| Name: _____ | _____ | _____ | _____ |
| (c) Generate multiple paths to [learning] | | | |
| Artifacts: | | | |
| Name: _____ | _____ | _____ | _____ |
| Name: _____ | _____ | _____ | _____ |
| #3. Responsibility for managing and monitoring student learning | | | |
| (a) Call on multiple methods to meet goals | | | |
| Artifacts: | | | |
| Name: _____ | _____ | _____ | _____ |
| Name: _____ | _____ | _____ | _____ |
| (b) Orchestrate learning in group settings | | | |
| Artifacts: | | | |
| Name: _____ | _____ | _____ | _____ |
| Name: _____ | _____ | _____ | _____ |
| (c) Place premium on student engagement | | | |
| Artifacts: | | | |
| Name: _____ | _____ | _____ | _____ |
| Name: _____ | _____ | _____ | _____ |
| (d) Regularly assess student progress | | | |
| Artifacts: | | | |
| Name: _____ | _____ | _____ | _____ |
| Name: _____ | _____ | _____ | _____ |
| (e) Are mindful of principal objectives | | | |
| Artifacts: | | | |
| Name: _____ | _____ | _____ | _____ |
| Name: _____ | _____ | _____ | _____ |
| #4. Think systematically about one's practice and learn from experience | | | |
| (a) Are continually making difficult choices that test judgment | | | |
| Artifacts: | | | |
| Name: _____ | _____ | _____ | _____ |
| Name: _____ | _____ | _____ | _____ |

*(continued)*

**Figure 4.5** *(continued)*

| Core proposition, supporting standards, and items | Organization | Form and quality | Evidence of understanding |
|---|---|---|---|
| (b) Seek advice of others and draw on education research and scholarship to improve practice | | | |
| Artifacts: | | | |
| Name: _____ | _____ | _____ | _____ |
| Name: _____ | _____ | _____ | _____ |
| #5. Are members of learning communities | | | |
| (a) Contribute to school effectiveness by collaborating with other professionals | | | |
| Artifacts: | | | |
| Name: _____ | _____ | _____ | _____ |
| Name: _____ | _____ | _____ | _____ |
| (b) Work collaboratively with parents | | | |
| Artifacts: | | | |
| Name: _____ | _____ | _____ | _____ |
| Name: _____ | _____ | _____ | _____ |
| (c) Take advantage of community resources | | | |
| Artifacts: | | | |
| Name: _____ | _____ | _____ | _____ |
| Name: _____ | _____ | _____ | _____ |

**Figure 4.5**    *(continued)*

an informal self-check of the entire collection of items. The checklists offers a good way to determine the status of the working portfolio and to establish goals for "missing" standards. In addition, the working portfolio should be analyzed to help determine whether there is a need to diversify the different kinds of artifacts. For example, there may be a tendency to rely too heavily on curriculum units as representative of many standards. The artifacts analysis chart in figure 4.6 can be used for this purpose. Check marks and/or dates could be entered to record the range of artifacts in support of the five core propositions and 17 supporting standards.

For the showcase portfolio, any self-evaluation scheme should incorporate explicit content and quality criteria. Because the showcase portfolio represents one's professional profile, it should receive careful scrutiny. The rubric rating form in figure 4.7 can be used by inservice physical education teachers to evaluate their showcase

portfolios. The list of portfolio contents would vary depending on the purpose of the portfolio.

## CLOSING STATEMENT

The professional portfolio provides a way for inservice physical education teachers to bring distinction to their achieved competence. Through the working and showcase portfolios, accomplished teachers can document their knowledge, skills, dispositions, beliefs, and practices. The showcase portfolio can be used to satisfy evaluation procedures, monitor goals, guide career paths, and enhance new job opportunities. Advanced professional standards for experienced teachers are recommended as the basis for organizing the professional portfolio. Also, techniques for managing the portfolio include several storage options, organizational tools, reflections, self-assessment, and conferences. In addition, the selection of artifacts from a wide

| Kind of artifact (e.g., lesson plans) | Name of artifact (e.g., series on movement exploration) | Core propositions/supporting standards | | | | | | | | | | | | | | |
|---|---|---|---|---|---|---|---|---|---|---|---|---|---|---|---|---|
| | | 1 | | | | 2 | | | 3 | | | | | 4 | | 5 | | |
| | | a | b | c | d | a | b | c | a | b | c | d | e | a | b | a | b | c |
| | | | | | | | | | | | | | | | | | | |
| | | | | | | | | | | | | | | | | | | |
| | | | | | | | | | | | | | | | | | | |
| | | | | | | | | | | | | | | | | | | |
| | | | | | | | | | | | | | | | | | | |
| | | | | | | | | | | | | | | | | | | |
| | | | | | | | | | | | | | | | | | | |
| | | | | | | | | | | | | | | | | | | |
| | | | | | | | | | | | | | | | | | | |
| | | | | | | | | | | | | | | | | | | |
| | | | | | | | | | | | | | | | | | | |
| | | | | | | | | | | | | | | | | | | |
| | | | | | | | | | | | | | | | | | | |
| | | | | | | | | | | | | | | | | | | |
| | | | | | | | | | | | | | | | | | | |
| | | | | | | | | | | | | | | | | | | |
| | | | | | | | | | | | | | | | | | | |
| | | | | | | | | | | | | | | | | | | |
| | | | | | | | | | | | | | | | | | | |
| | | | | | | | | | | | | | | | | | | |
| | | | | | | | | | | | | | | | | | | |
| | | | | | | | | | | | | | | | | | | |
| | | | | | | | | | | | | | | | | | | |
| | | | | | | | | | | | | | | | | | | |
| | | | | | | | | | | | | | | | | | | |
| | | | | | | | | | | | | | | | | | | |
| | | | | | | | | | | | | | | | | | | |
| | | | | | | | | | | | | | | | | | | |
| | | | | | | | | | | | | | | | | | | |
| | | | | | | | | | | | | | | | | | | |

**Figure 4.6** The artifacts analysis chart is used to manage the documentation of each teaching standard.

## Showcase Portfolio Rating Form

Name: _____ Date: _____

### Portfolio contents

Components of the professional portfolio should be verified according to the following indicators:

✔ = Fully developed        – = Included but incomplete        0 = Not included

_____ Cover letter

_____ Table of contents and/or index

_____ Biographical sketch

_____ Resume

_____ Certification/licensing documents

_____ Letters of recommendation

_____ List of relevant courses

_____ Artifacts representing the teaching standards

Comments: _____

_____

_____

_____

_____

_____

_____

### Portfolio quality

The professional portfolio should evidence an acceptable level of quality. Use the following scale to rate each characteristic and artifact:

2 = High quality; above expectation

1 = Satisfactory quality; meets expectation

0 = Low quality; below expectation

_____ Organization

_____ Layout/visual appeal

_____ Creativity/expressiveness

_____ Spelling, punctuation, grammar

_____ Artifact #1: _____

_____ Artifact #2: _____

_____ Artifact #3: _____

_____ Artifact #4: _____

_____ Artifact #5: _____

_____ Artifact #6: _____

_____ Artifact #7: _____

_____ Artifact #8: _____

_____ Artifact #9: _____

_____ Artifact #10: _____

_____ Artifact #11: _____

_____ Artifact #12: _____

_____ Artifact #13: _____

_____ Artifact #14: _____

_____ Artifact #15: _____

_____ Artifact #16: _____

**Figure 4.7**  Form that can be used for self-rating of the inservice teacher's showcase portfolio.

range of possibilities should consider the type of portfolio and the professional teaching standards. Finally, evaluative feedback about the professional portfolio can be derived from colleagues through reflection, conferences, and performance ratings and from self-analysis through artifacts review and application of established criteria.

# SAMPLE INSERVICE PROFESSIONAL PORTFOLIO SYSTEM

To synthesize the information presented in this chapter, a sample portfolio system is provided for use as a practicing physical education teacher. Although the system is hypothetical in nature, the portfolio elements are applicable to actual physical education settings at the inservice level. The system incorporates the concepts and principles advanced in this chapter. It is structured in the form of a manual for professional growth. The manual could be used independently by physical educators or by any school committed to improving and bringing distinction to the successful practices of physical educators.

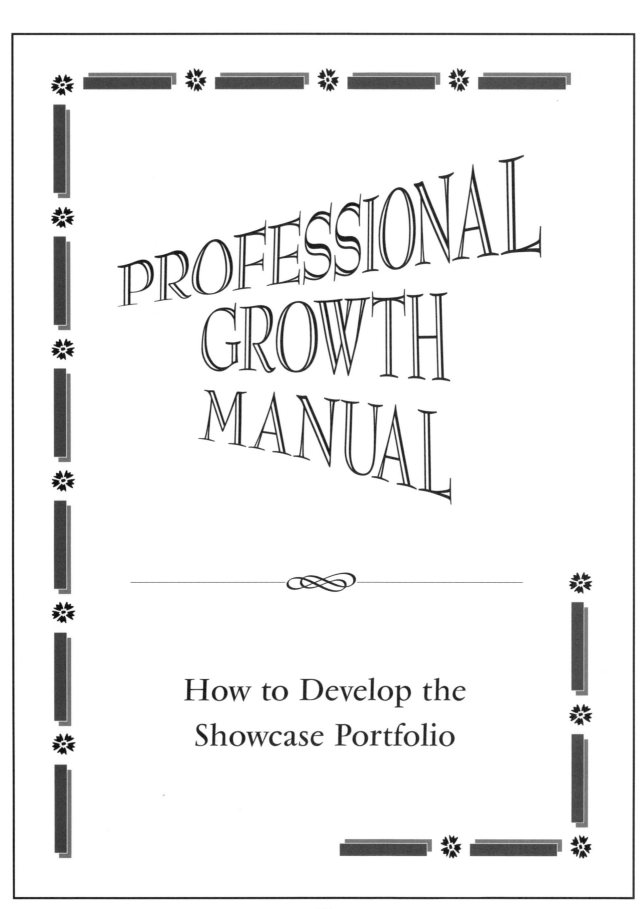

# PROFESSIONAL GROWTH MANUAL

How to Develop the
Showcase Portfolio

# Professional Growth Manual

**CONTENTS**

# I. RATIONALE AND PURPOSES

As a practicing, professional physical educator, your desire to achieve certain teaching goals and to pursue your own professional growth are commendable. Accomplished teachers continually look for ways to improve and bring distinction to their successful practices. Because your effectiveness often goes unrecognized and unrewarded, a process is needed to document growth and achieved competence in the complex act of teaching—the professional portfolio.

For experienced teachers, the incentives for maintaining effectiveness are professional success and personal satisfaction. Although the skills, dispositions, beliefs, and practices that characterize effective physical education teachers are substantial, they need to be documented. The process of gathering information about your work through portfolios can be a rewarding experience. However, given the real-world demands on physical education teachers, some solid reasons are needed for spending time and energy on portfolios. Therefore, the primary purpose of the professional portfolio is to verify the wide range of knowledge, skills, and dispositions acquired through teaching experience, professional development, advanced training, and reflection. Secondary purposes are to (1) grow professionally, (2) monitor goals, and (3) satisfy evaluation procedures.

# II. ORGANIZATION

The ongoing, systematic collection of teaching-related artifacts, including student work samples, is referred to as a "working" portfolio. It serves as the repository from which items are selected for the "showcase" portfolio, a customized overview of your professional abilities as a physical educator. Ideally, the showcase portfolio could be organized around some universal set of teaching competencies. Fortunately, performance categories that describe teaching proficiency do exist. These categories, known as core propositions, are supported by teaching standards that have widespread acceptance and general applicability. The showcase portfolio should be organized around these core propositions and standards, as follows (National Board for Professional Teaching Standards, 1994):

**Core Proposition 1: Teachers are committed to students and their learning**

   a. Teachers recognize individual differences in their students and adjust their practice accordingly.
   b. Teachers have an understanding of how students develop and learn.
   c. Teachers treat students equitably.
   d. Teachers' mission extends beyond developing the [psychomotor] capacity of their students.

**Core Proposition 2: Teachers know the subjects they teach and how to teach those subjects to students**

   a. Teachers appreciate how knowledge in their subjects is created, organized, and linked to other disciplines.
   b. Teachers command specialized knowledge of how to convey a subject to students.
   c. Teachers generate multiple paths to [learning].

**Core Proposition 3: Teachers are responsible for managing and monitoring student learning**

    a.  Teachers call on multiple methods to meet their goals.

    b.  Teachers orchestrate learning in group settings.

    c.  Teachers place a premium on student engagement.

    d.  Teachers regularly assess student progress.

    e.  Teachers are mindful of their principal objectives.

**Core Proposition 4: Teachers think systematically about their practice and learn from experience**

    a.  Teachers are continually making difficult choices that test their judgment.

    b.  Teachers seek the advice of others and draw on education research and scholarship to improve their practice.

**Core Proposition 5: Teachers are members of learning communities**

    a.  Teachers contribute to school effectiveness by collaborating with other professionals.

    b.  Teachers work collaboratively with parents.

    c.  Teachers take advantage of community resources.

## III. MANAGEMENT

You must assume responsibility for storing, maintaining, and updating your professional portfolio. You need to decide how you will handle the logistics of portfolios (i.e., method of construction, how and where to store the portfolio, when to manage it, and how to analyze it). These aspects are covered in the following sections.

### A. Storage

The actual container for collecting artifacts is a matter of personal preference. Some options include notebooks, expanding and accordion files, hanging files, large file box, folders, satchels, pockets for electronic documents, large notebook divided into sections, and file drawers in a cabinet. The working portfolio may require considerable space because it serves as an artifacts repository. Items for the showcase portfolio would be drawn from this collection. Because the showcase portfolio is a more concise representation of accomplishments, the number of items is limited. Thus, an accordion file or satchel is all that may be needed.

### B. Tools

You may be good at collecting work samples and exhibits but need help in managing the portfolio. These organizational tools may be helpful: (1) dividers (separate artifacts according to teaching standards or incomplete works), (2) color codes (code entries with colored dots, colored files, or markers), (3) artifact registry (record the date, item, and reason for either adding or removing an item), (4) work log (list activities and decisions about the portfolio with dates), (5) table of contents (categories and subcategories of items), and (6) Post-it™ Notes (attach to each artifact to identify standard and explain why it was collected).

### C. Reflection

Each collected artifact should be thoughtfully examined and labeled to reveal its meaning and value to the working portfolio. By reflecting on your work samples and exhibits, you get to know why an item was collected for a particular standard. The cover sheet on the next page can be used and should remain with those items selected for the showcase portfolio.

### D. Self-Assessment

The collection of artifacts should be reviewed to make sure that teaching standards are well-documented. Missing areas should be kept in mind as professional activities are completed. The checklist can be used. The specific teaching standards that support each core proposition should be considered. Where artifacts are needed, indicate your goal for filling the void and a target completion date.

## IV. ITEM SELECTION

Ultimately, you must decide what is included and excluded from your professional portfolio. Most artifacts are derived from school and community activities, professional development experiences, teacher-made materials, and curriculum plans that include units and lesson plans. A broad array of artifacts is available for the working portfolio. As an experienced physical educator, you will have numerous alternatives from which to select, including the following:

1. Statement of philosophy
2. Goals statement
3. Videotape of teaching
4. Teacher-made instructional materials
5. Lesson plans
6. Unit plans
7. Integrated units
8. Technology resources
9. Student works
10. Case studies
11. Community and extracurricular involvement descriptions
12. Professional growth activities list
13. Professional readings list
14. Awards, honors, and commendations
15. Letters
16. Photographs
17. Logs and journals
18. Reflections and self-assessments

The task of selecting items for the showcase portfolio should focus on the established teaching standards. There should be a strong link between the standards and the artifacts selected to represent them. The following is a list of the *minimum* expectations for the showcase portfolio relative to the core propositions and standards.

1. *Commitment to students and their learning*
   - Performance checklist for students who exhibit difficulty in a movement or sport skill

# REFLECTION COVER SHEET

## for Showcase Portfolio Artifacts

Name: _____ Date: _____

Standard: _____

Name of item: _____

Source: _____

Rationale statement: _____

_____

_____

_____

_____

_____

_____

_____

_____

_____

_____

_____

_____

_____

_____

_____

_____

_____

_____

_____

_____

_____

_____

_____

_____

_____

# ARTIFACTS SELF-CHECK

## for the Showcase Portfolio

Name: _____ Date: _____

| Core propositions | Good | OK | Artifacts needed |
|---|---|---|---|
| 1. Is committed to students and their learning | | | Goal:<br><br><br>Target date: |
| 2. Knows subject and how to teach it | | | Goal:<br><br><br>Target date: |
| 3. Is responsible for managing and monitoring student learning | | | Goal:<br><br><br>Target date: |
| 4. Thinks systematically about practices and learns from experiences | | | Goal:<br><br><br>Target date: |
| 5. Is a member of learning communities | | | Goal:<br><br><br>Target date: |

- Case study showing a student's development in a physical education unit
- Frequency index scale for an affective behavior (e.g., cooperation, tolerance, interpersonal relationships)

2. *Knowledge of subject and how to teach it*
   - Integrated unit plan with at least two other subject areas
   - Teacher-made rating scales
   - Videotape showing at least three kinds of instructional strategies (e.g., guided discovery, practice, role play, cooperative learning)

3. *Responsibility for managing and monitoring student learning*
   - Student work samples showing multiple methods
   - Assessment procedures for cognitive, affective, and psychomotor learning
   - Lesson plans that link objectives with learning activities and performance standards

4. *Think systematically about practices and learn from experiences*
   - Organization schemes for learning areas (e.g., gymnasium, outdoor field)
   - Results of an action research project
   - Annotated list of professional readings over the past year

5. *Member of learning communities*
   - Motor development component from three IEPs
   - Handouts used for "Parents Night"
   - Materials written as a member of a curriculum development team

## V. FEEDBACK AND SELF-ASSESSMENT

During the progressive stages of portfolio development and refinement, periodic reviews not only are essential, but they are natural to any system directed toward professional growth. Evaluative criteria should focus on the portfolio's *content* and *quality*. Feedback from colleagues and self-analysis are the best sources for evaluation.

### A. Feedback From Colleagues

Because practicing teachers may be involved in their own professional growth plans, they are qualified to review the work of others. Several feedback constructs can be used with the showcase portfolio—reflection, conferences, and performance rating. Colleagues who provide feedback should be experienced, trustworthy, and willing to offer objective, constructive information.

In the same way that you engage in self-reflection, *reflection* by colleagues serves as a valuable cross-check. With the established teaching standards as the basis, the reflection sheet can be used.

*Conferencing* with colleagues offers another way to acquire feedback and, at the same time, foster relationships in a collaborative environment. The focus should be on the teaching standards and how they document accomplishments and professional competence. Conferences should compare your perceptions and your colleague's opinion regarding (1) overall strength as a physical education teacher, (2) artifacts that represent "holistic" abilities and dispositions toward teaching,

# COLLEAGUE REFLECTION SHEET

## of the Showcase Portfolio

To: _____

From: _____

1. What teaching standard is documented most effectively? Why?

2. What teaching standard is documented least effectively? Why?

3. What artifacts made an impression on you? Why?

4. What artifacts need the most work? Why?

5. What is your overall impression of the organization and presentation of artifacts?

Signed: _____  Date: _____

(3) how the portfolio verifies that the teaching standards have been met, and (4) what standards need further justification as revealed by the portfolio. Colleagues could focus their feedback around answers to the following statements:

The part of the portfolio I like best is _____ because . . .

The part I'm not really clear about is _____ because . . .

The part you need to tell me more about is . . .

You could improve your portfolio by . . .

My overall impression is . . .

Assuming a truly professional relationship exists, a colleague can also provide a more formal *performance rating* of the showcase portfolio. Its review should consider the established teaching standards and general criteria such as organization and form and quality of documentation. The rating form that follows can be used for this purpose.

## B. Self-Analysis

The previous self-assessment provided an informal self-check of the working portfolio to establish goals for "missing" standards. For the showcase portfolio, you should also try to diversify the kinds of artifacts selected. There may be a tendency to rely too heavily on one kind over another, such as curriculum units. The chart that follows can be used to record, with check marks and/or dates, the range of artifacts in support of the five core propositions and 17 supporting standards.

# RATING FORM

## for Showcase Portfolio

Name: _____

Reviewer: _____

Rating scale:     + = impressive     ✔ = acceptable     0 = needs work

| | *Organization and form* Clear layout; Writing mechanics; Visual appeal | *Quality of documentation* Expressiveness; Explicit link to standard |
|---|---|---|
| *Commitment to students and their learning* | | |
| Item 1: _____ | _____ | _____ |
| Item 2: _____ | _____ | _____ |
| Item 3: _____ | _____ | _____ |
| *Knowledge of subject and how to teach it* | | |
| Item 1: _____ | _____ | _____ |
| Item 2: _____ | _____ | _____ |
| Item 3: _____ | _____ | _____ |
| *Responsibility for managing and monitoring student learning* | | |
| Item 1: _____ | _____ | _____ |
| Item 2: _____ | _____ | _____ |
| Item 3: _____ | _____ | _____ |
| *Think systematically about practices and learn from experiences* | | |
| Item 1: _____ | _____ | _____ |
| Item 2: _____ | _____ | _____ |
| Item 3: _____ | _____ | _____ |
| *Member of learning communities* | | |
| Item 1: _____ | _____ | _____ |
| Item 2: _____ | _____ | _____ |
| Item 3: _____ | _____ | _____ |

# ANALYSIS CHART

## for Showcase Portfolio Artifacts

| Kind of artifact | Name of artifact | Core propositions/supporting standards | | | | | | | | | | | | | | |
|---|---|---|---|---|---|---|---|---|---|---|---|---|---|---|---|---|
| | | 1 | | | | 2 | | | 3 | | | | | 4 | | 5 | | |
| | | a | b | c | d | a | b | c | a | b | c | d | e | a | b | a | b | c |
| | | | | | | | | | | | | | | | | | | |
| | | | | | | | | | | | | | | | | | | |
| | | | | | | | | | | | | | | | | | | |
| | | | | | | | | | | | | | | | | | | |
| | | | | | | | | | | | | | | | | | | |
| | | | | | | | | | | | | | | | | | | |
| | | | | | | | | | | | | | | | | | | |
| | | | | | | | | | | | | | | | | | | |
| | | | | | | | | | | | | | | | | | | |
| | | | | | | | | | | | | | | | | | | |
| | | | | | | | | | | | | | | | | | | |
| | | | | | | | | | | | | | | | | | | |

# References

Batzle, J. (1992). *Portfolio assessment and evaluation: Developing and using portfolios in the classroom.* Cypress, CA: Creative Teaching Press.

Bloom, B. (Ed.). (1956). *Taxonomy of educational objectives, handbook I: Cognitive domain.* New York: David McKay.

Bruininks, R.H. (1978). *Bruininks-Oseretsky test of motor proficiency.* Circle Pines, MN: American Guidance Service.

Burke, K. (1994). *How to assess authentic learning.* Palatine, IL: IRI/Skylight.

Burke, K., Fogarty, R., & Belgrad, S. (1994). *The mindful school: The portfolio connection.* Palatine, IL: IRI/Skylight.

Campbell, D.M., Cignetti, P. B., Melenyzer, B.J., Nettles, D.H., & Wyman, R.M. (1997). *How to develop a professional portfolio: A manual for teachers.* Boston: Allyn & Bacon.

Carnegie Task Force on Teaching as a Profession. (1986). *A nation prepared: Teachers for the 21st century.* New York: Author.

Chittenden, E. (1991). Authentic assessment, evaluation, and documentation of student performance. In V. Perrone (Ed.), *Expanding student assessment* (pp. 22-31). Alexandria, VA: Association for Supervision and Curriculum Development.

Cooper Institute for Aerobics Research. (1992). *FitnessGram test administration manual.* Dallas: Author.

Darling-Hammond, L. (Ed.). (1992). *Model standards for beginning teacher licensing and development: A resource for state dialogue.* Washington, DC: Council of Chief State School Officers, Interstate New Teacher Assessment and Support Consortium.

DeFina, A.A. (1992). *Portfolio assessment: Getting started.* New York: Scholastic Professional Books.

Educational Testing Service. (1992). *The praxis series: Professional assessments for beginning teachers.* Princeton, NJ: Author.

Educational Testing Service. (1995). *Praxis III: Classroom performance assessments—orientation guide.* Princeton, NJ: Author.

Franck, M., Graham, G., Lawson, H., Loughrey, T., Ritson, R., Sanborn, M., & Seefeldt, V. (1992). *Outcomes of quality physical education programs.* Reston, VA: National Association for Sport and Physical Education.

Gardner, H. (1993). *Multiple intelligences: The theory in practice.* New York: HarperCollins.

Graham, G., Castenada, R., Hopple, C., Manross, M., & Sanders, S. (1992). *Developmentally appropriate physical education practices for children.* Reston, VA: National Association for Sport and Physical Education, Council on Physical Education for Children.

Harrow, A.J. (1972). *A taxonomy of the psychomotor domain.* New York: David McKay.

Hopple, C.J. (1995). *Teaching for outcomes in elementary physical education: A guide for curriculum and assessment.* Champaign, IL: Human Kinetics.

Kendall, J.S., & Marzano, R.J. (1996). *Content knowledge: A compendium of standards and benchmarks for K-12 education.* Aurora, CO: Mid-continent Regional Educational Laboratory.

Kimeldorf, M. (1994). *A teachers guide to creating portfolios.* Minneapolis: Free Spirit Publishing.

Krathwohl, D.R., Bloom, B. S., & Masia, B.B. (1964). *Taxonomy of educational objectives, handbook II: Affective domain.* New York: David McKay.

Lambdin, D. (1997). Computer organized physical education (COPE). *Journal of Physical Education, Recreation & Dance, 68*(1), 25-29.

Marmo, D. (1994, April). *'Sport'folios — On the road to outcome-based education.* Paper presented at the AAHPERD National Convention, Denver.

McTighe, J., & Ferrara, S. (1994). *Assessing learning in the classroom.* Washington, DC: National Education Association.

Meisels, S.J., Dichtelmiller, M., Dorfman, A., Jablon, J.A., & Marsden, D.B. (1993). *The work sampling system resource guide.* Ann Arbor, MI: Rebus Planning Associates.

Melograno, V. J. (1994). Portfolio assessment: Documenting authentic student learning. *Journal of Physical Education, Recreation & Dance, 65*(8), 50-55, 58-61.

Melograno, V.J. (1996). *Designing the physical education curriculum.* Champaign, IL: Human Kinetics.

Melograno, V.J. (1997). Integrating assessment into physical education teaching. *Journal of Physical Education, Recreation & Dance*, 68(7), 34-37.

Moersch, C., & Fisher, L.M. (1995). Electronic port-folios — some pivotal questions. *Learning and Leading with Technology*, 23(2), 10-15.

Mohnsen, B. S. (1995). *Using technology in physical education*. Champaign, IL: Human Kinetics.

Murphy, S., & Smith, M. (1992). *Writing portfolios: A bridge from teaching to assessment*. Markham, ON: Pippin Publishing Limited.

National Board for Professional Teaching Standards. (1994). *What teachers should know and be able to do*. Southfield, MI: Author.

National Board for Professional Teaching Standards. (1996). *An invitation to national board certification*. Southfield, MI: Author.

National Commission on Excellence in Education. (1983). *A nation at risk: The imperative of educational reform*. Washington, DC: U.S. Government Printing Office.

National Commission on Teaching & America's Future. (1996). *What matters most: Teaching for America's future* (summary report). Woodbridge, VA: Author.

Perrone, V. (Ed.). (1991). *Expanding student assessment*. Alexandria, VA: Association for Supervision and Curriculum Development.

Rink, J., Dotson, C., Franck, M., Hensley, L., Holt-Hale, S., Lund, J., Payne, G., & Wood, T. (1995). *National standards for physical education: A guide to content and assessment*. St. Louis: Mosby.

Rudner, L.M., & Boston, C. (1994). Performance assessment. *The ERIC Review*, 3(1), 2-12.

Ryan, J.M. (1995). *Current practices and procedures in testing, measurement, and assessment*. Reston, VA: National Association of Secondary School Principals.

Strand, B.N., & Wilson, R. (1993). *Assessing sport skills*. Champaign, IL: Human Kinetics.

Tannehill, D., Faucette, N., Lambert, L., Lambdin, D., McKenzie, T., Veal, M., & Saville, M.E. (1995). *National standards for beginning physical education teachers*. Reston, VA: National Association for Sport and Physical Education.

Tierney, R.J., Carter, M. A., & Desai, L.E. (1991). *Portfolio assessment in the reading-writing classroom*. Norwood, MA: Christopher-Gordon Publishers.

U.S. Department of Education. (1991). *America 2000: An education strategy*. Washington, DC: Author.

Wichita State University College of Education. (1995). *Professional portfolio handbook*. Wichita, KS: Author.

Zessoules, R., & Gardner, H. (1991). Authentic assessment: Beyond the buzzword and into the classroom. In Perrone (Ed.), *Expanding student assessment* (pp. 47-71). Alexandria, VA: Association for Supervision and Curriculum Development.

# About the Author

Vincent J. Melograno has been a professor in the Department of Health, Physical Education, Recreation, and Dance at Cleveland State University since 1971. He is also the chairperson of the department, a position that he previously held from 1974 to 1987. He has held several administrative positions within the College of Education as well.

Melograno, who earned his doctoral degree in physical education from Temple University, is the author of *Designing the Physical Education Curriculum* (Human Kinetics, 1996), now in its third edition; a coauthor of a book on physical fitness for college-aged adults; and the writer of numerous book chapters, journal articles, and monographs. He is a member of several professional organizations, including the American Alliance for Health, Physical Education, Recreation and Dance (AAHPERD) and the International Association for Physical Education in Higher Education (AIESEP). In 1993 he was selected for the "International Who's Who in Sport Pedagogy Theory and Research" by AIESEP.

Melograno lives in Shaker Heights, Ohio, and enjoys tennis, fitness training, and softball.

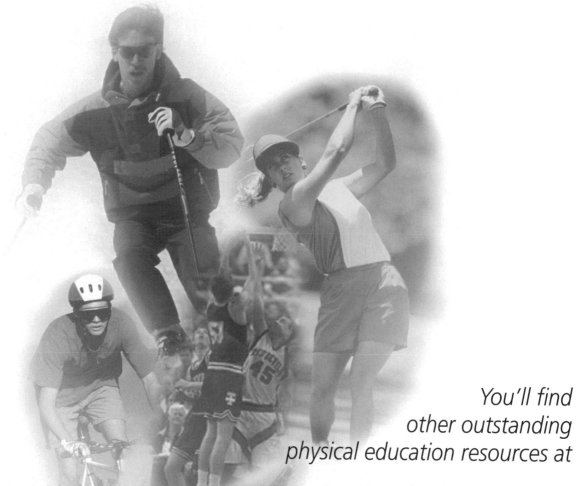